™

References for the Rest of Us! ®

BESTSELLING BOOK SERIES

Are you intimidated and confused by computers? Do you find that traditional manuals are overloaded with technical details you'll never use? Do your friends and family always call you to fix simple problems on their PCs? Then the For Dummies® computer book series from Hungry Minds, Inc. is for you.

For Dummies books are written for those frustrated computer users who know they aren't really dumb but find that PC hardware, software, and indeed the unique vocabulary of computing make them feel helpless. For Dummies books use a lighthearted approach, a down-to-earth style, and even cartoons and humorous icons to dispel computer novices' fears and build their confidence. Lighthearted but not lightweight, these books are a perfect survival guide for anyone forced to use a computer.

> *"I like my copy so much I told friends; now they bought copies."*
>
> *— Irene C., Orwell, Ohio*

> *"Quick, concise, nontechnical, and humorous."*
>
> *— Jay A., Elburn, Illinois*

> *"Thanks, I needed this book. Now I can sleep at night."*
>
> *— Robin F., British Columbia, Canada*

Already, millions of satisfied readers agree. They have made For Dummies books the #1 introductory level computer book series and have written asking for more. So, if you're looking for the most fun and easy way to learn about computers, look to For Dummies books to give you a helping hand.

T0370390

1/01

Internet Explorer 6

FOR DUMMIES®

by Doug Lowe

Internet Explorer 6 For Dummies®

Published by
Wiley Publishing, Inc.
909 Third Avenue
New York, NY 10022
www.hungryminds.com
www.dummies.com

Library of Congress Control Number: 2001092739

ISBN: 0-7645-1344-3

10 9 8 7 6 5 4 3 2 1

1O/RT/QZ/QR/IN

Distributed in the United States by Wiley Publishing, Inc.

Distributed by CDG Books Canada Inc. for Canada; by Transworld Publishers Limited in the United Kingdom; by IDG Norge Books for Norway; by IDG Sweden Books for Sweden; by IDG Books Australia Publishing Corporation Pty. Ltd. for Australia and New Zealand; by TransQuest Publishers Pte Ltd. for Singapore, Malaysia, Thailand, Indonesia, and Hong Kong; by Gotop Information Inc. for Taiwan; by ICG Muse, Inc. for Japan; by Intersoft for South Africa; by Eyrolles for France; by International Thomson Publishing for Germany, Austria and Switzerland; by Distribuidora Cuspide for Argentina; by LR International for Brazil; by Galileo Libros for Chile; by Ediciones ZETA S.C.R. Ltda. for Peru; by WS Computer Publishing Corporation, Inc., for the Philippines; by Contemporanea de Ediciones for Venezuela; by Express Computer Distributors for the Caribbean and West Indies; by Micronesia Media Distributor, Inc. for Micronesia; by Chips Computadoras S.A. de C.V. for Mexico; by Editorial Norma de Panama S.A. for Panama; by American Bookshops for Finland.

For general information on Wiley's products and services please contact our Customer Care Department within the U.S. at 800-762-2974, outside the U.S. at 317-572-3993 or fax 317-572-4002.

For sales inquiries and reseller information, including discounts, premium and bulk quantity sales, and foreign-language translations, please contact our Customer Care Department at 800-434-3422, fax 317-572-4002, or write to Wiley Publishing, Inc., Attn: Customer Care Department, 10475 Crosspoint Boulevard, Indianapolis, IN 46256.

For information on licensing foreign or domestic rights, please contact our Sub-Rights Customer Care Department at 212-884-5000.

For information on using Wiley's products and services in the classroom or for ordering examination copies, please contact our Educational Sales Department at 800-434-2086 or fax 317-572-4005.

For press review copies, author interviews, or other publicity information, please contact our Public Relations Department at 317-572-3168 or fax 317-572-4168.

For authorization to photocopy items for corporate, personal, or educational use, please contact Copyright Clearance Center, 222 Rosewood Drive, Danvers, MA 01923, or fax 978-750-4470.

About the Author

Doug Lowe lives in sunny Fresno, California (where the motto is "Keep the lights on if you can"), with his wife, Debbie; daughters Sarah and Bethany (Rebecca moved out!); and female golden retrievers Nutmeg and Ginger. He works full-time creating outstanding literary works, such as *Internet Explorer 6 For Windows For Dummies,* and wonders why he hasn't yet won a Pulitzer Prize or had one of his books made into a movie by Steven Spielberg. Doug realizes that a few years ago it wouldn't have been technically possible, but now that we have the technology to create a startlingly realistic computer-generated Dummies Man, John Kilcullen's people should call Steven's people really soon before someone else steals the idea.

If we can't convince Steven, we can always tell him that Stanley Kubrick had been secretly working on the project since 1992.

Doug spends most of his spare time (which amounts to about three full hours per month) driving his daughters around. Hiking is also a favorite hobby, so much so that Doug really would like to write *Hiking For Dummies* or *Backpacking For Dummies* but hasn't had the time to write a proposal yet because these computer books just keep coming up. Maybe someday.

Dedication

This book is dedicated to Rebecca, Sarah, and Bethany.

Author's Acknowledgments

Just when I think that I'm finished and can leave for vacation, I remember that there's one thing left to write: the acknowledgments! It's always a pleasure to take a few moments to thank the many people who helped along the way. I'll start with project editor and copy editor Rebecca Whitney, who saw this project through from start to finish and turned my senseless prose into the finished book you now hold in your hand. She also corrected all my spelling errors and other silly mistakes.

Thanks also to Mark Chambers, for his excellent technical review. Many technical tips and caveats mentioned in these pages were inspired by his review.

I also want to thank my good friends Jerry and Dianne McKneely, for helping out with the MSN Messenger and NetMeeting material. They may be the only two people on the entire Internet who will chat with me.

Oh, and thanks also to James Orr. He didn't have anything to do with this book, but I promised I'd mention him somewhere.

This book borrows heavily from the previous edition, *Internet Explorer 5.5 For Dummies,* so I want to thank the crew that helped with that one, too: project editor Dana Lesh, copy editors Beth Parlon and Rebekah Mancilla, and technical editor Allen Wyatt.

Publisher's Acknowledgments

We're proud of this book; please send us your comments through our Wiley Online Registration Form located at www.dummies.com.

Some of the people who helped bring this book to market include the following:

Acquisitions, Editorial, and Media Development

Project Editor: Rebecca Whitney

Acquisitions Editor: Steven H. Hayes

Technical Editor: Mark L. Chambers

Editorial Manager: Mary C. Corder

Editorial Assistants: Amanda Foxworth, Jean Rogers

Production

Project Coordinator: Nancee Reeves

Layout and Graphics: Joyce Haughey, Gabriele McCann, Jackie Nicholas, Brian Torwelle, Jeremey Unger

Proofreaders: John Greenough, Angel Perez, Jean Rogers

Indexer: TECHBOOKS Production Services

General and Administrative

Wiley Publishing, Inc.: John Kilcullen, CEO; Bill Barry, President and COO; John Ball, Executive VP, Operations & Administration; John Harris, Executive VP and CFO

Wiley Technology Publishing Group: Richard Swadley, Senior Vice President and Publisher; Mary Bednarek, Vice President and Publisher, Networking; Walter R. Bruce III, Vice President and Publisher; Joseph Wikert, Vice President and Publisher, Web Development Group; Mary C. Corder, Editorial Director, Dummies Technology; Andy Cummings, Publishing Director, Dummies Technology; Barry Pruett, Publishing Director, Visual/Graphic Design

Wiley Manufacturing: Ivor Parker, Vice President, Manufacturing

Wiley Marketing: John Helmus, Assistant Vice President, Director of Marketing

Wiley Production for Branded Press: Debbie Stailey, Production Director

Wiley Sales: Michael Violano, Vice President, International Sales and Sub Rights

◆

The publisher would like to give special thanks to Patrick J. McGovern, without whom this book would not have been possible.

◆

Contents at a Glance

Cartoons at a Glance

By Rich Tennant

"Guess who found a Kiss merchandise site on the Web while you were gone?"

page 289

"I like getting complaint letters by e-mail. It's easier to delete than to shred."

page 127

"Just how accurately should my Web site reflect my place of business?"

page 7

"What I'm looking for are dynamic Web applications and content, not Web innuendoes and intent."

page 37

"This is amazing. You can stop looking for Derek. According to an MSN search I did, he's hiding behind the dryer in the basement."

page 225

Cartoon Information:
Fax: 978-546-7747
E-Mail: richtennant@the5thwave.com
World Wide Web: www.the5thwave.com

Table of Contents

Introduction

•••

*D*on't you hate it when, just about the time you figure out a game, someone goes and changes the rules on you?

That happens on the Internet all the time, and it has happened again. Just when you thought that you had the Internet all figured out, Microsoft has the nerve to throw a new version of your trusted friend Internet Explorer at you. Ready or not, here comes Internet Explorer 6!

Fear not! — for you have found the perfect companion book to Internet Explorer 6. With this book in hand, you'll have no trouble deciphering the main features of Internet Explorer 6 and mastering your Internet domain.

This book tackles all the important Internet Explorer subjects in plain English and with no pretense. No lofty prose here. The language is friendly. You don't need a graduate degree in computer science to get through it. I have no Pulitzer ambitions for this book, but it would be cool if it were made into a movie starring Harrison Ford.

I even occasionally take a carefully aimed potshot at the hallowed and sacred traditions of Internetdom, just to bring a bit of fun to an otherwise dry and tasteless subject. If that doesn't work, I throw in an occasional lawyer joke.

Why Another Internet Book?

Unfortunately, when it comes right down to it, Internet Explorer — like the Internet itself — isn't as easy to use as *they* would have you believe. Alas, Internet Explorer is nothing more than a computer program, and, like any computer program, it has its own commands to master, menus to traverse, icons to decipher, nuances to discover, and quirks to work around. Bother.

Oh, and then take the Internet itself. Frankly, the Internet is a sprawling mess. It's filled with klutzy interfaces, programs that don't work the way they should, and systems that were designed decades ago. Finding the information you need on the Internet can be like the proverbial search for a needle in a haystack. The Internet is everything they say it is — except easy to use.

That's why you need this book to take you by the hand and walk you step-by-step through all the details of using Internet Explorer 6. This book doesn't bog you down with a bunch of puffed-up technojargon that makes you feel like your head is about to explode. Instead, this book spells out what you need to know in language that promises not to rap your urge to know more.

Sure, plenty of books about the Internet already crowd the computer section of your local bookstore. Hungry Minds, Inc., even has several excellent books available: *The Internet For Dummies,* 7th Edition (by John R. Levine, Carol Baroudi, and Margaret Levine Young), is an especially good general introduction to the Internet. But if you are using — or are planning to use — Internet Explorer, you need to know more than generic Internet stuff. You need to know specifically how to use the features of Internet Explorer 6. Many of these features are unique to Internet Explorer 6 and are not found in any other web browser.

How to Use This Book

The beauty of this book is that you don't have to read it through from start to finish. You wouldn't dare pick up the latest Clancy or Grisham novel and skip straight to page 173. But with this book, you can. That's because this book works like a reference. You can read as much or as little of it as you need. You can turn to any part of the book, start reading, and then put the book down after finding the information you need and get on with your life.

On occasion, this book directs you to use specific keyboard shortcuts to get things done. I indicate these key combinations like this:

Ctrl+Z

This line means to hold down the Ctrl key while pressing the Z key and then release both together. Don't type the plus sign.

Sometimes, I tell you to use a menu command. For example, you may see something like this:

File⇨Open

This line means to use the keyboard or mouse to open the File menu and then choose the Open command.

Whenever I describe a message or information you see onscreen, it looks like this:

`Are we having fun yet?`

Anything you are instructed to type appears in bold, like so: Type **puns** in the field. You type exactly what you see, with or without spaces.

Internet addresses (technically known as *URLs*) appear like this: www.whatever.com.

Another little nicety about this book is that when I tell you to click one of those little toolbar buttons on the Internet Explorer screen, a picture of the button appears in the margin. Seeing what the button looks like helps you find it onscreen.

This book rarely directs you elsewhere for information — just about everything you need to know about using Internet Explorer is in here. However, two other books may come in handy from time to time. The first is *Windows XP For Dummies,* by Andy Rathbone (published by Hungry Minds, Inc.), which is helpful if you're not sure how to perform a Windows XP task, such as copying a file or creating a new folder. The second book is *The Internet For Dummies,* 7th Edition (I referred to it earlier in the Introduction), which is helpful if you decide to venture into the dark recesses of the Internet.

Foolish Assumptions

I'm making only three assumptions about you:

- You use a computer.
- You use Windows XP or one of its predecessors: Windows Millennium Edition, Windows 98, or even Windows 95.
- You access (or are thinking about accessing) the Internet with Internet Explorer 6.

Nothing else. I don't assume that you're a computer guru who knows how to change a controller card or configure memory for optimal usage. These types of technical chores are best handled by people who like computers. Hopefully, you're on speaking terms with such a person. Do your best to keep it that way.

How This Book Is Organized

Inside this book are ample chapters arranged into five parts. Each chapter is broken down into sections that cover various aspects of the chapter's main subject. The chapters have a logical sequence, so reading them in order makes sense (if you're crazy enough to read this entire book). But you don't have to read them that way. You can flip open the book to any page and start reading.

The following sections give you the lowdown on what's in each of the seven parts.

Part I: Preparing for an Internet Exploration

The two chapters in this part deal with really introductory stuff: what the Internet is and how to get connected to it. Part I is the place to start if you haven't visited the Internet before and you're not sure what the World Wide Web is, what www.microsoft.com means, or how to connect your computer to the Internet.

Part II: Embarking on a World Wide Web Adventure

This part is the heart and soul of the book. Its chapters show you how to use the basic features of Internet Explorer to untangle the World Wide Web. You find out how to surf the Web like a pro using the Internet Explorer 6 Web browsing features, how to look up information on the Web, how to build a library of your favorite Web sites so that you don't always have to hunt them down, and how to get help when you're stuck. You can also read about setting up your computer to download the Web pages you're most interested in by using offline synchronization while you sleep.

Part III: Getting Connected with Outlook Express

The chapters in this part show you how to use Outlook Express, the e-mail program that comes with Internet Explorer. With Outlook Express, you can send and receive e-mail, set up an address book, and participate in Internet newsgroups. You also find out how to use MSN Messenger, the Microsoft instant-message program that lets you talk online with your friends.

Part IV: Customizing Your Explorations

The chapters in this part show you how to configure Internet Explorer by tweaking its options so that it suits your working style. This stuff is best read by people who like to show their computers who's the boss.

You'll also find a chapter here about creating your own home page on the Internet.

Part V: The Part of Tens

This wouldn't be a *For Dummies* book if it didn't include a collection of chapters with lists of interesting snippets: Ten Tips for Using Internet Explorer Efficiently and Ten Things That Sometimes Go Wrong, for example.

Glossary

People use so much technobabble when they discuss the Internet that I've decided to include an extensive glossary of online terms, free of charge. With this glossary in hand, you can beat the silicon-heads at their own game.

Icons Used in This Book

As you read all this wonderful prose, you occasionally encounter the following icons. They appear in the margins to draw your attention to important information.

Uh-oh, some technical drivel is about to come your way. Cover your eyes if you find technical information offensive.

This icon points out traps you may fall into if you're not careful. Heed these warnings and all shall go well with you, with your children, and with your children's children.

Pay special attention to this icon — it points to some particularly useful tidbit, perhaps a shortcut or a way of using a command that you may not have considered.

This icon points out important information to definitely remember as you use the Internet Explorer features being discussed. The information may not be totally new to you; it may just remind you of something you've temporarily forgotten.

This icon points out a new feature of Internet Explorer 6 for those Internet Explorer 5 veterans in the audience.

Where to Go from Here

The Internet is an exciting new computer frontier, and Internet Explorer is hands-down the best way to experience the Internet. So where do you go from here? Disney World, of course!

If you can't get to Disney World, try the next best thing: Hop online and start exploring the Internet. With this book at your side, you can visit the world from your desktop. Bon voyage!

Part I
Preparing for an Internet Exploration

The 5th Wave — By Rich Tennant

"Just how accurately should my Web site reflect my place of business?"

In this part . . .

The Internet is one of the best things to happen to computers since the invention of the On button. Everyone and his uncle are going online these days. Even television commercials are in on the act — the number of ads that flash Internet addresses at the end is amazing. The Internet promises to revolutionize the way we do business, the way we buy cars, the way kids learn at school — even the way we shop for groceries.

The two chapters in this part give you a gentle introduction to the Internet. In Chapter 1, you get a crash course on what the Internet is and why everyone is so excited about it. In Chapter 2, you find out how to get yourself connected so that you don't miss out on all the excitement.

Chapter 1

Welcome to the Internet

In This Chapter

▶ A mercifully brief description of the Internet

▶ A rational explanation of why you should give a hoot about the Internet

▶ An overview of the different faces of the Internet

*O*nce upon a time, seven stranded castaways were lost on a desert isle somewhere in the Pacific. They were cut off from civilization: no television, no newspapers, and worst of all — gasp — no Internet access! What would they do?

Fortunately, they had a genius among them: a professor, who figured out a way to access the Internet by using an old radio, a few coconut shells, and electricity generated by a makeshift stationary bicycle. The professor set up a Web page announcing the location of the island, but the hapless first mate, Gilligan, somehow managed to crash the server only moments before a Coast Guard sailor was about to access the crew's home page.

So what's the point of this story? Simply that just about everyone — even the crew of the *S.S. Minnow* — is cruising the Internet these days. If you want to join the tour but you're afraid that you know even less about the Internet than Gilligan, this chapter is for you. It provides a brief introduction to what the Internet is and why you would want to use it. So grab your sailor cap and let's get going!

What Is This Internet Thing?

The *Internet* is an enormous computer network that links tens of millions of computers all across the planet. The Internet lets you, while sitting at your own, private computer in a small town in Iowa, access computers in Moscow or Geneva or Tokyo or Washington, D.C. The Internet is the most exciting thing to happen to computers since the invention of the mouse.

The Internet is sometimes referred to as the *information superhighway*. It is supposed to enable every man, woman, and child in the United States — indeed, on the entire planet — to access instantly and without error every conceivable bit of information that has ever been discovered.

Unfortunately, the information superhighway is, at best, only a promise of what the future holds. Accessing the Internet still requires a fairly major investment in computer equipment. (A decent computer for accessing the Internet still costs close to $750 or more, although prices are coming down all the time.) And although an enormous amount of information is available on the Internet, the entire contents of the Internet amount to only a tiny fraction of human knowledge, and the information that is there is haphazardly organized, difficult to sift through, and often unreliable.

Still, a tiny fraction of all human knowledge is worth having, even if it's poorly organized. And that's why the Internet has become so popular: People love to surf the Web (I explain what the Web is later in this chapter), hoping to glean some useful bit of information that may make their investment of online time and money worthwhile.

Plus, the Internet is just downright fun.

The Internet: A Network of Networks

The Internet is a network of networks. The world is filled with computer networks. Large and small businesses have networks that connect the computers in their offices. Universities have networks that the students and faculty can access. Government organizations have networks. Many experienced computer users have even set up networks in their own homes. And online services such as CompuServe, America Online, and The Microsoft Network are themselves large computer networks.

The Internet's job is to connect all these networks to form one gigantic meganetwork. In fact, the name *Internet* comes from the fact that the Internet allows connections among distinct computer networks.

The Internet consists of several hundreds of thousands of separate computer networks. These networks, in turn, connect millions of computers to one another.

Who Invented the Internet?

First, the simple answer: Not Al Gore.

Is the Internet really as big as they say it is?

The simple fact is that no one really knows just how big the Internet is. That's because no one really owns the Internet. But several organizations make it their business to try periodically to find out how big the Internet is. The science is far from exact, but these organizations are able to come up with reasonable estimates.

One of the best-known Internet surveys is the Internet Domain Survey, sponsored twice a year by the Internet Software Consortium. In January 2001, the Internet Domain Survey found that more than 109 million computers were connected to the Internet. Compared with the January 2000 survey, the 2001 survey shows that the Internet grew by just over 50 percent in that one year. During the year 2000, more than 37 million computers were added to the Internet — about one computer every .85 seconds. Or, put another way, during the 9.87 seconds it took Maurice Green to win the gold medal in the 100 meter dash at the Olympic games in Sydney, Australia, 11 more computers joined the Internet.

If you find these figures interesting, you can check the results of the latest Internet Domain Survey by visiting the Internet Software Consortium Web site at www.isc.org.

Now for the answer that you would get if Ken Burns decided to make a 16-hour PBS documentary about the Internet. For maximum effect, play some melancholy violin music in the background as you read the rest of this section.

In the summer of 1969, the four mop-topped singers from Liverpool were breaking up. The war in Vietnam was escalating. Astronauts Neil Armstrong and Buzz Aldrin walked on the moon. And the Department of Defense built a computer network named ARPANET to link its defense installations with several major universities throughout the United States. ARPANET was designed to enable the Defense Department computer to communicate even in the event of a nuclear attack.

In the early 1970s, ARPANET was getting difficult to manage, so it was split into two networks: one for military use, named MILNET, and the other for nonmilitary use. The nonmilitary network retained the name ARPANET. To link MILNET with ARPANET, a new method of connecting networks, named *Internet Protocol* (or just *IP*, for short), was invented.

The whole purpose of IP was to enable these two networks to communicate with one another. Fortunately, the designers of IP realized that it wouldn't be too long before other networks wanted to join in the fun, so the designers designed IP to allow for more than two networks. In fact, that ingenious design allowed for tens of thousands of networks to communicate via IP.

The decision was a fortuitous one because the Internet quickly began to grow. By the mid-1980s, the original ARPANET reached its limits. Just in time, the National Science Foundation (NSF) decided to get into the game. NSF had built a network named NSFNET to link its huge supercomputers.

(*Supercomputers* are those behemoth computers — the kind of computers that, even today, fill entire rooms and are used to calculate the orbits of distant galaxies, discover new prime numbers, and outwit chess masters like Kasparov.)

NSFNET replaced ARPANET as the new background for the Internet. Around that time, such magazines as *Time* and *Newsweek* began writing articles about this new phenomenon called the Internet, and the Net (as it became nicknamed) began to grow like wildfire. Soon NSFNET couldn't keep up with the growth, so several private commercial networks took over the management of the Internet backbone. The Internet has grown at a dizzying rate ever since, and who knows how long this frenetic growth rate will continue.

If the story of the Internet has a moral, it is that the Internet has probably been so successful precisely because it's not strictly a commercial or government venture. No one is really in charge of the Internet. Instead, the Internet sprang up pretty much on its own. No rules dictate who can and who cannot join the Internet. Kinda warms your cockles, doesn't it?

The Many Faces of the Internet

The Internet is not a single, monolithic entity that has a consistent look and feel for all its services. Quite the contrary — over the years, many different services have sprung up on the Internet, each with its own style and appearance. Microsoft Internet Explorer has features that enable you to access most, but not all, of these services.

The World Wide Web

The most popular Internet venue is the *World Wide Web,* usually called *the Web,* for short. The Web is to the Internet what Windows is to DOS: a graphical interface to what would otherwise be a bland and boring place. The Web enables you to view the information that is available on the Internet using neatly formatted text, stunning pictures, and gee-whiz special effects, such as sounds, animations, and videos.

Information on the World Wide Web is organized into documents called *pages.* A single Web page can be as short as one word, or it can contain hundreds of lines of text. Most pages contain no more information than you can comfortably squeeze on an 8½-x-11-inch printed page.

Each page on the Web can contain text, graphics, sounds, videos, and — most important — links to other Web pages with related information. For example, a page that contains information about frogs may contain links to other pages with information about princes, Muppets, or hallucinogenic substances.

A *Web site* is a collection of pages related to a particular subject and kept on a single computer, known as a *Web server.* Every Web site has a *home page,* which is the starting point for accessing the pages that are available at the Web site. The home page has *links* that let you access the Web site's other pages in an organized fashion.

Besides links to other pages at the same Web site, a Web page can also have links to pages that live on different Web sites. Thus, clicking a link may take you to an entirely different Web site that's located halfway around the world from the one you were accessing, without jet lag, airsickness, or even a noticeable hesitation!

That's the neat thing about surfing the Web: You can travel the world without leaving your home — and without long-distance charges! Your Internet Service Provider charges you a flat monthly or hourly rate, whether you're retrieving data from a Web site four miles or four *thousand* miles from your computer.

To access the Web, you need a special program called a Web browser. A *Web browser* knows how to display the special formats and codes used to send information over the World Wide Web. The Web browser reads these special codes over the Internet and translates them into fancy displays and beautiful pictures for your screen. The browser also enables you to follow links from one Web page to another by simply clicking the link.

Just as you can choose among many different word processing or spread-sheet programs, you have your choice of many different Web browsers to use. Internet Explorer 6 is the latest and greatest Web browser program from Microsoft. Figure 1-1 shows Internet Explorer in action, displaying a page from the World Wide Web.

Internet Explorer isn't the only Web browser on the block, of course. Another popular Web browser is Netscape Navigator. Netscape and Microsoft are in a neck-and-neck race to see who can create the best browser software — kind of like the way the Republicans and Democrats are in a race to see who can create the best campaign-reform proposals. Obviously, this book is about exploring the Internet using Internet Explorer. If you use Netscape Navigator, you should probably be reading *Netscape Navigator 6 For Dummies,* by Paul Hoffman (published by Hungry Minds, Inc.), instead.

Web browsers, such as Internet Explorer, aren't limited to accessing just the World Wide Web. In fact, you can access most of the other parts of the Internet directly from Internet Explorer or from programs that come with Internet Explorer.

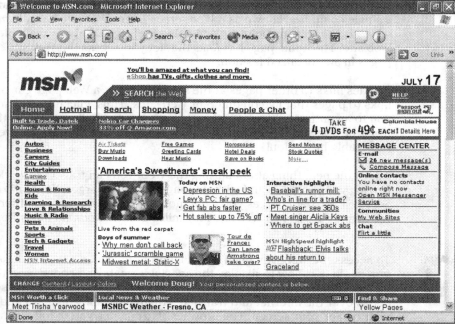

Figure 1-1:
Internet
Explorer
displays
pages
from the
Internet's
World
Wide Web.

Electronic mail

Electronic mail (usually called *e-mail*) enables you to exchange private messages with any other e-mail user on the Internet, no matter where in the country or world that user lives. Unlike with the postal service, Internet e-mail is delivered almost instantly. And unlike with Federal Express, you don't have to pay $13 for fast delivery. In fact, Internet e-mail is probably the least expensive, yet most efficient, form of communication available.

E-mail is not just for sending short notes to your friends, either. You can use e-mail to send entire files of information to co-workers. For example, I used Internet e-mail to send the document files for this book to my editor at Hungry Minds, Inc., and she, in turn, used e-mail to send me back corrections and technical questions.

Many programs are available for reading Internet e-mail. Internet Explorer 6 comes with a handy e-mail program named Outlook Express. It's a scaled-down version of a more complete e-mail program named Microsoft Outlook, which is included as a part of Microsoft Office. Although Microsoft Outlook has more features than Outlook Express, Outlook Express is more than adequate for most e-mail users.

Figure 1-2 shows Outlook Express in action. The program is so useful that I've devoted Part III of this book to showing you how to use it to access your e-mail.

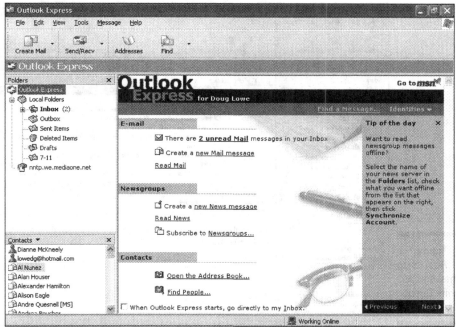

Figure 1-2:
Outlook
Express lets
you read
and send
e-mail.

Newsgroups

Newsgroups are online discussion groups — places where users with common interests gather to share ideas. Thousands of newsgroups exist, covering just about every topic imaginable. You can find newsgroups that discuss obscure computer topics, fan clubs for various celebrities, online support groups, and who knows what else.

Most Internet newsgroups are distributed over *Usenet,* a network of special server computers that contain the special software needed to handle newsgroups. As a result, you sometimes see the terms *Usenet* and *newsgroups* used together. However, you can access some newsgroups that aren't a part of Usenet.

As luck would have it, Outlook Express, the handy e-mail program that comes with Internet Explorer, is also adept at handling Internet newsgroups. Figure 1-3 shows Outlook Express accessing a newsgroup — in this case, the newsgroup happens to be devoted to the subject of everyone's favorite comic strip, *Peanuts.* I give you in Chapter 14 the ins and outs of using Outlook Express to participate in newsgroup discussions.

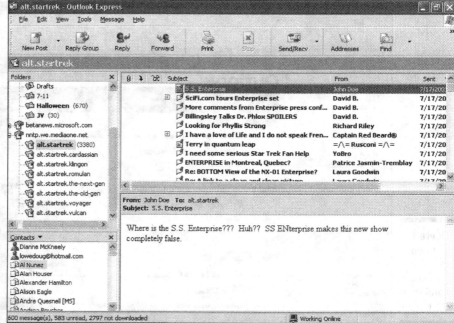

Figure 1-3:
Accessing
newsgroups
with Outlook
Express.

Don't be confused by the term *news* in newsgroups. Newsgroups are *not* a news service designed to give you accurate, up-to-date, and unbiased information about current events. Newsgroups are places where people with common interests can share opinions. In this sense, newsgroups are more like talk radio than a news program.

File Transfer Protocol

File Transfer Protocol — or FTP, as it is usually called — is the Internet equivalent of a network file server. FTP is the Internet's primary method of moving files around. Thousands of FTP sites make their files available for downloading. All you have to do is sign in to the FTP site, find the file you want to download, and click.

Internet Explorer has built-in support for FTP, so you can easily log in to an FTP site and download files to your computer. In fact, you don't have to do anything special to access FTP from Internet Explorer; you may not even be aware that you're using FTP.

Be warned: The Internet is not censored

No censorship exists on the Internet. If you look hard enough, you can find just about anything on the Internet — not all of it wholesome. In addition to information about fly fishing, knitting, and the solar system, you can find photographs of men and women in various states of dress and undress, often engaged in unmentionable acts that would make Hugh Hefner blush.

Unfortunately, you can't do much about the content on the Internet. A few years back, Congress tried to pass a law that would ban indecent content from the Internet, but the Supreme Court ruled such legislation unconstitutional. After all, indecency is an ambiguous concept, and the First Amendment pretty much prohibits Congress from banning any but the most obscene materials from publication in any medium.

However, just because Congress can't prevent people from publishing offensive material on the Internet doesn't mean that you have to view it. Microsoft, along with other Internet companies, has sponsored a voluntary system of ratings that lets you know whether an Internet site contains offensive material. Internet Explorer enables you to control whether you (or anyone in your household) can view such material. The solution's not perfect, but it does go a long way toward controlling the amount of offensive material kids are exposed to. In Chapter 16, I describe Internet Explorer controls for blocking this type of material, as well as other ways to filter out obnoxious or offensive Internet content.

Instant messages

Instant messaging is an online feature that lets you chat online — that is, you can exchange messages directly with other Internet users, kind of like a phone call with your computer. The most popular instant message service is America Online's AIM (which stands for *AOL Instant Messenger*).

Not to be outdone by America Online, Microsoft has its own instant-message service, known as MSN Messenger. *MSN Messenger* enables you to create a list of online friends with whom you can chat, either one-on-one or in small groups. Plus, MSN Messenger is integrated with a more sophisticated online chatting program named Microsoft NetMeeting, which sports advanced features, such as audio- and videoconferencing, a whiteboard on which you and your online friends can doodle, and more. I show you how to use MSN Messenger and Microsoft NetMeeting in Chapter 13.

Another form of online chatting is *Internet Relay Chat,* or *IRC.* Unlike instant-message services, such as AIM or MSN Messenger, IRC does not let you set up lists of friends to chat with. Instead, IRC hosts thousands of chat rooms, where anyone can join in on the discussion.

Chapter 2

Getting Connected with Internet Explorer

In This Chapter

▶ Finding out whether you're already connected to the Internet

▶ Getting connected, if you aren't so lucky

▶ Comparing various Internet pricing plans to get the best deal

▶ Setting up your Internet connection with the Internet Connection Wizard

*T*he hardest part about using the Internet is figuring out how to get connected to it the first time. After you figure that out, the rest is easy. (Well, *relatively* easy. Nothing about computers is completely easy!)

This chapter explores the various options for connecting your computer to the Internet using Internet Explorer 6. With luck, you may discover that you're already connected to the Internet and Internet Explorer is set up on your computer, so you can skip this chapter and get on with the fun. If you're not so fortunate, read on to find out how to get the job done.

You May Already Be on the Internet

It's true. You may have been on the Internet for years now and not realized it. And you may have already won $10 million from Publisher's Clearing House, and maybe tomorrow you'll get struck by lightning and your IQ will double.

Actually, the possibility that you already have access to the Internet isn't that outlandish. Here are some reasonable scenarios:

✔ If you subscribe to one of the major online services, such as America Online, CompuServe, or The Microsoft Network, you already have access to the Internet. Each of these online services provides a link to the Internet. In the past, online services provided only limited access to the Internet and were among the more expensive methods of connecting to the Net. But nowadays, the major online services offer full Internet access at competitive prices.

- ✔ If you use a computer at work and that computer is a part of a local area network (LAN) and the LAN is connected to the Internet, you may be able to access the Internet via the LAN. Talk to your resident network guru to find out.

- ✔ The computers at many schools are connected to the Internet. If you're a student, you may be able to bribe your teachers into letting you access the Internet. You may even get extra credit for using the Internet — especially if you use it to do your homework.

- ✔ Some public libraries have computers that are connected to the Net. With access at a public library, you may still be able to access free e-mail services, such as Hotmail, for your electronic mail.

- ✔ Cybercafés — once found only in trendy cities such as Seattle and San Francisco — have sprouted up around the country. At a cybercafé, you can surf the Web free while sipping a decaf latté and enjoying classical music.

If You're Not Already on the Internet

If you don't have access to the Internet through one of the sources listed in the preceding section, you have no alternative but to set up your own Internet access at home. Unfortunately, you can't do so without having to contend with at least some of the boring technical details.

Here are a few general tips I want to offer before I get into the details of setting up your Internet access:

- ✔ Upgrade to one of the latest and greatest versions of Windows: Windows Millennium Edition (I refuse to call it Windows Me) or Windows 2000 or Windows XP, if it's available by the time you read this book. One favorable feature about these new versions of Windows is that they have built-in support for the Internet and they come with Internet Explorer built in.

- ✔ If you plan on connecting to the Internet over the phone (as the overwhelming majority of people do), make sure that your computer is located near a telephone outlet.

- ✔ If you have a friend who already has access to the Internet, treat him to lunch and pick his brain (well, not literally). Find out what kind of modem he has, who his Internet Service Provider (ISP) is, how much he is paying for it, what he likes best about it, what he hates about it, what he would do differently, and whether he thinks John Travolta should go back to playing nice guys.

> ✔ If a friend happens to be a computer expert, see whether you can bribe
> her into helping you set up your Internet access. Don't offer cash;
> bartering is better. Offer to mow her lawn or wash her car.

First, You Need a Modem

The first thing you need to connect your computer to the Internet is a
modem. If your computer is brand new, you're lucky: It probably already has
a modem in it. In that case, all you have to do is plug the modem into the telephone jack by using a phone cord, and you're ready to go.

If your computer doesn't have a modem, you need to purchase and install
one yourself. Fortunately, you can stroll right down to your nearest electron-
ics superstore, computer superstore, or office-supply superstore and buy one
off the shelf for less than $50. If you shop around, you can probably find one
for as little as $20.

Modems come in a variety of speeds. The speed of a modem determines how
fast the modem can pump data through the phone line. Modem speed is measured in units called *bps,* which stands for *bits per second.* When you buy a
modem, make sure that you get a 56,000 bps modem, usually called a 56K
modem. (The term *baud* is sometimes used as a substitute for bps. Both have
pretty much the same meaning.)

If your computer has an older modem in it, watch out. Older modems may
not be fast enough to access the World Wide Web efficiently. If you're working
with an older, 14400 bps modem or — heaven forbid — a 2400 bps modem,
you should definitely replace it with a faster model. If you have a newer, 28.8K
or 33.6K modem, you can continue to use it. However, your Internet access
will be noticeably faster if you upgrade to a 56K modem.

Your modem must be connected to a phone line so that your computer can
access the outside world. Unfortunately, whenever you use the Internet, the
modem ties up your phone line. Anyone calling your number gets a busy
signal, and you can't use the phone to call out for pizza. If being deprived of
telephone privileges while you're online proves to be a problem, you can
always have the phone company install a separate phone line for your
modem. (Or you can use your cell phone to order pizza.)

If the thought of installing a modem nauseates you, pack up your computer
and take it to your friendly local computer shop. The folks there can sell you
a modem and install it for you for a small charge.

Or, You Can Take the Cable or DSL Plunge

If you plan on using the Internet frequently and don't mind spending a few extra dollars for Internet access, you may want to consider one of two relatively new methods of connecting to the Internet: cable and DSL. Cable Internet access works over the same cable that brings 40 billion TV channels into your home, whereas DSL is a digital phone service that works over standard phone lines. Both offer three major advantages over normal dial-up connections:

- Cable and DSL are much faster than dial-up connections. A cable connection can be anywhere from 10 to 200 times faster than a dial-up connection, depending on the service you get. And the speed of a DSL line is comparable to cable.

- With cable and DSL, you are always connected to the Internet. You don't have to connect and disconnect each time you want to go online. No more waiting for the modem to dial your Service Provider and listening to the annoying modem shriek as it attempts to establish a connection.

- Cable and DSL do not tie up your phone line while you're online. With cable, your Internet connection works over your TV cables rather than your phone cables, so your phone service is not affected. (The cable Internet connection doesn't affect your regular cable TV service, either.) As for DSL, the Internet connection operates over your existing phone line without disrupting your regular phone service. In other words, DSL allows your computer to talk to the Internet and your teenage daughter to talk to her boyfriend at the same time, over the same phone line.

Unfortunately, there's no such thing as a free lunch, and the high-speed, always-on connections offered by cable and DSL do not come without a price. For starters, you can expect to pay a higher monthly access fee for cable or DSL. In most areas, cable runs about $50 per month. The cost for DSL service depends on the access speed you choose. In some areas, you can get a relatively slow (but still faster than a 56K modem) DSL connection for as little as $30 a month. For higher access speeds, DSL can cost as much as $200 per month or more. (Of course, prices may come down by the time you read this chapter, so be sure to check.) When you consider cost, remember that the ISP is included with both DSL and cable (and is covered by their fees).

In addition, both cable and DSL connections require extra equipment. Both require that your computer have a special type of connection called an Ethernet port. If your computer doesn't have one, you need to add an Ethernet interface card. (Fortunately, you can get a relatively inexpensive

---

What about ISDN?

ISDN, which stands for *Integrated Services Digital Network*, is a digital phone service that was popular a few years ago as an alternative to dial-up connections. ISDN allows data to be sent about twice as fast as a conventional phone line — up to 128 Kbps (kilobits per second) rather than 56 Kbps. As an added plus, a single ISDN line can be logically split into two separate channels, so you can carry on a voice conversation while your computer is connected to the Internet.

ISDN is inferior to cable and DSL connections in many ways, however. For starters, it's slower. ISDN may be twice as fast as a regular dial-up

connection, but a cable modem or DSL connection is at least ten times as fast and often even faster than that. Plus, ISDN is not an always-on connection, like cable or DSL is. With ISDN, you must dial and connect to the Internet each time you want to use it, much as you do with a regular dial-up connection. And, ISDN is more expensive than cable or DSL. In short, ISDN is fast becoming a thing of the past. It was a good idea for its time, but its time has passed. If you're using ISDN for your Internet access, you may want to consider switching to cable or DSL.

Ethernet card for about $25.) Cable and DSL require, besides the Ethernet port, their own modems, which can cost several hundreds of dollars. (In many cases, the cable or DSL company provides you with the modem as a part of its service.)

DSL stands for *Digital Subscriber Line,* but that won't be on the test.

Next, You Need a Service Provider

An *Internet Service Provider,* or *ISP,* is a company that charges you, usually on a monthly basis, for access to the Internet. The ISP has a bunch of modems connected to phone lines that you can dial in to. These modems are connected to a computer system, which is in turn connected to the Internet via a high-speed data link. The ISP's computer acts as a liaison between your computer and the Internet.

Typically, an ISP provides you with the following services in exchange for your hard-earned money:

- ✔ **Access to the World Wide Web:** Most ISPs let you access any Web site on the Internet from your computer. Some ISPs provide built-in filtering software that automatically blocks access to pornography and other objectionable Web sites.

- ✔ **Electronic mail:** The ISP assigns you an e-mail address that anyone on the Internet can use to send you mail. You can use Microsoft Outlook Express, which comes with Internet Explorer, to access your e-mail. See Chapter 10 for more information.

- ✔ **Access to Internet newsgroups:** In newsgroups, you can follow ongoing discussions about your favorite topics. Read all about newsgroups in Chapter 14.

- ✔ **Software to access the Internet:** In many cases, this software includes Microsoft Internet Explorer. Or it may include a different web browser, such as Netscape Navigator. (If your ISP doesn't provide Internet Explorer, you can obtain it free from Microsoft after you set up your Internet connection. Find out how later in this chapter, in the section "Finally, You Need Internet Explorer.")

- ✔ **Technical support, the quality of which varies greatly:** If you have trouble with your Internet connection, try calling your ISP's technical support line. If you're lucky, an actual human being who knows something about computers will pick up the phone and help you solve your problem. Next best: You're put on hold, but someone eventually answers and helps you. Not so good: The technical support line is always busy. Worse: You get a recording that says "All our support engineers are busy. Please leave a message, and we'll get back to you." Yeah, right.

Basically, two types of companies provide access to the Internet: commercial online services, such as America Online, CompuServe, and The Microsoft Network, and independent Internet Service Providers. The following sections describe the pros and cons of both types of providers and the Internet access they provide.

Online services

All the major online services enable you to connect to the Internet. On the plus side, you gain access to unique content that's available only to members of the online service. On the minus side, you pay for this extra service. The following are the pricing plans of the three major online services:

- ✔ **America Online (AOL):** The most popular online service, more than 29 million people subscribe to AOL. AOL has several pricing plans. The standard monthly plan gives you unlimited access to AOL and the Internet for $23.90 per month; if you prepay 12 months, the rate drops to $19.95 per month. The light usage plan gives you three hours per month for $4.95, with each additional hour costing $2.50. And the limited usage plan gives you five hours for $9.95 per month, with each additional hour costing $2.95.

✓ **CompuServe:** Running second in online service popularity is CompuServe, which claims more than 2.8 million users. CompuServe has two pricing plans. The best-value plan gives you 20 hours per month for $9.95, with each additional hour costing $2.95. The unlimited plan gives you unlimited access for $19.95 per month. You can lower this amount to $17 per month if you pay an entire year in advance.

America Online owns CompuServe, but at least for now, AOL and CompuServe continue to operate as separate online services.

✓ **The Microsoft Network (MSN):** MSN is the Microsoft attempt to challenge America Online and CompuServe. MSN offers unlimited access for $21.95 per month.

If you opt to use an online service as your Internet Service Provider, you need to carefully select the correct pricing plan for the number of hours you intend to use the service. To make this point, Table 2-1 shows the monthly cost for each of the preceding plans for monthly usages of 10, 20, 40, and 60 hours. As you can see, the actual monthly cost varies tremendously depending on which plan you select.

Table 2-1	Pricing Plans Compared			
	Number of Hours			
Price Plan	*10*	*20*	*40*	*60*
America Online, standard	$23.90	$23.90	$23.90	$23.90
America Online, light usage	$22.45	$47.45	$97.45	$147.45
America Online, limited Usage	$24.70	$54.20	$113.20	$172.20
CompuServe, unlimited	$19.95	$19.95	$19.95	$19.95
CompuServe, best value	$9.95	$9.95	$68.98	$127.95
The Microsoft Network, unlimited	$21.95	$21.95	$21.95	$21.95

I hear too many horror stories about families who have signed up for America Online or CompuServe, expecting the monthly bill to be only $9.95, only to discover a $200 bill the first month. The problem is that the kids discover the Internet one evening and end up spending four or five hours online every night for two weeks before the parents catch on.

Are the online services worth it?

Because you can access the Internet in less expensive ways, this question naturally comes up: "Are the extra features you get with an online service worth the extra cost?" This may sound like a cop-out, but that question has no right or wrong answer. The answer depends on whether you use and benefit from the additional features provided by online services.

One major advantage of online services is their organization. The Internet is a sprawling mess, and sometimes it's hard to find what you want. In contrast, online services are well organized. Information in online services is neatly arranged according to topic. Not so on the Internet.

Another benefit you can probably expect from your online service is customer service support. CompuServe and America Online both have large support staffs that can help to make sure that you get on and stay on the Internet without lots of technical headaches. The quality of technical support that comes with an ISP varies greatly from one ISP to the next.

Still, if you subscribe to an online service and then discover that you use it only to access the Internet, you may be better off canceling your online service subscription and signing up with a simple Internet Service Provider instead.

My advice: If you sign up for an online service, always start off with an unlimited-access plan. This type of plan may cost you $10 or $15 more if you end up not using it as much as you expect, but that's better than paying $50 to $100 more for exceeding the limited-usage plan. And make sure that all family members, including the kids, understand how the pricing works.

Basic Internet Service Providers

The alternative to using a commercial online service is to sign up with a basic Internet Service Provider, or ISP. ISPs provide the same Internet access that online services do, but they don't provide their own additional content. ISPs are invariably less expensive than commercial online services because they don't have the added expense that results from providing their own proprietary services.

Technically, any company that provides you with Internet access is an ISP, including commercial online services. However, I prefer to use the term *ISP* to refer to a company that specializes in providing only Internet access without providing a separate online service of its own.

You can choose from nationally known service providers, such as EarthLink or AT&T WorldNet Service, or you can select a local ISP. To find the ISPs in your area, check the *Yellow Pages* under Computers – Online Services and Internet (or a similar heading).

The changing role of online services

The sudden growth of the Internet has had a profound impact on established online services like CompuServe and America Online. In the past, online services required you to use software provided by the online service to access the information available at the service. For example, to access America Online, you must use special software provided by America Online. CompuServe works the same way.

All that is changing, however. Online services are discovering that users prefer to choose access software — so the providers are slowly but surely moving their services to a format that provides users with online access by means of standard Internet web browsers, such as Netscape Navigator and Internet Explorer.

These developments don't mean that online services are becoming part of the World Wide Web or that you can look forward to free CompuServe or America Online access. The online services will continue to offer distinctive subscriber-only features, such as discussion forums, file libraries, stock-quote services, and reference databases.

The gradual change means a move toward using the same software to access an online service and the World Wide Web and picking which browser program you prefer to use to access your online service.

These changes are evolving slowly. You can't change all at once the software used by millions of subscribers. But the change is certain, and within a few years all the major online services will let you use Internet Explorer or any other web browser to access their content.

In fact, MSN is already at that point. The latest version of MSN is Web based so that you can move seamlessly between Internet Web sites and The Microsoft Network without changing browsers.

Most ISPs offer unlimited access for $15 to $20 per month. Some offer a limited-hours plan for slightly less (for example, 40 hours for $10). Either way, the cost of using an ISP is likely to be less than the cost of using a commercial online service unless you end up using the Internet for only a few hours each month.

Both America Online and CompuServe let you access their services for $9.95 per month, if you use your own Internet Service Provider. In other words, you can access America Online or CompuServe by dialing into your own ISP rather than by dialing one of the AOL or CompuServe access numbers.

Finally, You Need Internet Explorer

Naturally, before you can begin to use Internet Explorer, you must install it on your computer. This section explains how.

As you may know, Internet Explorer is free. You can download it from any of several sites on the Internet, and you can use it without charge. Microsoft places no restrictions on how you can use it: At home or at the office, Internet Explorer is completely free.

How can the good people at Microsoft afford to distribute Internet Explorer for free? Because they're hoping that the browser will catch on like wildfire. Internet Explorers 3, 4, 5, and 5.5 were huge successes. Microsoft hopes to build on that success by offering Internet Explorer 6 at the same irresistible rate.

For sure, Microsoft plans to make plenty of money from Internet Explorer — not by selling the browser itself, but rather by establishing Internet Explorer as the standard Internet browser used by more people than any other browser. Microsoft then plans to make its money by selling the development tools that Web authors and software developers need to create interesting content that is viewable only with Internet Explorer.

Here are some of the ways you can obtain Internet Explorer 6:

✔ If you already have Internet access and are using another program (such as Netscape Navigator or an earlier version of Internet Explorer), you can download Internet Explorer 6 from the Microsoft Web site at www.microsoft.com/ie. Note that the download for Internet Explorer can take several hours if you don't have a cable or DSL connection. Better go to the local video store and rent a movie before proceeding. Or start the download just before you go to bed. The download should be finished by morning.

✔ If your computer runs the latest version of Windows, known as Windows XP, you already have Internet Explorer 6.

✔ If you sign up with an Internet Service Provider that uses Internet Explorer as its default browser, you may get a CD with Internet Explorer on it. But make sure that the service uses the latest version of Internet Explorer; some ISPs offer only older versions of Internet Explorer.

Internet Explorer has been through several major revisions. The current version, Internet Explorer 6, is among the more powerful web browsers available. If you have an earlier version (5.5, 5, 4, 3, 2, or 1), be sure to upgrade to Version 6 as soon as possible. You can find Internet Explorer 6 available for download at www.microsoft.com.

If your computer already has Internet Explorer but you're not sure what version, you can easily find out. Start Internet Explorer by clicking the Internet Explorer icon on your desktop or on the Windows taskbar. Then choose Help⇨About Internet Explorer. This action summons a dialog box that tells you which version of Internet Explorer is installed on your computer.

After you download the Internet Explorer file, exit from your web browser, open the folder into which you downloaded the file, and double-click the file's icon. The Internet Explorer setup program then installs Internet Explorer for you. (Depending on the browser you use, Internet Explorer may automatically install itself after the download finishes. If so, just sit back and enjoy the ride.)

If you don't want to contend with an hours-long download, you can get Internet Explorer 6 on CD from most computer stores for about $5, or you can order it from Microsoft in the USA by calling 800-458-2048.

To install the downloaded Internet Explorer 6 on your computer, just follow the instructions that appear when you go to the Internet Explorer download page. If you get Internet Explorer 6 on a CD, insert the CD in your CD-ROM drive and follow the instructions that appear on-screen.

The Internet Explorer 6 Setup program asks you several questions before it installs Internet Explorer on your computer. For starters, the Setup program asks whether you want to install all of Internet Explorer or just part of it. You have two choices:

- ✔ **Typical Set of Components:** Installs just those parts of Internet Explorer that you'll probably use, in Microsoft's opinion. This is the easiest and fastest way to install Internet Explorer.

- ✔ **Customize Your Installation:** Lets you pick exactly which parts of Internet Explorer you want to install. Use this option if you're choosy.

If you have plenty of disk space on your computer and don't mind a long download (as in several hours long unless you have a DSL or cable connection), I suggest that you opt for the Customize Your Installation option, and then select any of the Internet Explorer components that you think you may need. If you select the typical installation, you can always return to the download page later and pick up the components you didn't install the first time.

If you have Windows 98, Windows Millenium Edition (also known as Windows Me), or Windows 2000 and an Internet connection, you can upgrade to Internet Explorer 6 by clicking the Start button and then choosing Settings⇨ Windows Update. Performing these steps takes you to the Windows Update site, which automatically offers to install new Windows features, including Internet Explorer 6.

Now You Can Set Up Your Internet Connection

In the old days, setting up a connection to the Internet was a complicated affair best handled by computer experts with pocket protectors and tape on their glasses. But with Internet Explorer 6 and newer versions of Windows, configuring your computer to connect to the Internet is a simple, straightforward process. All you have to do is run a special program that handles all the configuration details for you.

Depending on the version of Windows you're using, the connection wizard is named either the Internet Connection Wizard or the New Connection Wizard. Either wizard helps you get connected to the Internet.

To set up an Internet Connection in Windows XP, you use the New Connection Wizard, as described in the following steps:

1. **Gather the information you need to configure your Internet connection.**

   You need the following information, which your Internet Service Provider should be able to supply:

   - The name of your Internet Service Provider

   - The telephone number you dial to connect to the Internet

   - The name and password you must use to access the system

   - Your IP address, unless an IP address is assigned automatically each time you log on

   - The DNS server address, which looks like a bunch of numbers with periods where they don't belong, as in 123.4.56.789

   - Your e-mail address and the address of your e-mail server

   - The address of your Internet news server

2. **Fetch your Windows installation disks or CD.**

   You may not need these, but the New Connection Wizard sometimes asks for them. Better keep your disks handy just in case.

3. **Start the New Connection Wizard.**

   Click the Start button on the taskbar and choose All Programs⇨ Accessories⇨Communications⇨New Connection Wizard.Internet Explorer⇨Connection Wizard. The New Connection Wizard comes to life, showing the dialog box in Figure 2-1.

Figure 2-1:
The New
Connection
Wizard
greets you
with a
friendly
welcome
message.

Another way to start the New Connection Wizard is to double-click the Internet Explorer icon on your desktop. If you don't have an Internet connection already set up, Internet Explorer automatically starts the New Connection Wizard for you.

4. Click Next.

The next screen of the New Connection Wizard appears, as shown in Figure 2-2. This screen lists the various types of connections the New Connection Wizard can help you make.

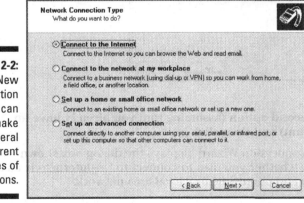

Figure 2-2:
The New
Connection
Wizard can
make
several
different
types of
connections.

5. **Select the Connect to the Internet option and click Next.**

The New Connection Wizard displays the screen shown in Figure 2-3, which describes three different ways it can help you set up an Internet connection:

- The first option enables you to set up a new Internet connection. Choose this option if you don't already have any type of Internet connection or an account with an Internet Service Provider. The Internet Connection Wizard uses your modem to dial in to a Microsoft computer that maintains a list of Internet Service Providers. A list of ISPs in your area appears, and you are granted the privilege of signing up with one of these providers and having your connection configured automatically.

- The second option lets you configure your Internet account manually.

- The third option lets you use a CD you have obtained from an Internet Service Provider to set up your connection.

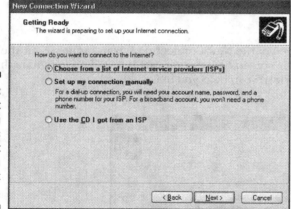

Figure 2-3:
The Internet
Connection
Wizard is
ready to set
up an
Internet
connection.

6. **Choose the second option (assuming that you already have an Internet account) and then click Next.**

The Internet Connection Wizard displays the dialog box shown in Figure 2-4, asking whether you plan to connect to the Internet via an ISP with a modem and phone line or a local area network.

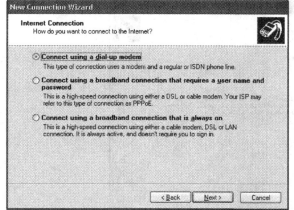

Figure 2-4:
The Internet Connection Wizard asks how you will connect to the Internet.

7. **Check the appropriate connection option and then click Next.**

    Assuming that you're connecting to an ISP via a telephone connection and a modem, the Wizard displays a dialog box similar to the one shown in Figure 2-5.

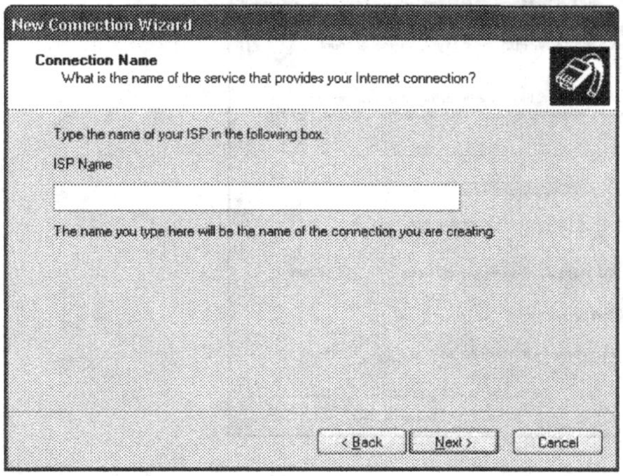

Figure 2-5:
Type a name for your connection.

8. **Type a name for your connection and then click Next.**

    The dialog box shown in Figure 2-6 appears.

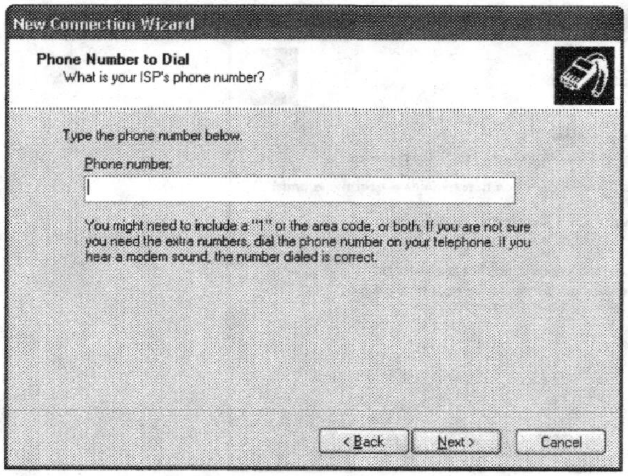

Figure 2-6:
The New
Connection
Wizard
wants to
know your
ISP's phone
number.

9. **Type the phone number for your service provider and then click Next.**

   The dialog box shown in Figure 2-7 appears next.

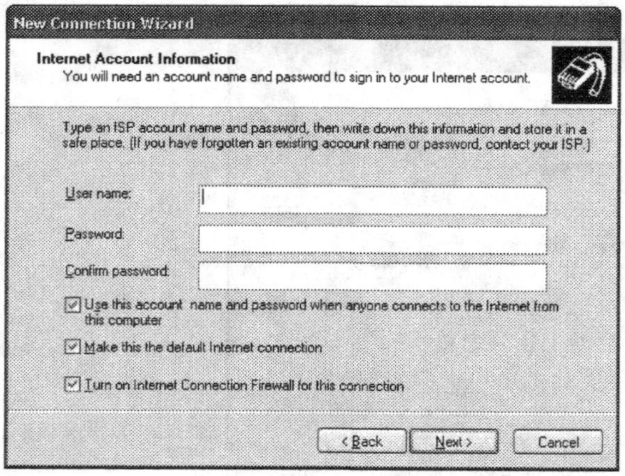

Figure 2-7:
The Internet
Connection
Wizard
wants to
know your
name and
password.

10. **Type your name and password and then click Next.**

    Your password isn't displayed when you type it, so you don't need to worry about anyone watching over your shoulder. If you click Next, the Internet Connection Wizard displays the dialog box shown in Figure 2-8.

Figure 2-8:
The New
Connection
Wizard has
done its job.

11. **Click Finish.**

    You're done with the New Connection Wizard. Now all that's left to do is to tell Outlook Express how to read your e-mail and newsgroups.

12. **Start Outlook Express by clicking the Start button on the Windows taskbar and then choosing E-mail: Outlook Express from the Start menu.**

    Outlook Express appears.

13. **Choose the Tools➪Accounts command.**

    This step summons the Accounts dialog box, as shown in Figure 2-9.

Figure 2-9:
The Internet
Accounts
dialog box
lets you
add mail
and news
accounts to
Outlook
Express.

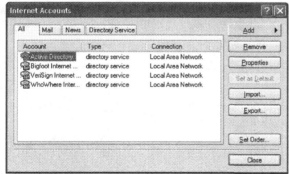

14. Click Add⇨Mail and configure your e-mail account.

This step summons a wizard that asks you for the information needed to set up your e-mail account. When asked, type your e-mail account information, clicking Next to move from one screen to the next, and click Finish when the Wizard reaches its last screen.

15. Click Add⇨News and configure your news account.

The wizard appears again, this time asking for information about your news account.

16. Click Close to dismiss the Accounts dialog box.

You're done!

Now, you can access the Internet by double-clicking the Internet Explorer icon that appears on your desktop. (If you opted to install the Active Desktop option when you installed Internet Explorer, you don't have to double-click the icon; a single click does the trick.) When the Connection Manager dialog box appears, click Connect and start exploring!

If you need to change any of the advanced settings for your Internet connection, click the Advanced button in Step 6 (refer to Figure 2-3) and then enter the information for the advanced settings you need. Do this only if your ISP uses a SLIP connection rather than a PPP connection or if your ISP tells you to set your browser to use a specific IP or DNS server address. The good news is that you don't have to know anything about what SLIP connections, IP addresses, or DNS server addresses mean. Just type the information your Internet Service Provider gives you and get on with it.

Part II
Embarking on a World Wide Web Adventure

The 5th Wave   By Rich Tennant

"What I'm looking for are dynamic Web applications and content, not Web innuendoes and intent."

In this part . . .

In this part of the book, you'll discover the basics of using Internet Explorer: how to start it, how to use it to browse the World Wide Web, how to look for and find the information you're interested in, how to keep track of your favorite places, and how to get help when you don't know what you're doing.

Part II is just the beginning of your Internet explorations. After you have these basics under your belt, you'll be ready to take on the most advanced topics covered in the last three parts of this book. But, as a great king once advised, it is best to begin at the beginning, and go on until you come to the end, and then stop. So sit back and prepare for Web Wonderland!

Chapter 3

Pushing Off

● ●

In This Chapter

▶ Starting Internet Explorer and understanding its screen

▶ Working with Explorer bars

▶ Understanding World Wide Web addresses

▶ Displaying pages on the World Wide Web

▶ Printing and saving Web pages

▶ Stopping a long download

▶ Finding information on a page

▶ Exiting Internet Explorer and disconnecting from the Internet

● ●

*A*fter you have your Internet connection in place and you've installed Internet Explorer, you're ready to begin your Internet explorations. This chapter shows you how to use the basic features of Internet Explorer to surf the Web. You won't gather intimate knowledge about all the nuances of using Internet Explorer — I save some of the more exotic features for later chapters. In this chapter, I focus on the foundation: how to start Internet Explorer and how to explore the Web, for example.

Starting Internet Explorer

The first step to surfing the Web using Internet Explorer is starting the program. You have at least three ways to start Internet Explorer:

Internet
Explorer

    ✔ Double-click the Internet Explorer icon that appears on your desktop, as shown in the margin. (If you don't have this icon on your desktop, you probably need to install Internet Explorer — read Chapter 2.)

If you or someone else has configured your Windows desktop to work in single-click mode, a single click of the Internet Explorer desktop icon is sufficient to start Internet Explorer.

✔ Click the Start button on the taskbar and then choose Internet: Internet Explorer.

✔ Click the small Launch Internet Explorer Browser icon that appears in the taskbar (as shown in the margin).

Whichever method you opt for, Internet Explorer grinds and churns for a moment. If you use a modem to connect to the Internet and you aren't already online, you're greeted by the Dial-up Connection dialog box, as shown in Figure 3-1. Type your user ID and password into the appropriate text boxes; click Connect to proceed.

Figure 3-1:
The Dial-up
Connection
dialog box.

After you click Connect, your computer automatically dials the phone number of your Internet Service Provider (ISP). If the modem volume is turned up, you hear a dial tone, two or three rings, and then a few moments of rather obnoxious squealing as the modems establish their connection.

After a connection is established, the Internet Explorer window appears and you're taken directly to your start page, as shown in Figure 3-2.

If you connect to the Internet via a cable modem, DSL connection, or high-speed network connection, you don't see the Dial-up Connection dialog box. Instead, Internet Explorer simply comes to life, as shown in Figure 3-2.

You can resize the Internet Explorer window just as you would any other window. I usually like to work with Internet Explorer maximized so that it fills the entire screen and displays as much of each Web page as possible. To maximize a window, click the Maximize button in the upper-right corner of the Internet Explorer window.

Figure 3-2:
Welcome to
Internet
Explorer 6!

After Internet Explorer dials into your ISP, you may be faced with a window in which you must type login information. For example, some ISPs require that you type your user ID and password, even though the Connection Manager knows your user ID and password. If your ISP tells you to type similar information, you have to follow its instructions.

Typing login information every time you access the Internet is a big-time hassle. Fortunately, Windows lets you create a special file, called a *dial-up script,* that supplies the information automatically whenever you dial up your ISP. Creating a dial-up script isn't rocket science, but it's a little more advanced than this chapter can handle. When you grow weary of typing this login information every time you call your ISP, skip to Chapter 18, which explains in detail how to create a dial-up script.

The Web page that appears when you start Internet Explorer may be different from the page shown in Figure 3-2, depending on how Internet Explorer is configured on your computer. If you would rather have Internet Explorer start with a different page, see Chapter 15 for instructions on changing the Internet Explorer home page.

Making Sense of the Internet Explorer Screen

Before I show you how to explore the Internet, later in this chapter, I want to pause for a moment to examine all the bells and whistles that Microsoft has loaded in the Internet Explorer window. Figure 3-3 shows the Internet Explorer window, maximized for your viewing pleasure, with some of the more important parts labeled for easy identification.

The following items on the Internet Explorer screen are worthy of note:

✔ **Title bar:** At the top of the window, the title bar always displays the name of the Internet page you are viewing. For example, in Figure 3-4 (shown in the following section), you can see that the title is "Welcome to MSN.com — Microsoft Internet Explorer."

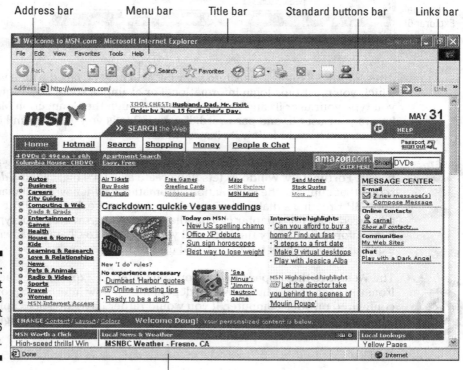

Address bar   Menu bar   Title bar   Standard buttons bar   Links bar

Status bar

Figure 3-3: The different parts of the Internet Explorer 6 window.

✔ **Menu bar:** Just as in any Windows program, the menu bar lives below the title bar. Internet Explorer's deepest secrets are hidden within the menus located on the menu bar.

✔ **Standard Buttons toolbar:** Beneath the menu bar is the Standard Buttons toolbar, which contains buttons you can click to perform common tasks. The purpose of each of these buttons is summarized in Table 3-1, but don't feel as though you need to understand these buttons at first. As you gain experience with Internet Explorer, the function of each of these buttons becomes apparent.

✔ **Address bar:** Beneath the Standard toolbar is the Address bar, which displays in the Address box the Internet address (or URL) of the page being displayed. You can click the down-arrow button on the right end of the Address box to see addresses of pages you recently visited, and you can type an Internet address in the Address box if you want to go to a specific Web page. (If you don't understand Internet addresses, don't worry. I explain them later in this chapter, under the heading "Understanding Web addresses.")

To the right of the Address box is the Go button, which you can click to cause Internet Explorer to go to the Web page indicated by the address you type in the Address box. Or, if you prefer, you can simply press the Enter key after typing an address.

✔ **Links toolbar:** Next to the Address bar is the Links toolbar, which houses a collection of frequently visited Web sites you can access with a single mouse click. For more information about the Links toolbar, see Chapter 5.

If a toolbar doesn't fit completely on the screen, Internet Explorer displays a double arrow in the upper-right corner of the toolbar. You can click the double arrow to display a menu that lists any toolbar buttons that don't fit in the Internet Explorer window.

✔ **Status bar:** The status bar, located at the bottom of the window, periodically displays useful information, such as what Internet Explorer is trying to do or how much progress it has made in downloading a large file.

One of the most useful things about the status bar is that a Secure Connection icon, which resembles a padlock, appears whenever you're viewing a page that uses encryption to protect sensitive data, such as credit card numbers or other confidential information. For more information about Internet privacy and security, see Chapter 17.

✔ **Scroll bars:** Located to the right and bottom of the window, the scroll bars appear and disappear as needed. Whenever Internet Explorer can't display on a single screen all the information on an Internet page, a scroll bar appears so that you can scroll to the hidden information.

Table 3-1	Buttons on the Internet Explorer Standard Buttons Toolbar
Button	**What It Does**
	Moves back to the most recently displayed page
	Moves forward to the page you most recently moved back from
	Cancels a time-consuming download
	Forces Internet Explorer to obtain a fresh copy of the current page
	Takes you to your start page
	Enables you to search the Internet quickly for topics of interest
	Displays a list of your favorite Internet locations
	Displays a list of sites you have recently visited
	Switches to the Outlook Express program so that you can send and receive e-mail
	Prints the current page
	Lets you edit the current Web page
	Lets you access a Microsoft Office 2000 discussion server
	Starts MSN Messenger for instant communications with your online friends

One other feature of the Internet Explorer screen that's important to know about but that isn't visible in Figure 3-3 is the Explorer bar. The Explorer bar is an area on the left side of the main Internet Explorer window area that comes and goes as needed. Internet Explorer has three different incarnations of the Explorer bar, known as the Search bar, Favorites bar, and History bar, which appear when you click the Search, Favorites, or History button on the Standard toolbar. You can see the Explorer bar in action in several places throughout this book.

Exploring the Explorer Bars

The leftmost area of the Internet Explorer window is sometimes taken over by *Explorer bars,* which appear to assist you with common tasks. The following list describes the most popular Explorer bars:

- ✔ **Search:** Helps you locate information on the Internet
- ✔ **Contacts:** Lists your address book contacts so that you can quickly send e-mail or an instant message
- ✔ **Favorites:** Lists the Web pages you visit frequently so that you can quickly access them
- ✔ **History:** Lists Web pages you have visited recently so that you can quickly return to them
- ✔ **Folders:** Lists folders on your computer so that you can quickly locate files

To summon an Explorer bar, choose the View➪Explorer Bar command and then choose from the list that appears the bar you want to use. Or, you can click the appropriate toolbar button to summon the Explorer bar without navigating through the menus. (Note that not all Explorer bars have a corresponding toolbar button.)

Figure 3-4 shows the Search bar in action. You can see how the Search bar takes up the left side of the Internet Explorer window.

If you want, you can enlarge or reduce the amount of window space occupied by an Explorer bar. Point your mouse at the border that separates the Explorer bar from the rest of the Internet Explorer window (the mouse pointer turns into a double-sided arrow when you're pointing at the border). Then, click the border and drag it to the left or right to change the size of the Explorer bar.

To get rid of the Explorer bar, click the small Close button that appears in the upper-right corner of the Explorer bar.

Figure 3-4:
The Search
bar in
action.

Internet Explorer comes configured with several other Explorer bars you may occasionally use:

- ✔ **Expedia:** Quick access to travel information
- ✔ **Search the Web:** Advanced search options
- ✔ **News:** News stories courtesy of MSN
- ✔ **Slate:** A popular online magazine
- ✔ **MSN Calendar:** A calendar datebook provided by MSN

You can download, besides these, even more Explorer bars from the Microsoft Web site by choosing the View⇨Explorer Bar⇨Add/Remove Explorer Bars command. It opens a separate window from which you can add or remove Explorer bars. Just follow the steps that appear in the window.

Oh, the Places You'll Go!

As the name Internet Explorer implies, its chief function is to enable you to explore the Internet. To do so, you need to know how to get around — that is, how to navigate from one Internet location to another. The following sections explain the Internet Explorer navigation features.

Understanding Web addresses

Just as every house in a neighborhood has a street address, every page on the World Wide Web has an Internet address. The Internet address of a Web page is also called a *Uniform Resource Locator* (or *URL*).

URLs are becoming commonplace in our society. Just think about how many times you've seen addresses such as www.whatever.com appear at the end of a television advertisement. These days, every company that advertises seems to have a Web page.

To use Internet Explorer effectively, you need to know the various parts that make up a typical URL Web address. Typing URLs isn't hard, but it takes some practice.

A URL consists of three parts, written as follows:

```
protocol://host_address/resource_name
```

- ✔ For World Wide Web pages, the *protocol* portion of the URL is always http (http stands for *Hypertext Transfer Protocol,* but you don't need to know that to use URLs).

- ✔ The *host address* is the Internet address of the computer on which the Web page resides (for example, www.dummies.com).

- ✔ The final part, the *resource name,* is a name assigned by the host computer to a specific Web page or other file. In many cases, the resource name contains additional slashes that represent directories on the host system. Most of the time, you can omit the resource name if you simply want to display the home page for a company's Web site.

Here are some examples of complete URLs:

```
http://www.yahoo.com
http://www.cbs.com/network/tvshows/mini/lateshow
http://vol.com/~infidel/halloween/halloween.html
```

Notice that all Web page addresses must be prefixed by http://. However, Internet Explorer cleverly adds the http:// automatically, so you don't have to type it yourself. Throughout this book, I leave off the http:// from any World Wide Web address.

Because Internet Explorer always lets you omit the protocol part (http://) and because you can often omit the resource name, the only URL component you usually need to worry about is the host address. Host addresses themselves consist of three components separated from one another by periods, usually called *dots:*

✔ The first part of the Internet address is usually www, to indicate that the address is for a page on the World Wide Web.

✔ The second part of the Internet address is usually a company or organization name, which is sometimes abbreviated if the full name is too long. Sometimes, this second part consists of two or more parts in itself, separated by periods. For example, in the address www.polis.iupui.edu, the second part is polis.iupui.

✔ The third and final part of an Internet address is a category that indicates the type of organization the name belongs to. The most common categories are

   • **gov:** Government agencies

   • **com:** Private companies

   • **edu:** Universities

   • **org:** Organizations

   • **net:** Networks

Putting these three address parts together, you get addresses, such as www.microsoft.com, www.nasa.gov, and www.ucla.edu.

Going to a specific page

What if a friend gives you the address of a Web page you want to check out? No problem. To visit a specific Web page for which you know the address, all you have to do is follow these simple steps:

1. **Click the mouse in the Address box, which you can find on the Address toolbar (refer to Figure 3-4).**

2. **Type the address of the Web page you want to retrieve.**

3. **Press Enter.**

Internet Explorer offers several time-saving features that can help you type Web addresses quickly:

✔ You don't have to type the www. that comes before most Web addresses and the .com that comes after most addresses. Instead, you can just type the middle portion of the Web address and then press Ctrl+Enter rather than just the Enter key. When you press Ctrl+Enter, Internet Explorer automatically adds http://www. and .com to your Web addresses.

Suppose that you want to go to the Microsoft Web site. You could do that by typing **www.microsoft.com** in the Address box and pressing the Enter key. Or, to save time, you could just type **microsoft** and press Ctrl+Enter. Internet Explorer changes microsoft to http://www.microsoft.com and then retrieves the page.

Note that this trick doesn't work for government or educational Web pages because their addresses end in .gov or .edu rather than in .com.

✔ A timesaving feature called AutoComplete keeps track of Web addresses you've recently typed. Then, AutoComplete watches as you type Web addresses and tries to anticipate which address you're typing. As soon as it thinks that it knows, it automatically fills in the rest of the address.

For example, if you recently visited www.microsoft.com and you type **www.mi**, AutoComplete automatically fills in www.microsoft.com as the complete address. If you visited www.yahoo.com and then type **www.ya**, AutoComplete fills in www.yahoo.com. If the address AutoComplete suggests is indeed the address you want to type, just press Enter. Otherwise, keep typing — the address AutoComplete suggests disappears the instant you type another letter.

✔ Internet Explorer keeps on the Address bar a list of Web sites you've recently visited. Just click the down-arrow that appears to the right of the Address bar to reveal this list, and then click the address you want to go to. (If you're allergic to your mouse, press Ctrl+down arrow to reveal the Address bar list.)

Many Web addresses are complicated — complicated enough that typing them without making a mistake is difficult. Fortunately, if you already have the Web address in another document, such as a word processing document or e-mail message, you can always copy and paste it into the Internet Explorer Address box. Assuming that Internet Explorer is already running and that you have opened in another window the document that contains the address you want to copy, you can paste the address into Internet Explorer by following these steps:

1. **From Internet Explorer, press Alt+Tab to call up the document or e-mail message that contains the address you want to copy.**

   You may have to press Alt+Tab several times to bring up the document, depending on what other programs are running.

2. **Highlight the entire address and then press Ctrl+C to copy the address to the Windows Clipboard.**

   If you're a mouse fan, you can choose Edit⇨Copy.

3. **Press Alt+Tab again to return to Internet Explorer.**

4. **Click in the Address box on the Address toolbar.**

5. **Press Ctrl+V to paste the address.**

   Or, you can use the Edit⇨Paste command.

6. **Press Enter.**

Following the links

The most popular method of navigating through the Internet is by following links. A *link* is a bit of text or a graphic on one Web page that leads you to another Web page. A link may lead to another page at the same Web site, or it may lead to a page at a different Web site altogether.

You can easily identify the text links on a Web page because they're underlined and displayed in colors different from the rest of the text. For example, Figure 3-2 is filled with links: Air Tickets, Buy Books, and Buy Music, for example.

In addition to text links, many Web pages contain *graphical links* — graphics you can click to jump to another Web page. Unlike text links, graphical links are not identified with a special color or underlining. But you can spot them by watching the mouse pointer as you glide it over the graphic. If the mouse pointer changes from an arrow to a pointing finger, you know that you've found a link.

In some graphical links, the page you're taken to depends on where in the graphic you click. For technical reasons you don't want to know, this type of graphical link is called an *image map*.

In most cases, Web page designers try to make their graphical links obvious by including text next to them. For example, Figure 3-5 shows the Web page for the National Park Service, which sports the following graphical links:

- ✔ National Park Service Museum Collections: American Revolutionary War
- ✔ Visit Your Parks
- ✔ And Bring Your National Parks Pass
- ✔ Links to the Past
- ✔ Nature Net
- ✔ Park Smart
- ✔ Info Zone

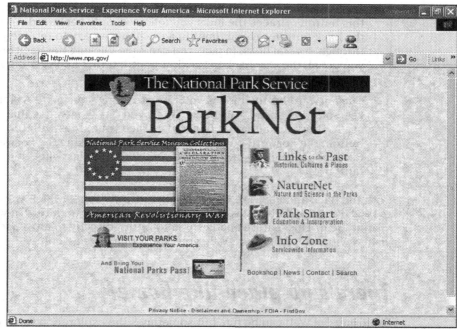

Figure 3-5:
The National
Park Service
home page
(www.nps.
gov).

You can tell where a link leads by moving the mouse pointer over it. This action displays a message on the status bar indicating the address of the page that is displayed if you click the link. For example, if you point the mouse at the Park Smart link on the National Park Service page, the status bar displays this message:

```
http://www.nps.gov/intersp/pksmart.htm
```

Yes, you can go back

Exploring links on the Web can be like exploring paths in the woods. You see a link that looks promising, so you take it. The page the link leads to has other links that seem interesting, so you pick one and take it. And so it goes until pretty soon you're lost. You should have marked your path with bread crumbs.

Fortunately, Internet Explorer lets you retrace your steps easily. Two buttons on the Standard Buttons toolbar exist for just this purpose:

✔ The Back button moves backward along the path you've taken. Clicking this button retraces the links you followed, only backward. You can click the Back button several times in a row if necessary to retrace your steps through several links. In fact, you can keep clicking the Back button until you get all the way back to the first page Internet Explorer displayed when you started it up.

✔ The Forward button moves you forward along your path. As long as you keep plowing ahead, this button is grayed out — meaning that you can't use it. However, after you begin to retrace your steps with the Back button, the Forward button becomes active. Clicking the Forward button takes you to the page where you were when you last clicked the Back button.

Both the Back and Forward buttons sport a down arrow, which you can click to reveal a list of Web pages you've recently visited in the order in which you visited them. This feature enables you to return directly to any page you've visited without having to retrace your steps one page at a time.

There's no place like home!

Exploring the Web can be fun, but sometimes the exploration turns out to be a wild goose chase. Fortunately, Internet Explorer can bail you out if you find yourself hopelessly lost, by transporting you instantly back to your *home page* — the page that pops up first when you start Internet Explorer. To transport yourself back to your home page, follow these simple steps:

1. **Click your heels together three times.**

2. **Say, "There's no place like home" three times.**

3. **Click the Home button (shown in the margin).**

If you prefer, you can skip Steps 1 and 2.

If you want to change your start page, may I recommend Chapter 15?

It's all history now

Internet Explorer automatically keeps track of the pages you've visited not only during your current Internet session, but also in past sessions. To quickly return to one of these pages, click the History button on the Standard Buttons toolbar. The History bar appears on the left side of the Internet Explorer window, as shown in Figure 3-6.

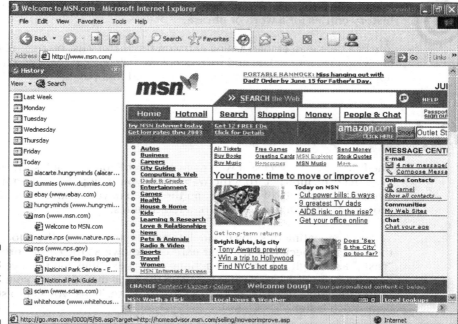

Figure 3-6:
Step right
up to the
History bar.

As you can see, the History bar lists the Web pages you've visited today and in past weeks. To return to a page, first click Today or one of the previous week's history folders. A list of Web sites appears, showing all previous stops on your Web page tour. You can then click the site you want to revisit.

If you have visited more than one page from a particular Web site, the History Bar organizes those pages under a folder icon that represents the site. For example, three pages are listed under the NPS (www.nps.com) Web site shown in Figure 3-6.

To make the History bar disappear, click the History button again or click the Close button in the upper-right corner of the History bar.

Don't forget that every place you visit is recorded in the History folder. Thus, the History folder provides a record of where you've been and what you've seen — and that can be incriminating!

If your kid denies that he's been sneaking peeks at www.playboy.com, pop up the History folder and find out. Pretty tricky, eh? (Of course, if your kid reads this book, he will know about this trick — and the next one. Better tear out this page before anyone else sees it.)

You can also click the Search icon at the top of the History bar to search your history entries for a word or phrase.

You can delete an embarrassing entry on the History list by right-clicking the entry you want to delete and then choosing Delete from the menu that appears. Poof! It's as though you never visited that page.

Refreshing a Page

The first time you access a Web page, Internet Explorer copies the entire page over the Internet from the Web site to your computer. Depending on the size and complexity of the page and the speed of your connection, this process can take a few seconds or a few minutes.

To avoid repeating this download, Internet Explorer saves the information for the page in a special area of your hard disk known as the *cache* (pronounced "cash," as though it's worth something). The next time you retrieve the same page from the Web, your computer gets the page directly from your hard disk rather than downloads it again from the Web site. Thus, you get to see the page much faster.

What happens if the page has changed since the last time you downloaded it? Most Web pages don't change very often, but some do. In fact, some pages change every day, and some change even more often. For example, pages that show trading information for a stock or the current bid price for an auction change frequently. For these types of pages, you can force Internet Explorer to refresh its view of the page.

 To refresh a page, all you have to do is click the Refresh button and then twiddle your thumbs while Internet Explorer downloads the page. Refreshing a page takes longer than grabbing it from your hard disk, but at least you know that the information is current.

If you prefer to cling to the keyboard, you can press F5 rather than click the Refresh button.

Internet Explorer has an Offline feature you can use to download new versions of a Web page automatically on a regular basis. You can find everything you need to know about this feature in Chapter 8.

Stop! Enough, Already!

Every once in a while, you wander into a Web page you could do without. The link that led you to the page may have looked interesting, but after you get there, the page isn't what you expected. According to Murphy's law, that page also is the page with a 800KB graphic that takes forever to download.

 Fortunately, you're not forced to sit and wait while a large graphic you don't want downloads. All you have to do is click the Stop button, and Internet Explorer cancels the download of the current page. The portion of the page that has already made it to your computer continues to be displayed, but anything that hasn't yet arrived won't. You can then click the Back button to go back to the preceding page.

If you're a keyboard junkie, you stop a page from downloading by pressing Esc.

If you're not sure whether a page has finished downloading, watch for these clues:

- ✔ The Windows flag logo that appears in the upper-right corner of the Internet Explorer window waves while the page is downloading. When the page is finished, the flag stops waving.

- ✔ The status bar displays the message Done when the page is finished. While the page is downloading, the status bar flashes various messages that indicate which parts of the page are being downloaded.

 Sometimes, you go to a page that appears to remain blank while a large graphic is downloading. In many cases, simply scrolling the page a bit reveals text that has already been downloaded to your computer, which (for some reason) Internet Explorer has yet to display. If you find yourself staring at a blank page that appears to be in the midst of downloading a large graphic, try clicking one of the scroll bars just to see whether any text is hiding.

Working in Full-Screen View

The Internet Explorer menus and toolbars are nice, but sometimes they get in the way — especially when you're viewing a Web page that is chock full of information. To see more of the Web and less of the Internet Explorer menus and toolbars, switch to full-screen view by choosing View➪Full Screen or pressing F11.

Figure 3-7 shows how the National Park Service Web page appears when displayed in full-screen view. As you can see, the menu bar, Address bar, and status bar have disappeared, and the Standard Buttons toolbar has been reduced to a smaller toolbar at the top of the screen. To return Internet Explorer to its normal view, press F11 again or click the Restore button that appears in the upper-right corner of the screen.

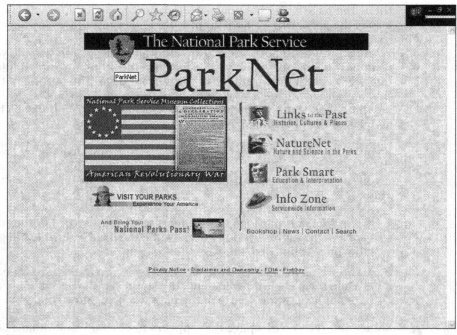

Figure 3-7:
Internet
Explorer in
full-screen
view.

Printing a Web Page

If you find a page with really interesting information that you want to have a hard copy of, all you have to do is print the page. Make sure that your printer's turned on and ready to go and then follow these steps:

1. **Choose File➪Print.**

   The Print dialog box appears, as shown in Figure 3-8.

2. **Stare at the Print dialog box for a moment.**

   If you have more than one printer at your disposal, make sure that the correct printer is selected. If you want to print more than one copy of the page, change the Number of Copies setting.

3. **Click OK.**

4. **Wait a moment while your printer grinds and whirls.**

A faster way to print a Web page — assuming that you want only one copy and you know that the correct printer has already been selected as your default printer — is to simply click the Print button on the toolbar.

Figure 3-8:
The Print
dialog box.

Opting for print options

The Options tab in the Print dialog box lets you control several aspects of how a Web page is printed. The first set of options are for pages that are laid out in two or more *frames,* which display content independently of one another. Internet Explorer gives you three options for dealing with frames:

✔ **As laid out onscreen:** Prints all the frames together, as they appear on the screen.

✔ **Only the selected frame:** Prints only the frame you've selected. This option is available only if you select a frame before calling up the Print dialog box.

✔ **All frames individually:** Prints separately all the frames that make up the page.

The Options tab also has two options related to links that appear on the page you're printing:

✔ **Print all linked documents:** Prints not only the current Web page, but also any pages that appear as links on the page you're printing

✔ **Print table of links:** Prints a list of all the links that appear on the page

Laying out your page

The File➪Page Layout command lets you tweak the appearance of your printed pages by summoning the dialog box shown in Figure 3-9.

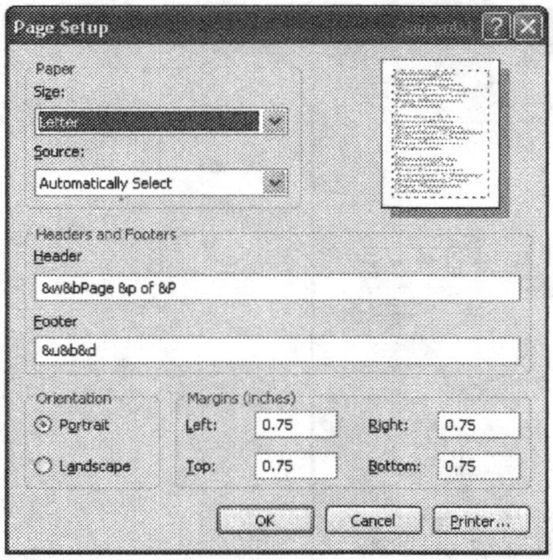

Figure 3-9:
The Page
Setup
dialog box.

The following paragraphs describe the page-layout options you can set from this dialog box:

- **Paper size:** The most common choices are Letter and Legal, but other page sizes are available. The important thing about this setting is to make sure that it corresponds to the type of paper you put in your printer. If you put letter-size paper in your printer but set this option to Legal, your pages don't print properly.

- **Paper source:** If you have more than one way to feed paper to your printer, this option lets you choose the one you want to use.

- **Header and Footer:** These fields let you set up information to be printed at the top and bottom of each page. The default settings for these options are to print the page title and page number in the header and the URL and the date in the footer.

  You can customize the information you want to appear in the header and footer, if you dare. Unfortunately, the road to customized headers and footers is paved with nerdy ampersand codes, such as &w, &p, and &b. Take a deep breath and look over the list of codes shown in Table 3-2. Then, twiddle with the header and footer fields if you can still see straight.

- **Portrait or Landscape:** This setting specifies the orientation of the printed pages, either Portrait (the long edge of the paper is vertical) or Landscape (the long edge of the paper is horizontal).

- **Margins:** You set the top, bottom, left, and right margins.

Table 3-2   Nerdy Codes You Can Use in a Page Header or Footer

Code	Explanation
&w	The window title, which is usually the title of the Web page.
&u	The URL (address) of the Web page.
&d	Short-format date.
&D	Long-format date.
&t	Time in regional format.
&T	Time in 24-hour format.
&p	Current page number.
&P	Number of pages in document.
&&	Prints an ampersand (&).
&b	The first time this code appears, the text that follows is centered. The second time the code appears, the text that follows is aligned with the right margin.

Using Print Preview

If you want to see how a page will appear on paper before you send it to your printer, choose the File⇨Print Preview command. A Print Preview screen appears, as shown in Figure 3-10.

The toolbar that appears at the top of the Print Preview screen sports buttons you can use to view the preview page, print the page, or return to Internet Explorer without printing the page. These buttons are listed for your enjoyment in Table 3-3.

Table 3-3   Buttons on the Print Preview Toolbar

Button	What It Does
Print...	Prints the page
▨	Summons the Page Setup dialog box
⇇	Goes to the first page of the printout
⇐	Goes to the preceding page

Continued

Table 3-3 *(continued)*

Button	What It Does
Page 2	Lets you go to a specific page
⇒	Goes to the next page
⇒⇒	Goes to the last page
🔍+	Zooms in for a closer look
🔍-	Zooms back out
75%	Selects the zoom factor
Help	Summons Help
Close	Closes the preview window without printing the page

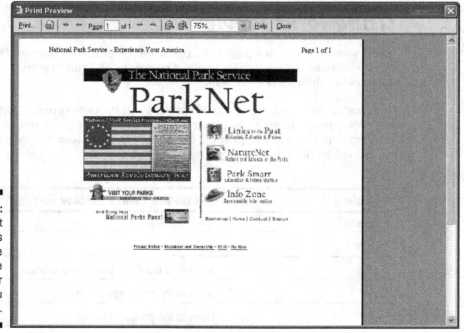

Figure 3-10:
Print Preview lets you see how a page will appear before you print it.

Changing the Font Size

If you consistently find that the text displayed on the Internet is too small, you may want to visit your ophthalmologist. On the other hand, if every once in a while you come across a page you have to squint at to see, the problem may not be with your eyes; it may be that the text is simply displayed too small.

Fortunately, Internet Explorer provides a simple solution for too-small text. To change the font size, choose View▷Text Size. This command leads to another menu that lists five font sizes: Largest, Larger, Medium, Smaller, and Smallest. Click the size you want.

 You can also use the Size button to change the font size. When you click the Size button, all the text on a page jumps to a larger size. Each time you click the Size button, the text size increases — until you get to the largest possible size. Clicking the Size button once more returns you to the smallest size.

Unfortunately, the Size button isn't normally displayed on the Internet Explorer Standard toolbar. To display the Size button, choose View▷Toolbars▷Customize. This command summons a dialog box that has two side-by-side list boxes. The one on the right lists the buttons that appear on your toolbar; the one on the left lists buttons you can add to the toolbar. Click the Size button in the left list box and click Add to add the Size button to the toolbar. Finally, click Close. The Size button now appears on your toolbar.

Saving a Web Page

You can save the contents of any Web page to a file on your computer by following these steps:

1. **Choose File▷Save As.**

   A dialog box like the one shown in Figure 3-11 appears.

2. **Select a suitable location for the file.**

   By default, Internet Explorer saves the file in your My Documents folder. If this isn't an appropriate location, you can browse your way to a better locale.

3. **Type in the File Name field a name for the file you want to save.**

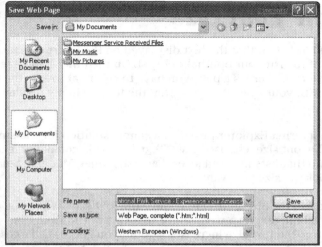

Figure 3-11:
The Save
Web Page
dialog box.

4. **Choose the file type in the Save As Type field.**

   You have four choices:

   - **Web Page, complete:** Saves all the files required to display the page, graphics and all
   - **Web Archive, single file:** Saves the Web page along with all its graphic and other elements as a single file, suitable for e-mailing to your friends
   - **Web Page, HTML only:** Saves the page complete with formatting but doesn't save auxiliary files, such as graphic or sound files
   - **Text File:** Saves the text without the formatting information

5. **Click the Save button.**

If you don't want to save the entire page as a text file, you can select the text you do want to save and then press Ctrl+C to copy it. Next, switch to a word processing program, such as Microsoft Word, open an existing document or create a new document, and then press Ctrl+V to paste the copied text into the document.

Finding Text

Sometimes, you stumble across a large page of text that you know contains some useful tidbit of information, but you can't seem to locate what you want among all those words. When this happens, you can use the Find command to locate text on the page. Simply follow these steps:

1. **Choose Edit⇨Find (or press Ctrl+F).**

   The Find dialog box appears, as shown in Figure 3-12.

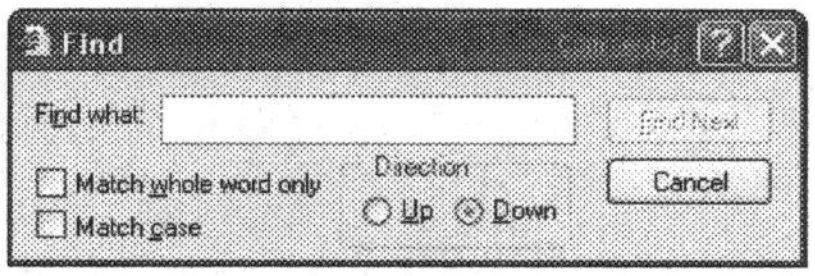

Figure 3-12:
The Find
dialog box.

2. **In the Find What text box, type the text you want to find.**
3. **Click Find Next.**

   Internet Explorer finds the first occurrence of the text on the current page. The Find dialog box remains active so that you can quickly find additional occurrences of the text.
4. **Keep clicking Find Next until you find the text you want.**
5. **Click Cancel to close the Find dialog box.**

Keep in mind that the Find command searches for text only on the current page; it doesn't search the Internet for other text references to what you're trying to find. To do that type of search, you must use one of the search services I describe in Chapter 4.

Exiting Internet Explorer

After you finish browsing the Web, you can exit Internet Explorer by using any of these techniques:

✔ Choose File⇨Close.
✔ Click the Close button, located in the upper-right corner of the Internet Explorer window. (It's the one with an X in it.)
✔ Press Alt+F4.

After closing Internet Explorer, you should disconnect from your Internet Service Provider. To do so, double-click the modem connection icon displayed in the right corner of the Windows taskbar to bring up the Connected dialog box, and then click the Disconnect button.

Some Internet Service Providers still insist on charging you for Internet access on an hourly basis. If your ISP charges you by the hour, be aware that connect-time charges continue to accumulate if you close Internet Explorer but forget to disconnect from your ISP. The extra time doesn't hurt if you pay a flat monthly rate with unlimited access, but if you're paying $2.50 or $2.95 per hour, you don't want to remain accidentally connected overnight!

2. In the right of the text box, type the ... you want to find

a. text_find.exe.

3. ...

4. ...

5. ...

Chapter 4

Searching the Web

● ●

In This Chapter

▶ Searching for information on the Web with the Internet Explorer Search bar

▶ Fooling with the Search bar

▶ Searching in the Address box

▶ Using search services, such as AltaVista, Lycos, and Yahoo!

● ●

Many people think of the Internet as a vast library of online information, but the Internet hardly resembles a library. Libraries are run by compulsive neat freaks known as *librarians,* whose mission in life is to make sure that, at least within their libraries, there is a place for everything and everything is in its place. Unlike a library, the Internet has no librarian. No single person or organization is officially in charge of what goes on the Internet. Anyone can put anything on the Internet, and no one is responsible for making sure that new entries are cataloged in any way, shape, or form.

Fortunately, all is not lost. Several excellent search services are available to help you locate information on the Internet. Although none of these services is truly comprehensive, several of them come pretty close. No matter what you're looking for, these services are likely to turn up a few Internet sites that pertain to your topic.

Internet Explorer has a built-in search feature, the Search bar, that makes searching the Internet simpler than ever. This chapter shows you how to use the Search bar to find the pages you're looking for.

Finding Stuff Fast

The easiest way to locate information on the Internet is to use the *Search bar*. This pane appears on the left side of the Internet Explorer window when you click the Search button on the Standard toolbar. The Search bar is designed to enable you to snoop around for information via a search service while simultaneously viewing a Web page.

The Search bar is a great time-saver. You can use it to look for Web pages, addresses, company or organization home pages, online encyclopedia articles, or newsgroup postings. Plus, the Search bar can search more than one search service for the information you're looking for. If the information doesn't turn up in one search service, odds are that you'll find it in another.

To use the Search bar, follow these directions:

1. **Click the Search button on the Standard toolbar.**

   The Search bar appears, as shown in Figure 4-1.

2. **Select the type of information you want to search for by clicking one of the options listed under Choose a Category for Your Search.**

   You can use the Search bar to search for Web pages, personal home or e-mail addresses, company home pages, or maps.

   You can click the More link to reveal two additional categories of searches: Look Up a Word and Find a Picture.

3. **Type in the text box next to the Search button the word or phrase you're looking for.**

   For example, type the word **arachnid** in the text box.

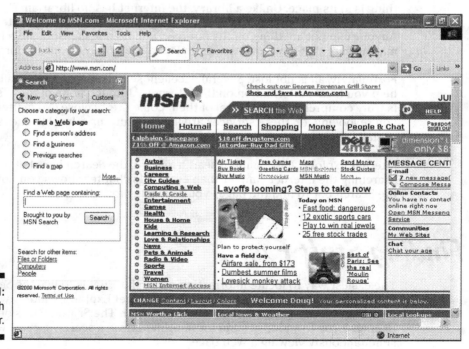

Figure 4-1:
The Search
bar.

4. Click the Search button.

Your search request is submitted to the first search service — for Web page searches, the MSN Search Web index is accessed first.

When the search service completes its search, the results of the search appear on the Search bar, as shown in Figure 4-2.

Figure 4-2: Eureka!

5. If you find something that looks promising, click it.

Internet Explorer displays on the right side of the Internet Explorer window the page you selected. Meanwhile, the Search bar remains visible on the left side of the window so that you can choose a different link.

6. If nothing looks promising, click the link for the next set of entries.

Each search service displays only a certain number of *hits* (found Web pages) at a time, typically 10 or 15. If none of the hits at the top part of the Search bar looks promising, scroll to the bottom of the Search bar and locate a link that says something along the lines of Next. Clicking this link displays additional results for the search.

7. If you still can't find what you're looking for, click the Next button (shown in the margin) at the top of the Search bar.

Doing this step switches you to another search service, which probably produces different results from the preceding search.

Here are some thoughts to keep in mind when searching:

 New

- ✔ If the search comes up empty, try again using a different search word or phrase. For example, try *spider* rather than *arachnid*. You can begin a new search by clicking the New button (shown in the margin), at the top of the Search bar.

- ✔ When picking search words, try to think of words that are specific enough that you don't end up with thousands of hits but general enough to encompass the topic you're trying to find.

- ✔ Most search services list results in sorted order, with the pages that most closely match your search criteria presented first. In particular, if you search with two words, the pages that contain both words are listed before pages in which just one of the words appears. For example, if you search for *Renaissance painting,* pages that contain both words — which are more likely to be about Renaissance paintings — appear before pages that contain the word *Renaissance* but not *painting* or pages that contain the word *painting* but not *Renaissance.*

- ✔ Each of the search services available from the Search bar has its own set of options for customizing your search. For example, you may be able to indicate whether the search should be case sensitive (so that *RAM* is not the same as *ram*) or whether to search for pages that contain all the words you type (so that if you search for Renaissance painting, you see only pages that contain both the words *Renaissance* and *painting*) or pages that contain any of the words you type (in which case you see pages that contain *Renaissance* but not *painting* and vice versa.)

Customizing the Search Bar

You can customize the search services used by the Search bar, and change the order in which search services are accessed, by clicking Customize on the Search bar's toolbar. This action brings up the Customize Search Settings page in a separate window, as shown in Figure 4-3.

The Customize Search Settings page has a separate section for each category of information you can search for from the Search bar. Within each category, you find one or more search services with check boxes and a list box that indicates the order in which the search services are used by the Search bar.

As you can see, some of the services listed are checked, and others aren't. To add or remove a service from the Search bar, just click the service's check box.

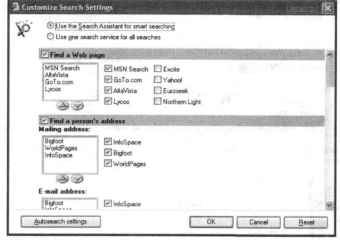

Figure 4-3:
The
Customize
Search
Settings
window.

To change the order in which the search services are accessed, first select the service whose order you want to change by clicking its entry in the list box. Then, click the up or down arrows that appear beneath the list box to move the service you selected.

At the bottom of the Customize Search Settings page, you find a list box that lists all the search categories. You can use this list box to change the order in which the search categories appear on the Search bar.

After you have finished playing with the search settings, click the Update button that appears at the bottom of the Customize Search Settings page to apply any changes you made to your Search bar.

Searching from the Address Bar

One of the niftier Internet Explorer features is *Autosearch,* a way to search the Internet quickly for specific information without even going to a search service. Simply type **Find** or **Go** or a question mark in the Address box, followed by the word or words you want to look up. For example, to search for *arachnid,* type **find arachnid**, **go arachnid**, or **? arachnid** in the Address box. Internet Explorer picks a search service to look up the word or phrase you typed and displays the results on the Search bar, as shown in Figure 4-4.

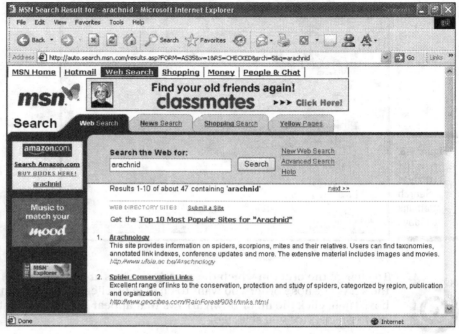

Figure 4-4:
Type **find arachnid** to search for spidery stuff automatically.

Notice that the Web address on the Address bar in Figure 4-4 has been changed from **find arachnid** to a long, almost incomprehensible address that searches the Microsoft Autosearch site for the word *arachnid*. Internet Explorer makes this change automatically.

You can customize the way Autosearch works by following these steps:

1. **Click the Search button.**

   The Search bar appears.

2. **Click the Customize button at the top of the Search bar.**

   The Customize Search Settings window appears (refer to Figure 4-3).

3. **Click the Autosearch Settings button at the bottom of the Customize Search Settings window.**

   The Customize Autosearch Settings dialog box appears, as shown in Figure 4-5.

4. **Choose the search service you want to use for Autosearch.**

   The drop-down list lets you choose from eight different search services. The default choice is MSN.

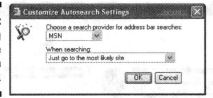

Figure 4-5:
Customizing
the
Autosearch
feature.

5. **Choose how you want the search results displayed.**

   The drop-down list gives you several choices: You can display the search results in the main browser window, go directly to the most likely page, or display the search results on the Search bar and go to the most likely page.

6. **Click OK to dismiss the Customize Autosearch Settings dialog box.**

   You're returned to the Customize Search Settings window.

7. **Click OK to dismiss the Customize Search Settings window.**

   You're done!

Using Popular Search Services

The Internet Explorer Search bar lets you quickly access nine popular search services. If you find the narrow confines of the Internet Explorer Search bar limiting, you can also access the search services directly. To work with a search service in the entire Internet Explorer window, type the service's Internet address in the Address box and press Enter.

Each of these services has its own peculiar approach to categorizing information and searching its database in response to your queries. As a result, you should experiment with the various services to determine which one best suits your needs.

AltaVista

www.altavista.com

AltaVista is a large and fast catalog of individual Web pages and Usenet discussion groups found throughout the Internet. The search network uses a special program, a *spider,* that automatically reads and catalogs 3 million Web pages every day. The AltaVista catalog lists tens of millions of Web pages. Figure 4-6 gives you a glimpse of the AltaVista home page.

Figure 4-6:
AltaVista.

One of the drawbacks of AltaVista is its huge size. Many searches return thousands (or even millions) of Web pages. For example, when I searched AltaVista for the word *arachnid,* it found 19,955 pages. As a result, you have to plow through pages and pages of results looking for Web sites that might contain the information you're looking for.

However, AltaVista does offer powerful advanced search capabilities. If you're a bit of a computer guru and want a powerful search tool, AltaVista is worth checking out.

EuroSeek

www.euroseek.com

As its name implies, EuroSeek is a search services that focuses on Web sites in Europe. One of the unique strengths of EuroSeek is its ability to operate in any of nearly 30 languages. So, if you're more comfortable searching in Bulgarian or Lithuanian, EuroSeek is the place to go. Figure 4-7 shows the EuroSeek home page.

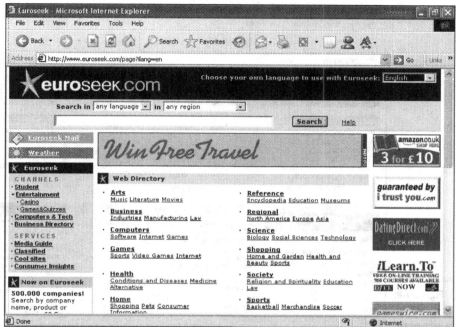

Figure 4-7:
EuroSeek.

Excite

`www.excite.com`

The Excite search service catalogs more than 50 million Web pages. In addition to this huge index of Web pages, Excite also features thousands of reviews prepared by the Excite services editorial staff; it also indexes Usenet newsgroup postings and classified ads. The Excite opening page appears in Figure 4-8.

Google

`www.google.com`

My personal favorite search site is Google. As you can see in Figure 4-9, the beauty of Google is its simplicity: the Search page isn't cluttered by a bunch of extraneous links, advertisements, and other paraphernalia. Instead, the Google page focuses on what it does best: search for words or phrases. And Google has a huge and fast database of Web pages to facilitate its searches.

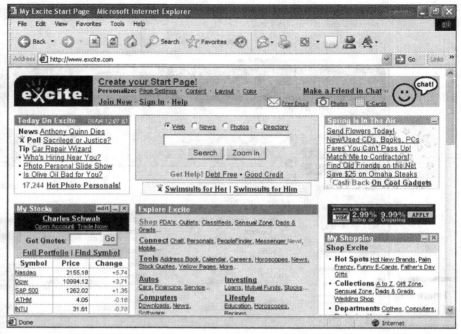

Figure 4-8:
Excite.

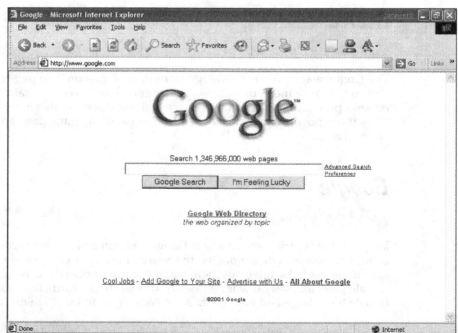

Figure 4-9:
Google.

That isn't to say that Google doesn't have other features. You can click the Advanced Search link to reveal advanced search options or click the Google Web Directory link to see a categorized directory of Web sites.

GoTo.com

```
www.goto.com
```

As Figure 4-10 shows, the GoTo.com home page isn't cluttered by advertisements, like most search services' home pages. That's because GoTo.com doesn't make its money by selling space for banner ads. Instead, advertisers pay GoTo.com for priority placement in its search results.

Lycos

```
www.lycos.com
```

Lycos is a huge Web index compiled by the computer nerds at Carnegie Mellon University. Lycos is primarily a keyword search tool, but it also includes categories you can browse. It's my personal favorite when I'm looking for obscure information. Figure 4-11 shows the Lycos opening page.

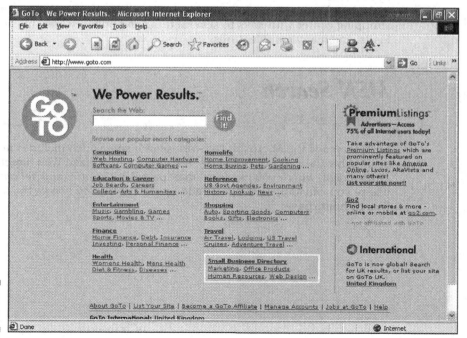

Figure 4-10:
GoTo.com

Figure 4-11:
Lycos.

Lycos includes such features as a travel guide that lets you reserve flights and a hotel room, view city maps or driving directions, and more; an online shopping center with links to several thousand online stores; music downloads; and many more features.

MSN Search

search.msn.com

MSN Search is the Microsoft Network search site, which includes not only a searchable database of Web sites, but also a categorized Web directory; *White Pages,* where you can look up personal addresses; and *Yellow Pages,* where you can look up business addresses. Figure 4-12 shows the MSN Search home page.

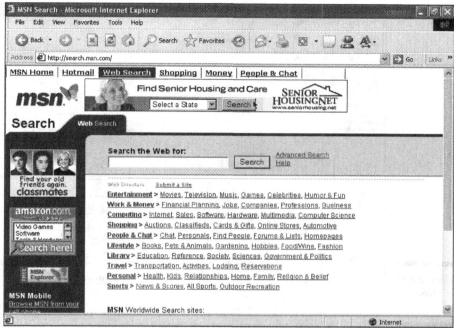

Northern Light

www.northernlight.com

Northern Light is possibly the largest Web index available, with more than 330 million entries in its database. In addition to a huge index of Web pages, Northern Light also features indexes of popular publications, such as *The Wall Street Journal, Business Week,* and *Fortune.* Figure 4-13 shows the Northern Light home page.

Yahoo!

www.yahoo.com

Yahoo! is one of the most popular Web directories around. Unlike search engines such as AltaVista and MSN Search, Yahoo! is a listing of tens of thousands of Web sites organized into categories, such as Arts & Humanities, Business & Economy, Computers & Internet, and Education. You can browse through the Yahoo! categories or search for specific pages by keyword. The Yahoo! opening page appears in Figure 4-14.

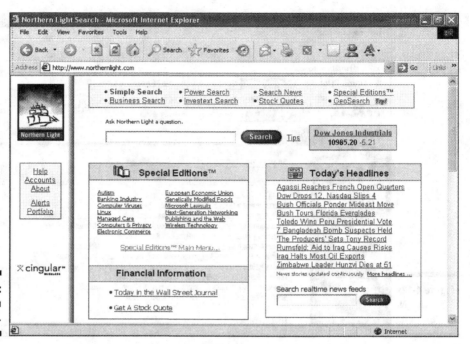

Figure 4-13:
Northern
Light.

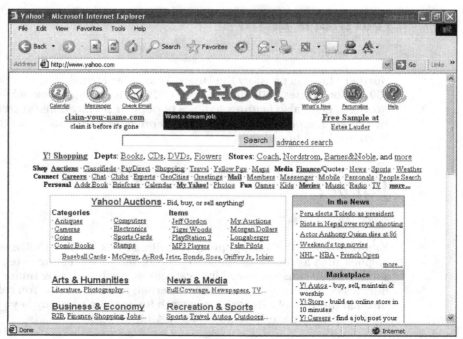

Figure 4-14:
Yahoo!

Yahoo! is excellent for searching categorized information, but its keyword search abilities aren't as strong as other services, such as Lycos or AltaVista.

Yahoo! was founded by two college students at Stanford University. Rumor has it that Yahoo! stands for Yet Another Hierarchical Officious Oracle, but the two student founders deny the allegation.

Chapter 5

Using Internet Explorer Features to Get Around the Web Quickly

*T*he World Wide Web offers millions of interesting destinations. Exploring them all just to see what's available would be fun, assuming that you could live long enough. But after you see a few hundred or a few thousand Web pages, you'll probably come to realize that not all Web pages are created equal. You soon settle on a few Web sites that are your personal favorites. This chapter shows you how to use two features of Internet Explorer that are designed to make it easier to access frequently visited pages: Favorites and the Links toolbar.

Playing Favorites

The Internet Explorer Favorites feature is designed to expedite travel to your favorite Web sites without your having to remember a bunch of Web addresses or navigate your way through link after link. The Favorites feature is basically a menu on the Internet Explorer menu bar that lists links to your favorite Web sites. You can add links to and remove links from the Favorites menu whenever you want. The following sections describe how to use the Internet Explorer Favorites feature.

Another popular term for Favorites is *bookmarks.* It's a Netscape word, how-ever, so you probably shouldn't use it in the presence of a Microsoft junkie.

Adding a Web page to the Favorites menu

To designate a Web page as one of your Favorites so that you can find it fast later, follow these steps:

1. **Browse your way to the page you want to add to your list of favorite pages.**

2. **Choose the Favorites➪Add to Favorites command.**

   The Add Favorite dialog box appears, as shown in Figure 5-1. The Name text box displays the name of the Web site you want to add to your Favorites menu.

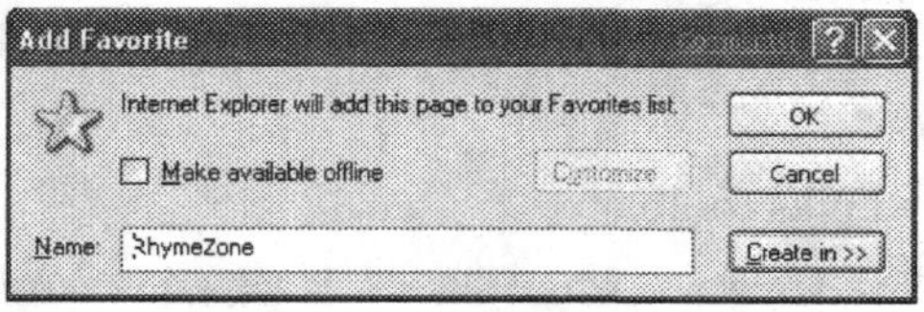

Figure 5-1:
The Add
Favorite
dialog box.

3. **Change the Web site's name in the Name box if you want.**

   In many cases, the name proposed by Internet Explorer is acceptable. If you want to change the name, you can do so by typing a new name in the Name field.

4. **Click OK.**

   Internet Explorer adds the Web page to your Favorites menu.

The Make Available Offline check box in the Add Favorite dialog box enables you to *synchronize* to a Web page so that you're automatically notified whenever the Web page changes. For now, leave this option unchecked. I show you how to use the Make Available Offline option in Chapter 8.

Going to one of your favorite places

After you add your favorite Web pages to your Favorites menu, you can open the menu to jet away to any of the pages it contains. Here's how:

1. **Choose Favorites from the menu bar.**

   The Favorites menu reveals your list of favorite places, as shown in Figure 5-2. Your Favorites menu undoubtedly contains a different collection of links than mine, so don't panic if your Favorites menu doesn't match the one shown in Figure 5-2.

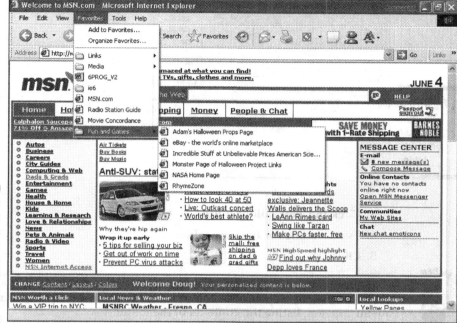

Figure 5-2:
The
Favorites
menu
contains
your list of
favorite
places.

2. **Select the Web page you want to view, and off you go.**

   Notice that the Favorites menu shown in Figure 5-2 includes several submenus that contain my favorite Web pages organized into categories.
   You can find instructions for setting up submenus like these in the next
   section, "Using Favorites folders."

Using Favorites folders

If you keep adding pages to the Favorites menu, pretty soon it becomes so
full of links to your favorite sites that you can't find anything. To ease crowd-
ing on the Favorites menu and to help you organize your favorite links,
Internet Explorer enables you to create separate folders in which you can
categorize your favorite sites.

To create a Favorites folder in which to place a link to the Web page you're
viewing, follow these steps:

1. **Choose Favorites⇨Add to Favorites.**

   The Add Favorite dialog box appears.

2. **Click Create In.**

   The Add Favorite dialog box expands, as shown in Figure 5-3.

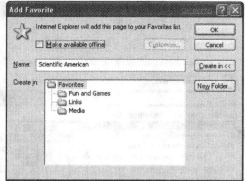

Figure 5-3:
Adding a
page to a
Favorites
folder.

3. **Click the New Folder button.**

4. **Type a name for the new folder.**

5. **Click OK.**

The folders within the Favorites menu appear as menu items with arrows next to them. If you point the mouse to one of these menu items, a second menu appears, listing the contents of the folder.

If you want to place a link to a Web page in an existing folder, follow these steps:

1. **Choose Favorites⇨Add to Favorites.**

   The Add Favorite dialog box appears.

2. **Click Create In.**

   The Add Favorite dialog box expands.

3. **In the Create In list, select the folder in which you want to store the new link.**

4. **Click OK.**

Organizing your Favorites

Eventually, your Favorites menu becomes filled with Web links that no longer hold your interest, are out of date, or just need to be reorganized. When you reach this point, it's time to roll up your sleeves and reorganize your Favorites. Fortunately, Internet Explorer provides a command just for this purpose.

To organize your Favorites, choose the Favorites➪Organize Favorites command. The Organize Favorites dialog box appears, as shown in Figure 5-4.

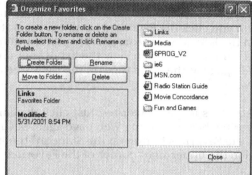

Figure 5-4:
The
Organize
Favorites
dialog box.

The buttons in the Organize Favorites dialog box enable you to create, rename, move around, and delete items in your Favorites folders.

✔ To create a new folder, click the Create Folder button. Doing this creates a new folder named, naturally, New Folder. Type a new name for the folder and then press Enter.

✔ To rename a page or a folder, select the page or folder and click the Rename button. Type a new name for the page or folder and then click OK.

✔ To move a page or a folder to another folder, select the page or folder. Click the Move to Folder button and then click the folder to which you want to move the page or folder. (To simply change the position of a folder or page on the Favorites list, you can click just the page or folder and then drag it to a new location.)

✔ To delete a page or a folder, select the page or folder and then click the Delete button. A dialog box appears, asking whether you're sure that you want to delete the folder or page; click Yes.

You can also right-click items in the Organize Favorites dialog box to summon a shortcut menu that contains options for deleting or renaming pages or folders.

If you're a Netscape user, you can quickly transfer bookmarks from Netscape into Internet Explorer Favorites (or vice versa) by choosing the File➪Import and Export command. Choosing this command summons the Import/Export Wizard, which walks you step-by-step through the process of exchanging favorites between Internet Explorer and Netscape Navigator.

Using the Favorites button on the Standard toolbar

The Favorites button on the Standard toolbar works a little differently from the Favorites menu. When you click the Favorites button, a separate Favorites bar appears on the left side of the Internet Explorer window, as shown in Figure 5-5. This bar enables you to view the list of your favorite Web pages while viewing a Web page at the same time on the right side of the Internet Explorer window.

To display any of the Web pages in your Favorites, just click the link for the page. To remove the Favorites bar so that the Web page again occupies the entire window, just click the Favorites button on the Standard toolbar again, or click the Close button in the upper-right corner of the Favorites bar.

At the top of the Favorites bar are two buttons:

✔ **Add**: Summons the Add Favorite dialog box so that you can add a page to your Favorites.

✔ **Organize:** Summons the Organize Favorites dialog box so that you can organize your Favorites.

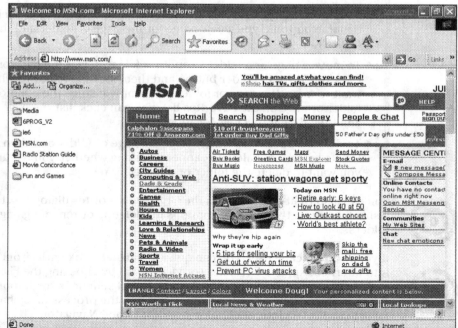

Figure 5-5:
The
Favorites
bar.

Using the Links Toolbar

Internet Explorer Favorites are a great way to keep track of all the Web pages you visit periodically. However, Internet Explorer provides an even more convenient method of quickly visiting a select group of your favorite Web sites: the Links toolbar. The Links toolbar enables you to place Web site links on a toolbar that's always available at the click of a mouse.

Accessing the Links toolbar

Ordinarily, the Links toolbar is covered up by the Address toolbar. To reveal the Links toolbar, double-click the word *Links* near the upper-right corner of the Internet Explorer window. The Links toolbar appears, as shown in Figure 5-6.

To display one of the pages on the Links toolbar, just click its button. To show the Address toolbar again, double-click the word *Address* to the left of the Links toolbar.

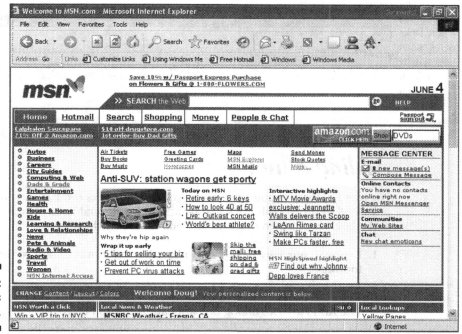

Figure 5-6:
The Links
toolbar.

Depending on the number of links you create for the Links toolbar and the size of the Internet Explorer window, Internet Explorer may not be able to squeeze all your links onto the visible portion of the Links toolbar. If not, you can click the right arrow that appears in the upper-right corner of the Links toolbar to display a menu of the additional links.

Here are two other ways you can position the Links toolbar:

✔ You can position the Links toolbar beneath the Address toolbar so that both toolbars are visible at the same time. To do so, click the word *Links* and hold down the mouse button. Then, drag the toolbar down until the Links toolbar pops into place beneath the Address toolbar; then release the mouse button.

✔ You can position and adjust the size of the Links and Address toolbars so that both are visible and share the same line, as shown in Figure 5-7. Just drag the Links toolbar left rather than down. As you drag the Links toolbar to the left, the Address toolbar is resized automatically to make room for the Links toolbar.

Figure 5-7:
The Address and Links toolbars can live side by side, in perfect harmony.

Adding a link

Internet Explorer enables you to customize the Links toolbar by removing any or all of the default links and by adding additional links of your own. To add a link of your own to the Links toolbar, follow these steps:

1. **Browse your way to the Web page that you want to add to the Links toolbar.**

2. **Choose the Favorites➪Add to Favorites command.**

   The Add Favorite dialog box appears (refer to Figure 5-1).

3. **Click the Create In button.**

   The Add Favorite dialog box expands to show your Favorites folders (refer to Figure 5-3).

4. **Click the Links folder.**

5. **Click OK.**

The page you displayed in Step 1 is added to the Links toolbar. If the page doesn't appear on the Links toolbar, you can click the small right-pointing arrow that appears at the right edge of the toolbar. This action displays a menu that lists those links that don't fit in the visible portion of the Links toolbar.

 You can quickly add the currently displayed page to the Links toolbar by dragging the page icon (as shown in the margin) from the Address bar to the Links toolbar.

Removing a link

To remove a link from the Links toolbar, follow these steps:

1. **Call up the Favorites⇨Organize Favorites command.**

   The Organize Favorites dialog box appears (refer to Figure 5-4.)

2. **Double-click the Links folder.**

   The Links folder appears, showing all the links that are on your Links toolbar.

3. **Select the link you want to remove.**

4. **Click the Delete button.**

   A dialog box appears, asking whether you really want to delete the link.

5. **Click Yes.**

You're done! The link you deleted is removed from the Links toolbar.

 Another way to delete a link is by right-clicking the link on the Links toolbar and then choosing the Delete command from the pop-up menu that appears. A dialog box appears, asking whether you're sure that you want to delete the link. Click Yes, and the link is deleted.

Chapter 6

Download This!

*O*ne of my favorite scenes from *The Wizard of Oz* is when Dorothy and the Scarecrow go through the apple orchard. When Dorothy picks an apple from one of the trees, the tree comes to life, grabs the apple back, slaps Dorothy on the hand, and says "How'd you like to have someone come along and pick something off you?"

The Internet is filled with Web pages that are like apple trees, with goodies you can pick. The technical term for picking something off a Web page is *downloading*. The main difference between downloading a file from a Web page and picking an apple from one of the apple trees in Oz is that when you download a file from a Web page, the page doesn't take the file back or slap you.

The word *download* means to copy a file from a computer on the Internet to your computer. You may not realize it, but you download files every time you use the Internet. Every Web page you view is made up of one or more files that Internet Explorer downloads to your computer and displays on your screen.

Many Web pages contain links to additional files you can download. You can download many different kinds of files. Pictures, songs, movies, documents, and other computer programs are the most popular.

Downloading Pictures

Millions of pictures are available for you to download from the Internet. When you have downloaded a picture, you can then use the picture in another program, such as Word, Publisher, or PowerPoint. Or, you can just enjoy the picture by viewing it on your computer, printing the picture, or using the picture as your Windows desktop wallpaper.

The hardest part about downloading pictures is finding the pictures you want to download. Here are a few tips to get you started in your quest for online pictures:

✔ When you use a search service to look for pictures, include words such as *image, picture, photograph,* or *painting* to narrow your search to specific types of images. For example, a search for *Mona Lisa painting image* gives you more pages with images of the actual painting than a search for just *Mona Lisa.*

✔ Some search services, including Lycos, Excite, and AltaVista, have special image indexes that let you search for pictures.

✔ Use a search page such as Yahoo (www.yahoo.com) or Google (www.google.com) to search for *image collection.* You can also search for specific types of collections, such as *Civil War image collection* or *NASA image collection.*

✔ For photographic collections, search for *stock photography.* One of the best online sources for stock photography is Corbis (www.corbis.com) The complete Corbis collection includes more than 65 million images, but only about 2 million of them are available on the Internet.

✔ If you're looking for historical photos, start at the Library of Congress American Memory collection at memory.loc.gov. It contains more than 7 million images you can download.

✔ When you find an image you like, make sure that you get the best available version of the image. Many Web pages show just a thumbnail version of a picture. You can click the thumbnail or a nearby link to get a larger version of the picture, which looks better if you enlarge it.

✔ Most images you can find on the Internet are protected by copyright laws. For more information about copyrights, see the sidebar "Is it legal?" later in this chapter.

Saving an image

Strictly speaking, when you see a picture on a Web page, saying that you want to download the picture isn't accurate because you already have. The fact that you can see the picture in Internet Explorer means that you have already downloaded it. The trick is figuring out how to separate the picture from the rest of the Web page and save the picture as a separate file on your hard disk so that you can access it later.

Fortunately, saving a picture as a file is easy. Just follow these steps:

1. **Move the mouse pointer over the picture and click the right mouse button.**

   A pop-up menu appears.

2. **Choose the Save Picture As command.**

   A standard Save As dialog box appears.

   For Internet Explorer 6, Microsoft has made the first two steps of this procedure a bit easier by introducing the Image toolbar. For more information, see the next section, cleverly titled "Using the Image toolbar."

3. **Navigate to the folder in which you want to save the file.**

   The default folder is named My Pictures. Change to another folder only if you have good reason to save the picture in a folder other than My Pictures. (For example, if you're downloading a bunch of pictures for a project, you may want to save the pictures in a separate folder.)

4. **Type a new filename for the file if you don't like the one that is supplied.**

   In many cases, the name is okay. But often the file will has a name like b1992ah8nk382.jpg. In that case, type a more meaningful name for the picture.

5. **Click the Save button.**

   The picture is copied to your hard disk.

Other commands appear on the pop-up menu when you right-click a picture. These commands include

- ✔ **E-Mail Picture:** Starts your e-mail program and creates a message with the picture attached. All you have to do is fill in the address of the person you want to send the picture to and click Send.

- ✔ **Print Picture:** Prints a copy of the picture on your printer.

- ✔ **Go to My Pictures:** Opens your My Pictures folder so that you can work with the pictures you've saved.

- ✔ **Set As Background:** Makes the picture your desktop wallpaper. For more information, see the section "Wallpapering your computer," later in this chapter.

Using the Image toolbar

Internet Explorer 6 has a new Image toolbar that appears when you move the mouse pointer over a picture. The Image toolbar contains buttons that duplicate many of the commands on the pop-up menu that appears when you right-click a picture:

- ✔ This button saves the image as a file on your hard disk. It's the same as right-clicking an image and choosing Save As, as described in the first two steps of the procedure in the preceding section, "Saving an image."

- ✔ This button prints the image.

- ✔ This button lets you e-mail a copy of the image to a friend. (For this process to work, your friend must have a program that can display the image file. If your friend is using Internet Explorer 6, the image is displayed directly in Outlook Express when she opens the message. Otherwise, your friend may need to save the image to disk and view it with a separate program.)

- ✔ This button opens the My Pictures folder so that you can play with your pictures. For more information, see the section "Using the My Pictures folder," later in this chapter.

Dealing with large pictures

Internet Explorer 6 has a new feature that automatically reduces the size of large pictures so that they fit in the Internet Explorer window. That way, you don't have to use the scroll bars to see the entire picture.

You can tell that a picture has been reduced in size by moving the mouse pointer over the picture. When you do, the button shown in the margin appears in the lower-right corner of the picture. Click this button to enlarge the picture to its full size.

When you enlarge a picture, the button changes its appearance a bit, as shown in the margin. Click the button again to shrink the picture so that it again fits in the window.

Wallpapering your computer

If you find a picture you like so much that you want to see it every day, why not make it your Windows desktop wallpaper? To do so, right-click the image and then select Set As Wallpaper. The picture instantly becomes your wallpaper.

Internet Explorer saves the picture as a file named Internet Explorer Wallpaper, in your Windows folder. If you would rather choose your own name for the file, use the Save Picture As command as described in the preceding steps and save the picture in the C:\Windows folder. (For Windows 95, you have to save the picture as a BMP file, but Windows 98 or higher can use JPEG pictures as wallpaper.) Then, right-click your desktop, choose the Properties command, and choose the file you saved from the list of image files to use for your wallpaper.

Beware of copyright protections when you save a graphic. Many images, especially artwork, photographs, and company logos, are copyrighted. If you save a graphic that may be protected by copyright law, be sure to get the owner's permission before you use the graphic.

Using the My Pictures folder

Internet Explorer 6 uses a special My Pictures folder to store pictures you've downloaded. The My Pictures folder displays little thumbnail images of all your pictures and includes special picture-handling commands in a task pane on the left side of the window.

You can open the My Pictures folder by clicking the Open My Pictures Folder button on the Image toolbar. Or, you can click the My Documents icon on your desktop and then click the My Pictures icon. Either way, the My Pictures folder appears, as shown in Figure 6-1.

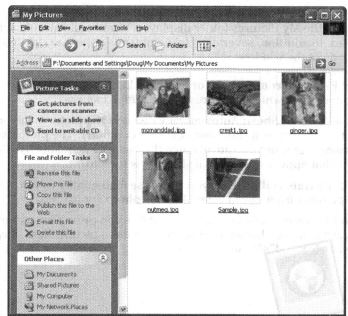

Figure 6-1:
The My
Pictures
folder.

Is it legal?

I'm not an attorney, and I don't play one on TV. So I don't give you legal advice about whether a particular image or other file is copyrighted or whether you have to get permission to use a file in a particular way, such as on your Web site, in a school report, or in a business brochure. But I want to clear up a few frequently misunderstood points about copyrights:

✔ The absence of a copyright notice doesn't mean that an item isn't copyrighted. Copyright law doesn't require that the owner of a creative work display a copyright notice to protect his or her copyright works. So if you find a beautiful photograph that has no copyright notice, don't assume that you can freely copy the photograph.

✔ Many older works, such as Shakespeare and the *King James Bible,* are considered public domain. However, specific editions based on a public domain work can be copyrighted.

✔ To use a copyrighted work, you must get permission from the person who owns the copyright, not the person you obtained the work from. If you see a picture on a Web page, don't assume that the person who created the Web page owns the picture's copyright. The person who created the Web page may well be using the picture illegally.

✔ The concept of "fair use" allows you to use excerpts from a copyrighted work without permission for the purposes of criticism, parody, news reporting, or teaching. However, fair use is often misunderstood and abused. For example, fair use does not allow a teacher to copy an entire chapter from a book so that students don't have to purchase the book. Nor does it allow a church to project the words to a song on a screen.

Notice how the My Pictures folder displays a thumbnail view of each of your image files. In addition, several useful commands appear in the task pane on the left side of the window:

✔ **Get Pictures from Camera or Scanner:** Lets you scan pictures from a scanner or download pictures from a digital camera.

✔ **View As Slide Show:** Automatically displays the pictures in your My Pictures folder as a slide show on your computer. The pictures advance automatically, or you can advance the pictures manually by clicking buttons that appear on a special slide show toolbar.

✔ **Order Prints Online:** Lets you purchase high-quality prints of your digital pictures from one of several online photo companies.

✔ **Print Pictures:** Calls up a wizard that lets you print your pictures. The wizard lets you choose from several common picture sizes, including 8"x10", 5"x7", 4"x6", and 3.5" x 5".

Clicking a picture in the My Pictures folder activates a special Image Preview feature, as shown in Figure 6-2. Buttons on the bottom of the Image Preview window let you call up other pictures from the My Pictures folder, zoom in or out, rotate the picture, and delete, print, or copy the picture to another location.

Figure 6-2:
Ginger.

Downloading a File

You can download, besides images, many other types of files from the Internet: sounds, movies, and other media files; document files, such as Word, Excel, or PowerPoint documents; and program files.

To download a file, just follow these steps:

1. **Find a Web site that contains a file you want to download.**

   You may have to use one of the search services described in Chapter 4. Usually, a search leads you to a page that includes a link you can click to download the file. This link usually, but not always, gives you some indication of how large the file is.

2. **Click the link to download the file.**

   Internet Explorer grinds and churns for a moment. Eventually, the dialog box shown in Figure 6-3 appears.

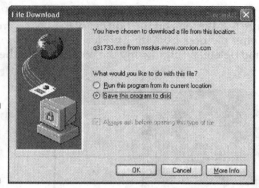

Figure 6-3:
The File
Download
dialog box.

3. **Make sure that the Save This Program to Disk option is selected and then click OK.**

   If you want to run the program immediately after you download it, click the Run This Program from Its Current Location option instead. When you choose this option, a copy of the program isn't permanently saved on your hard disk, so you should use this option only if you need to run the program just this one time. If you need to run the program more than once, choose the Save This Program to Disk option instead.

   Assuming that you chose the Save This Program to Disk option, a Save As dialog box appears. (If you chose Run This Program from Its Current Location instead, you can skip ahead to Step 5.)

4. **In the Save As dialog box, select the folder in which you want the file to be saved. Then click Save.**

   A dialog box displays a progress bar that enables you to monitor the download progress, as shown in Figure 6-4.

Figure 6-4:
Downloading
a file.

5. **Wait until the download is finished.**

   When the download finishes, the download progress dialog box informs you that the download is complete. (The title bar of this dialog box changes to Download Complete so that you know that the download has finished.)

6. **Click Close.**

   If you chose the Save This Program to Disk option in Step 3, you're done. If you chose the Run This Program from Its Current Location option instead, the program you downloaded runs immediately.

The Download Complete dialog box offers two additional buttons you can click:

Open: Opens the file you just downloaded

Open folder: Opens the folder in which you saved the file

Here are some pertinent points to ponder when performing a download:

✔ You should always make sure that you have enough disk space on your hard drive before downloading a large file. Nothing is more frustrating than discovering that you have only 3MB of free disk space an hour after you begin a 4MB download.

✔ To check your free disk space, you can double-click the My Computer icon on your desktop and then click the icon for your Drive C. The My Computer window displays on the status bar at the bottom of the window the amount of free space on Drive C.

✔ You don't have to twiddle your thumbs while the file is downloading. In fact, as I write this section, I'm downloading a 4MB file from the Internet. To continue with other work, simply click anywhere outside the File Download dialog box. The dialog box kindly steps out of the way, allowing you to work with other programs while the download continues. You can even use Internet Explorer to browse other Web sites while the download takes its sweet time.

Dealing with Zipped Files

To make downloads faster, some Web sites store large files in a compressed format known as zip. A *zip file* is a single file that contains one or more files that have had any and all wasted space squeezed out of them. Before you can use a downloaded zip file, you must unzip it to extract the compressed files from the zip file.

In previous versions of Windows and Internet Explorer, you had to get a separate program to handle this unzipping chore. Fortunately, Windows XP includes a built-in unzip feature that takes almost all the hassle out of working with zip files.

Windows XP treats a zip file as though it were a folder. That makes sense, when you think about it. Zip files contain one or more compressed files, and folders also contain one or more files. When you open a zip file in Windows XP, the zip file is treated as though it were a folder, and all the compressed files in the zip file appear as files in the folder. The files are automatically compressed, so you don't have to run a special program to uncompress them.

To use a downloaded zip file, click Open when the Download Complete dialog box appears. The zip file is opened as a folder, as shown in Figure 6-5.

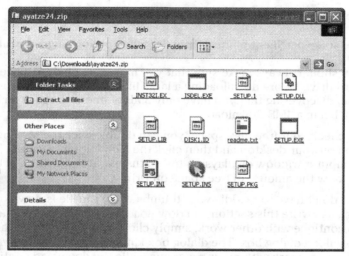

Figure 6-5:
The contents of a zip file.

After you have opened a zip file, you can do several things with it:

- ✔ If the file you downloaded is a program, you can install the program by clicking the icon for the Setup program, usually named Setup.exe.

- ✔ You can open any other program or document in the zip file by clicking the icon for the file you want to open.

- ✔ You can uncompress all the files in the zip file and copy them to another folder by clicking the Extract All Files command in the Folder Tasks pane on the left side of the window.

Some zip files are password protected. To access the files in a password-protected zip file, you must supply the correct password when prompted.

Working with FTP

FTP, which stands for *File Transfer Protocol,* is an Internet file server that lets you access libraries of files which you can download. Once upon a time, in the early days of the Internet, FTP was the main method of downloading files. Nowadays, most download libraries use Web pages. However, you may occasionally need to download a file from an FTP site.

Here are a few things you need to know about FTP sites before you start playing with them:

✔ Like Web sites, FTP sites have Internet addresses. FTP site addresses begin with **ftp://** instead of **http://**, but Internet Explorer can automatically add the **ftp://** so that you don't usually need to type it.

✔ All FTP sites require that you log in before you can use them. However, many sites allow you to log in as an anonymous user without supplying a password. This is called *anonymous login* and may give you only limited access to the files available at the site. If an FTP site does not allow anonymous login, you have to get a user ID and password from the FTP site's administrator.

✔ All FTP sites have a *home directory*, which is the first directory you see when you log in to the site. Most FTP sites have additional directories you can access. These directories work just like folders on your computer's hard drive.

Accessing an FTP site

FTP support is built in to Internet Explorer, so you don't have to use a separate FTP program to download files from an FTP site. To access an FTP site, just type the address of the FTP site into Internet Explorer's Address bar and press Enter. You'll be taken to the FTP site's home directory, as shown in Figure 6-6.

If the FTP site doesn't accept anonymous logins or requires you to log in with a user ID and password for full access to the files you want, choose File➪Login As to summon the Login As dialog box, as shown in Figure 6-7. Type your username and password and click Login to log in to the FTP server.

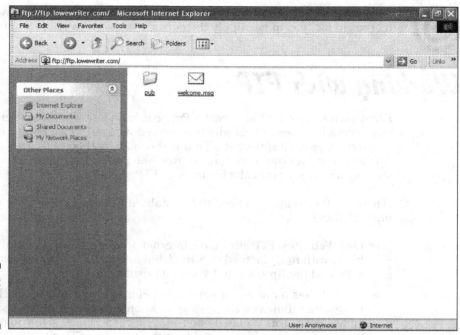

Figure 6-6:
Accessing
an FTP site.

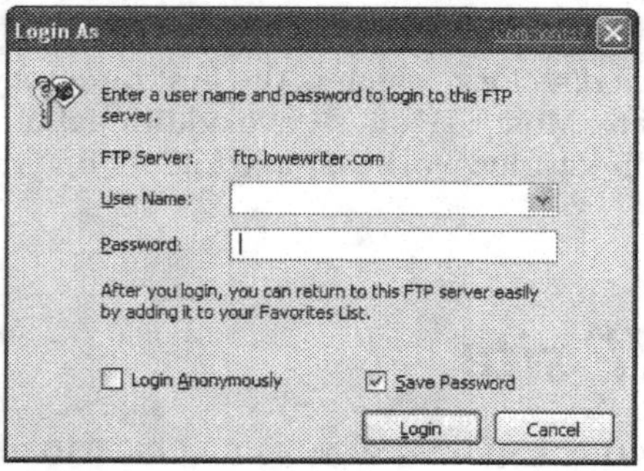

Figure 6-7:
Logging in.

TIP

Most FTP sites send a welcome message when you log in. Internet Explorer
doesn't automatically display this message, but you can view it by choosing
Help⇨FTP Server Welcome Message.

To download a file from an FTP site, right-click the file and choose the Copy
to Folder command. This command summons a dialog box listing the folders
on your hard disk. Select the folder you want to copy the file to and click OK.

Uploading files

Some FTP sites allow you to upload files as well as download files. If you want to upload a file to an FTP site, follow these steps:

1. **Open the FTP site and go to the directory to which you want to upload the file.**

   If you're not sure how, reread the preceding section, "Accessing an FTP site."

2. **Open your My Documents folder and navigate to the folder that contains the file you want to upload.**

   If necessary, minimize the Internet Explorer window and any other open windows so that you can click the My Documents icon on your desktop.

3. **Select the file you want to upload.**

4. **Choose Copy This File in the File and Folder Tasks pane on the left side of the My Documents window.**

   A dialog box labeled Copy Items appears.

5. **Select the FTP server you opened in Step 1.**

   The FTP server appears under My Network Places in the Copy Items dialog box. You may need to click the little plus sign next to My Network Places to see the FTP server.

6. **Click Copy.**

   The file is uploaded to the FTP server.

Finding Lost Downloads

Almost everyone who has downloaded files from the Internet has had the frustrating experience of not being able to find the file after downloading it. Here are some tips for locating a lost download:

- ✔ If you can remember the filename but can't remember the folder in which you saved the file, click the Start button and choose Search. Then type the name of the file and click the Search Now button. Windows searches your entire hard disk for the file.

- ✔ If you've lost an image file, start up Internet Explorer, right-click an image, and choose Save Picture As. Note the folder that the Save Picture As dialog box calls up. That's probably the folder where your lost picture is hiding. Click Cancel to close the Save Picture As dialog box without saving the picture.

✔ If you've lost a program or other download file, repeat the steps you took to download the file up to the point where the Save As dialog box appears. Then make a note of what folder comes up: That's probably where the file is. Click Cancel to close the Save As dialog box without downloading the file again.

✔ If you chose the Run This Program From its Current Location option when you downloaded the program, the program may have been automatically deleted from your hard disk. In that case, you have to download the program again. This time, use the Save This Program to Disk option.

Chapter 7

The Media Is the Message

*M*ultimedia is all the rage these days. Just ask any computer salesperson. He'll tell you that your next computer needs a DVD drive, a 25-inch monitor, a studio-quality sound card and surround-sound speakers, a scanner, and a videocamera. And that's just to play games! You need even better equipment if you actually need to *use* multimedia, not just play with it.

With the advent of high-speed cable and DSL connections, the Internet has joined the multimedia bandwagon. A splashy Web page used to be one that had a few pictures. Now, splashy Web pages have fancy animations, a soundtrack, and perhaps even a movie. It won't be long before the smell of popcorn can be sent (sorry) over the Internet.

This chapter is a brief overview of the multimedia capabilities of Internet Explorer 6. If you've read Chapter 6, you already know about working with pictures. This chapter focuses on sounds, movies, and other types of media. Prepare to be dazzled!

What Is Multimedia?

Strictly speaking, *multimedia* means information that is presented using more than one form of media. In the old days, most information available on the Internet was in the form of text — a single, basic type of media. However, in addition to text, the Internet deftly handles other types of media, most notably pictures, sounds, and movies.

Pictures

You've no doubt already encountered many different types of pictures in your Web explorations, and most of your graphic-viewing sessions have probably gone by without incident. Although picture files can be stored in dozens of formats, the two most popular file formats are GIF and JPEG. Internet Explorer handles both these file formats easily — all you have to do is sit back and watch.

For more information about viewing pictures and saving them on your hard drive, refer to Chapter 6.

Sounds

Sounds on the Internet used to be limited to collections of short sound files featuring quotes from *Star Trek* and *Monty Python* movies. Now, sound on the Internet includes everything from fancy sound effects to complete recordings of popular music.

Several different types of sound file formats are popular:

- **WAV:** The basic sound file format used by Windows. WAV files have decent fidelity, but they tend to be a bit large for sounds that are more than a few seconds long. For example, a complete CD-quality song can easily require 30 or 40 MB. That's a bit long for an Internet download, even with a high-speed cable or DSL connection.

- **AIFF:** Sound files for Macintosh computers, similar to WAV files.

- **MP3:** A compressed sound format that is almost miraculously able to save high-quality sounds in a fraction of the amount of space required for an equivalent WAV file. For example, that same song that required 30 or 40 MB in a WAV file can be shrunk to 3 or 4 MB in an MP3 file, and sounds just as good.

- **Real Audio:** A format that lets you play files in real time, as you download them. With a Real Audio file, you don't have to wait until the file has finished downloading before you can play it. Instead, you just listen to the file as it downloads. Real Audio is a popular format for online radio stations, but it's kind of like AM radio: The quality is not quite as good as MP3 files, and the music is sometimes interrupted by network problems.

- **WMA:** Windows Media Audio files, the latest and greatest standard for sound files from Microsoft. WMA files can contain sounds recorded with a variety of quality standards using a variety of different compression and decompression methods, referred to as *codecs*. (*Codec* is short for *compressor-deco*mpressor.)

✔ **MIDI:** A special type of sound file that doesn't actually contain sounds but instead contains instructions that tell the synthesizer in your sound card how to play instrumental music. MIDI files are very small when compared with WAV or MP3 files. For example, a MIDI file that plays *Sweet Adeline* may be only about 2K.

Video

The four most popular formats for video on the Internet are

✔ **AVI:** The Microsoft video format for Windows.

✔ **QuickTime:** The Apple video format for Macintosh computers, but also available for Windows and becoming very popular on Windows computers.

✔ **MPEG:** The video version of MP3. MPEG is the format used for DVD movies, but don't get all excited: most MPEG movies you find on the Internet are not even close to DVD quality.

✔ **Real Video:** A streaming-video format that lets you watch movies without waiting for them to download first, and the movie is subject to frequent interruptions.

Flash

Another type of multimedia you encounter on the Web are Flash animations. A *Flash animation* is a graphic animation created using a special program named Macromedia Flash, created by (you guessed it) a company named Macromedia.

Although Macromedia Flash is an expensive program, you don't have to own it to view Flash animations. All you need is the free Macromedia Flash Player. When you view a Web page that has a Flash animation, you also find a link that lets you download and install the free Flash player. After you've installed the player, you can view Flash animations on sites throughout the Internet.

Streaming media

A type of media that is becoming more and more popular is streaming media. *Streaming media* is audio or video media that you can watch in real time, like radio or television, only on your computer. With a high-speed Internet connection such as cable or DSL, you can use your $2,000 computer to listen to the radio so that you can throw away that $20 clock radio that has been sitting on your desk for years.

To listen to local radio stations, you're better off using a separate radio receiver. But streaming media does something that a regular radio can't: It lets you listen to radio stations around the world. So, if you don't have a good classic rock station in your city, you can find one on the Internet.

Streaming media works for video, too, although the reception isn't the quality you get from cable TV and the picture is small.

Playing a Sound or Movie

If you find a Web site that includes a link to a sound or movie file, click the link to download and play the file. Depending on how the link is set up, the media file may play within the current Internet Explorer window, or it may open a separate window to play the file. You may also be asked questions such as what kind of connection you have to the Internet and what media player you want to use to play the file.

Figure 7-1 shows Internet Explorer playing a media file — in this example, the theatrical trailer for the movie *Pearl Harbor* (www.pearlharbor.com). The video is displayed in a separate window along with a set of media controls that you can use to control the playback.

Figure 7-1:
Playing a
movie.

Although the exact appearance of different media players differs, most have controls that resemble those found on a VCR:

✔ **Play:** Starts the media from the current location.

✔ **Pause:** Temporarily stops playback. Click Play again to resume.

✔ **Stop:** Stops the playback and rewinds the media file to the beginning.

|◀◀   ✔ **Skip back:** Rewinds to the beginning of the file.

◀◀   ✔ **Rewind:** Rewinds the file.

▶▶   ✔ **Fast Forward:** Advances forward through the file.

▶▶| ✔ **Skip forward:** Skips to the next media file.

Most media players also include a volume control, and some allow you to adjust the size of the picture for video files.

Using the Media Bar

Internet Explorer 6 includes a built-in media player that appears on a separate Media bar when you play certain types of media files. Figure 7-2 shows the Media bar in action. It appears whenever you play a media file in an Internet Explorer window, but you can also summon it whenever you want by choosing the View⇨Explorer Bar⇨Personal Bar command.

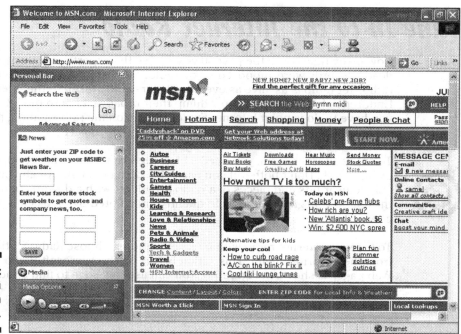

Figure 7-2:
The Media bar in action.

The buttons at the bottom of the Media bar let you control the media play-back, as shown in Table 7-1.

Table 7-1	Buttons on the Media Bar
Button	*What It Does*
▶	Plays the media file
■	Stops the media file
◀◀	Rewinds the file
▶▶	Fast-forwards the media file

Tune In to the Internet Radio

How many times over the past 50 years have the experts said that radio is dead? Records were supposed to kill radio. Television was supposed to kill radio. Yet radio is as alive as ever, and has recently taken to the Internet. Hundreds of radio stations now dump their broadcasts onto the Internet. All you have to do is point Internet Explorer at an online radio station, plug in some headphones, close your door, and enjoy the music.

To enjoy Internet radio, you need a high-speed Internet connection, such as cable or DSL. Don't bother if you use a dial-up modem. Although you may be able to hear bits and pieces of a radio broadcast with a dial-up connection, the sound gets garbled and is frequently interrupted by breaks in your connection.

To listen to Internet radio with Internet Explorer, choose Radio Station Guide from the Favorites menu. This action brings up the Microsoft Radio Tuner Web page, as shown in Figure 7-3. You can use this page to find a radio station you want to listen to.

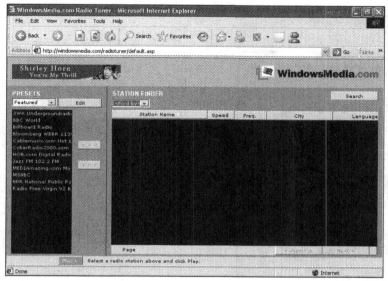

Figure 7-3:
The
Microsoft
Radio Tuner
Web page.

To find a radio station, start by using the Find By drop-down list to indicate how you want to search the available radio stations. Most likely, you want to search by format. When you set the Find By control to Format, a drop-down list appears that enables you to choose one of more than 30 different station formats, such as Classic Rock, Jazz & Blues, or Talk Radio. Pick the format you want and a list of stations appears.

For example, Figure 7-4 shows the list of classic rock stations that were available when I wrote this chapter. (Stations come and go, so the list may be different when you try it.)

Other search options include band (broadcast band — AM, FM, or Internet only — not musical groups), language, location, call sign, frequency, and keyword.

To listen to a station, double-click the station you want to tune in. What happens next varies from station to station. You may be taken directly to the Windows Media Player to listen to the station, or a separate window may appear in which a media player appears. You may be asked to register by supplying your e-mail address and other information, such as your zip code or age.

To stop listening to a radio station, either click the Stop button in the station's player or close the station's window.

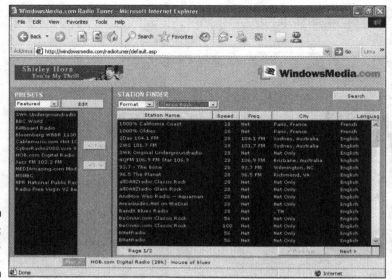

Figure 7-4:
Classic rock
stations.

The Radio Tuner page lets you set up a list of presets so that you can easily find your favorite stations. To create a preset for a station, first choose My Presets from the drop-down list in the Presets section of the Radio Tuner page. Then, click the station you want to create a preset for and click the Add button (the one with the three less-than signs, as shown in the margin).

Chapter 8

Working Offline

In This Chapter

▶ Viewing Web pages offline

▶ Changing your offline viewing options

▶ Getting your offline pages in synch

*O*ne of the major annoyances of the Internet is that you always have to be connected online to access the Web. That requirement can be a major hassle for folks who have to share the computer phone line with a teenager or for those who want to tote a laptop computer to the park and access the Web while watching kids play on a swing.

The Internet Explorer offline browsing feature comes in handy in those circumstances. The *offline browsing feature* lets you designate certain pages for offline browsing, which means that you can access those pages even if your computer isn't connected to the Internet.

Offline browsing works by keeping a copy of your offline pages on your computer's own hard disk. That way, if you want to visit a page without connecting to the Internet, Internet Explorer can retrieve a copy of the page from your hard disk without connecting to the Internet.

Obviously, if the online version of a Web page changes, the offline copy of the Web page becomes outdated. Fortunately, the offline browsing feature lets you *synchronize* the offline copy of a Web page with the online copy by downloading an updated version of the page to your hard drive. You can synchronize your offline pages manually, or you can tell Internet Explorer to automatically synchronize your pages on a regular basis — for example, every day at 2 a.m., when your teenager isn't using the phone (well, maybe).

If you have a permanent connection to the Internet, such as through a cable modem, DSL service, or a network at work, the Internet Explorer offline features aren't of much use to you because you're always online. But if you use a dial-up connection to access the Internet, pay attention to the features presented in this chapter.

Making a Page Available Offline

Suppose that you discover a Web site you want to visit often, but you don't want to connect to the Internet every time you visit the page. Here is the procedure for setting up a page for offline browsing:

1. **Browse your way to the site you want to view offline.**

   For example, I like to follow the exploits of the Fresno State softball team, whose home page is at `www.fansonly.com/schools/fres/sports/w-softbl/fres-w-softbl-body.html`.

2. **Choose the Favorites⇨Add to Favorites command.**

   This command summons the Add Favorite dialog box, as shown in Figure 8-1.

Figure 8-1:
The Add
Favorite
dialog box.

3. **If you don't like the name provided in the Name field, change the name.**

   Most of the time, the name is acceptable, so you can usually skip this step.

4. **Choose the Make Available Offline option in the Add Favorite dialog box.**

   This option configures the Web page properly so that you can view it offline.

   If you want, at this point you can click the Customize button. This action fires up the Offline Favorites Wizard, which lets you set up a schedule for automatically synchronizing the page and tweaks a few other offline settings. If you use the wizard, follow its instructions until you're returned to the Add Favorite dialog box.

5. **Click OK.**

The Add Favorite dialog box vanishes. Internet Explorer immediately synchronizes your offline copy of the Web page. This action may take a few moments, so be patient. While the Web page is synchronizing, a dialog box appears and lets you know that the page is being synchronized. The dialog box vanishes after the page is synchronized.

6. **You're done.**

You have now successfully set up the page for offline viewing.

 If you want to remove a page from your collection of offline pages, choose Favorites⊅Organize Favorites. Then, in the Organize Favorites dialog box, click the page you no longer want to access offline and uncheck the Make Available Offline option.

Viewing Web Pages Offline

To view Web pages offline, disconnect your computer from the Internet if it's connected. Then, start up Internet Explorer. Doing so summons the Dial-up Connection dialog box, as shown in Figure 8-2.

Figure 8-2:
The Dial-up
Connection
dialog box.

Normally, you type your user ID and password in the Dial-up Connection dialog box and then click the Connect button to connect your computer to the Internet. To work offline, click the Work Offline button instead. This action starts Internet Explorer in Offline mode, as shown in Figure 8-3. When Internet Explorer is in Offline mode, the title bar reads [Working Offline].

Figure 8-3:
Internet
Explorer is
working
offline.

To access an offline page, just select the page from your Favorites menu.

Internet Explorer continues in Offline mode until you disable Offline mode by choosing the File⇨Work Offline command.

If you close Internet Explorer while working in Offline mode, you're returned to Offline mode the next time you start Internet Explorer. After you set Internet Explorer to work in Offline mode, Internet Explorer always starts up in Offline mode until you choose File⇨Work Offline again to disable Offline mode.

Synchronizing Your Offline Pages

To bring your offline Web pages up-to-date, start up Internet Explorer and connect to the Internet. Next, follow these steps:

1. **Choose Tools⇨Synchronize.**

   Doing so summons the Items to Synchronize dialog box, as shown in Figure 8-4.

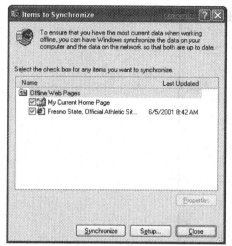

Figure 8-4:
The Items to
Synchronize
dialog box.

2. **Select the pages you want to synchronize.**

   Initially, all your offline pages are selected. Click the check box next to any Web page that you do not want to synchronize to deselect that item.

3. **Click Synchronize.**

   Internet Explorer proceeds to download fresh copies of each of the pages you selected. This process takes awhile, so now is a good time to fetch a cup of coffee. A dialog box appears and keeps you informed of Internet Explorer's progress. When all the pages are synchronized, Internet Explorer briefly displays a `Synchronization complete` message. Then, the progress dialog box disappears.

If you want to set up Internet Explorer so that it automatically synchronizes your pages on a regular basis, choose the Tools⇨Synchronize command to summon the Items to Synchronize dialog box; then click Setup. The Synchronization Settings dialog box appears, as shown in Figure 8-5.

The Synchronization Settings dialog box lets you set up three types of automatic updates for your offline Web pages:

✔ **Logon:** Lets you select pages that are automatically updated whenever you log on to the Internet.

✔ **On Idle:** Lets you select pages that are automatically updated whenever your computer is idle. For example, you can tell Internet Explorer to begin synchronizing your offline pages whenever your computer has been idle for more than 15 minutes.

✔ **Scheduled:** Lets you set up a schedule for regularly synchronizing your offline pages. For example, you can have your computer automatically start up the Internet and synchronize your offline pages every day at 2 a.m.

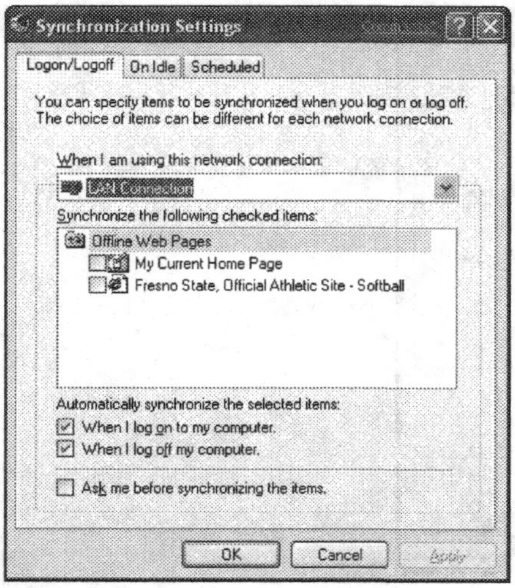

Figure 8-5:
The
Synchroniz-
ation
Settings
dialog box.

You can change the settings for an offline page by selecting the page in the Items to Synchronize dialog box and then clicking the Properties button. This action brings up the Properties dialog box, as shown in Figure 8-6. In this dialog box, you can click the Schedule tab to set up a schedule for synchronizing the page or press the Download tab to specify details of how you want the page to be downloaded, such as whether you want to also download pages linked to the offline page and whether you need to use a password to access the page.

Figure 8-6:
The
Properties
dialog box
for an offline
page.

Chapter 9

Getting Help While You Explore

* *

In This Chapter

▶ Calling for help

▶ Getting assistance with the Internet Explorer Help features

▶ Using Windows troubleshooters

▶ Finding help on the Internet

* *

*I*magine that you have a pet Internet guru who sits at your side while you surf the Web, ready and willing to answer your questions with straightforward responses spoken in plain English, gently but firmly correcting you when you make silly mistakes, never giggling at you behind your back. All you have to do is supply a steady stream of pizza and soda, let him or her out twice a day, and absorb the wisdom of the master.

The next best thing to having your own, personal Internet guide is using the built-in Help features of Internet Explorer. No matter how lost you become while exploring the Internet, help is but a few keystrokes or mouse clicks away.

Summoning Help

Internet Explorer comes with an excellent built-in Help system that can probably answer your most burning questions about the Web and Internet Explorer. You can summon this help in any of the following ways:

✔ **Press F1.** This action catapults you into the Internet Explorer Help system.

✔ **Choose Help⇨Help Topics.** This menu command is the mouse lover's equivalent to pressing F1.

✔ **Click the question mark icon.** Dialog boxes often have a question mark icon near the upper-right corner (as shown in the margin). Click this icon to transform the mouse pointer into a big question mark. You can then click any field in the dialog box to call up specific help for that field.

Getting to Know the Help Window

When you call up the Internet Explorer Help system, a separate window, like the one shown in Figure 9-1, appears. The Help window is divided into three main areas: a toolbar at the top, a contents area at the left, and the Help text on the right. As you can see, the contents portion of the Help window has four tabs across the top labeled Contents, Index, Search, and Favorites. All four tabs access the same Help information, but in a different fashion. The Contents tab groups Help topics by category, whereas the Index tab lists all Help topics in alphabetical order. The Search tab lets you look up Help information based on the word you type. The Favorites tab lets you create your own customized list of the Help topics you access most often.

Figure 9-1:
The Help
window.

Scanning the Contents

Clicking the Contents tab in the Help window displays a window that lists Internet Explorer Help topics by category. As Figure 9-1 shows, each category has a closed-book icon next to it. To expand a category, double-click the book icon. The Help topics associated with that category appear, and the closed-book icon changes to an open book. In addition, a category may include sub-categories, which may themselves have additional subcategories.

Notice that individual Help topics (as compared with categories that contain several topics) are represented by an icon that resembles a page with a big question mark. To display an individual Help topic, click the icon for the topic you want to display. The Help information for the topic appears on the right side of the Help window, and the contents remain visible on the left. For example, Figure 9-2 shows the Help contents after you open the Finding the Web Pages You Want category and click the topic Listing Your Favorite Pages for Quick Viewing.

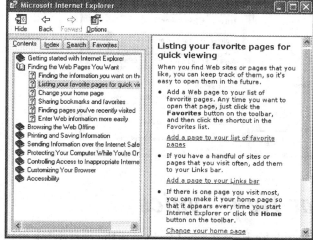

Figure 9-2:
Help
Contents
with a
category
expanded.

Many Help topics include links to other Help topics. For example, the Help topic shown in Figure 9-2 includes three links to other related topics: Add a Page to Your List of Favorite Pages, Add a Page to Your Links Bar, and Change Your Home Page. These links work just like the links in a Web document: Click once to follow the link.

Back

When you have followed a link to another Help topic, you can click the Back button on the Help toolbar to return to the preceding page.

Scanning the Index

The Help index, as shown in Figure 9-3, lists all the Internet Explorer Help topics in alphabetical order. To get help on a particular Help topic, scroll through the list of Help topics. When you find a topic that interests you, click the topic to display the appropriate Help page.

To find a Help topic quickly, type the first few letters of the topic in the text box that appears at the top of the Index tab. Doing this automatically scrolls the index to the topic you're interested in.

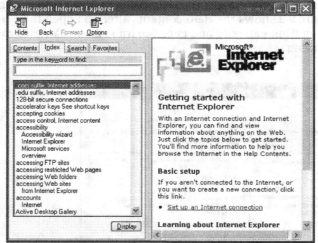

Figure 9-3:
The Help
index is a
list of Help
topics in
alphabetical
order.

Searching for Help Topics

You can also search for Help topics by clicking the Search tab in the Help
dialog box, typing a word or phrase, and then clicking the List Topics button.
Doing so displays a list of all the Help topics containing the word or phrase
you typed. For example, Figure 9-4 shows the results of a search for the word
favorites. Double-click any of the topics listed to display the Help topic.

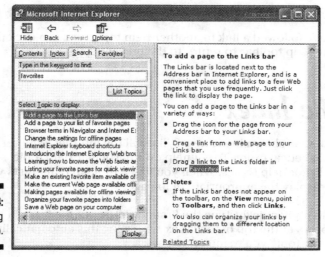

Figure 9-4:
Searching
for help.

Listing Your Favorite Help Topics

If you find yourself returning to a particular Help topic over and over again, you can add that Help topic to the Favorites tab so that you can call it up quickly when you need it. Figure 9-5 shows the Favorites tab with a few of my favorite Help topics added.

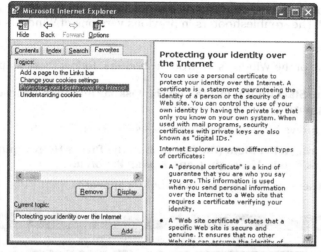

Figure 9-5:
These are a few of my favorite Help pages.

To add a Help topic to the Help Favorites, just follow these steps:

1. **Use the Contents, Index, or Search tabs to call up the Help topic you want to add to Favorites.**

2. **Click the Favorites tab.**

3. **Click the Add button.**

That's all there is to it.

To display a topic you've added to Help Favorites, click the Favorites tab and then double-click the topic you want to display. (If double-clicking gives you cramps, you can just click the topic once to select it and then click the Display button.)

To remove a Help topic from Favorites, click the Favorites tab, click the topic you want to remove, and click the Remove button.

Troubleshooting at Your Fingertips

If you don't find the clue you're looking for in the Internet Explorer Help feature, you may find the answer buried within the Help files that come with Windows. In fact, the Windows Help system includes several special troubleshooting features that can walk you through typical causes of common problems.

In this section, I show you how to conjure up the troubleshooters for Windows XP. The troubleshooters in previous versions of Windows are similar.

To fire up one of the Windows XP troubleshooters, follow these steps:

1. **Click the Start button located on the taskbar and then choose Help and Support.**

   The Windows XP Help page appears, as shown in Figure 9-6.

2. **Click Fixing a Problem (the last item in the Pick a Help Topic list), and then pick Email, Messaging, and Faxing Problems.**

   A list of several Internet troubleshooters appears.

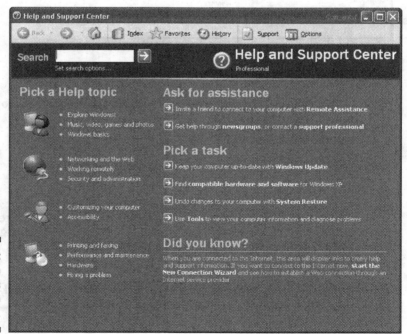

Figure 9-6:
The
Windows
XP Help
screen.

3. **Choose the troubleshooting topic that interests you.**

   For example, if you're having trouble with your modem, click Modem Troubleshooter. Figure 9-7 shows the Modem troubleshooter.

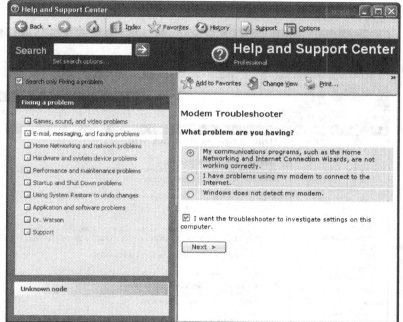

Figure 9-7:
The Modem troubleshooter.

4. **To use the troubleshooter, answer each of the troubleshooter's questions by clicking the appropriate button.**

   With luck, the troubleshooter leads you to the solution you seek.

Getting Help Online

If you can't find help for a specific problem in the Internet Explorer Help files, you can always turn to your online comrades on the Internet. The first place to check for online help is Microsoft's own Web page that's devoted to Internet Explorer technical support. You can call up this Web page by starting Internet Explorer and then choosing Help⇔Online Support. Or, you can manually navigate to the Internet Explorer technical support Web site at support.microsoft.com.

The Internet Explorer Support home page, as shown in Figure 9-8, provides up-to-date information about the latest releases of Internet Explorer. This Web page also includes links to pages that list frequently asked questions (FAQs), known problems with Internet Explorer, and other helpful information.

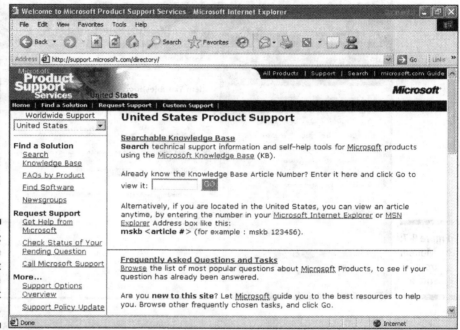

Figure 9-8: The Microsoft online support page.

Part III

Getting Connected with Outlook Express

The 5th Wave   By Rich Tennant

"I like getting complaint letters by e-mail. It's easier to delete than to shred."

In this part . . .

Internet Explorer comes with a companion program known as Outlook Express, a handy e-mail program that lets you send and receive electronic messages to and from your friends on the Internet. The chapters in this part show you how to use the basic features of Outlook Express, such as creating new mail messages, reading mail you have received, dealing with attachments, and setting up an address book that contains the e-mail addresses of the people you frequently exchange mail with. In addition, you'll learn how to use some of the more advanced Outlook Express features, such as adding an automatic signature to the end of your messages, setting up mail filters to screen out junk mail, accessing newsgroups, and working with more than one e-mail account.

You'll also learn how to use Outlook Express to access the free Microsoft e-mail service (Hotmail) and how to use MSN Messenger and NetMeeting to chat with your online buddies.

Chapter 10

E-Mailing with Outlook Express

*O*ne of the most common reasons people dare to venture forth onto the Internet is to use electronic mail — *e-mail,* as it's called. E-mail lets you exchange messages with your Internet-connected friends and colleagues. E-mail is much faster than regular mail, even mail delivered by Mr. McFeeley, the bespectacled mailman on *Mr. Rogers' Neighborhood* ("Speedy delivery!").

Sending an e-mail message is much like sending a letter through regular mail. In both cases, you write your message, put an address on it, and send it off through an established mail system. Eventually, the recipient of the message receives your note, opens it, reads it, and (if you're lucky) answers by sending a message back.

But e-mail offers certain advantages over regular mail. For example, e-mail arrives at its destination in a matter of minutes, not days. E-mail can be delivered any day of the week, including Sundays. And, as a special bonus, no way yet exists for your great-aunt to send you a fruitcake through e-mail.

About the only reason that the post office exists any more, other than transporting fruitcake, is that e-mail works only when both the sender and the receiver have computers connected to the Internet. In other words, you can't send e-mail to someone who isn't on the Internet.

Internet Explorer comes with a handy e-mail program named Outlook Express, which is a scaled-down version of the more powerful Outlook program that comes with Microsoft Office. Outlook Express handles not only

Internet e-mail, but also newsgroups. (You can find out about newsgroups in Chapter 14.) In this chapter, I focus on using Outlook Express for reading and sending e-mail.

Outlook Express and its older sibling, Microsoft Outlook, are not the only e-mail programs available. Fortunately, all e-mail programs can get along with one another, so you can use Outlook Express to exchange e-mail with your friends, whether they're using Outlook Express or Outlook or any other e-mail program.

Starting Outlook Express

As with all Windows programs, you can start Outlook Express a few different ways. Here are some of the more popular methods:

✔ Click Outlook Express on the Start menu. The exact location of Outlook Express on the Start menu depends on the version of Windows you're using. In Windows XP, you find Outlook Express near the top of the Start menu, under the heading E-Mail. In other versions of Windows, you can start Outlook Express by choosing Start⇨Programs⇨Internet Explorer⇨ Outlook Express. You may also find Outlook Express as a separate entry on the Start menu or on the Start⇨Programs menu.

✔ Click the Launch Outlook Express button on the Quick Launch toolbar, which is on the Windows taskbar, right next to the Start button.

If you don't see an icon for Outlook Express on the Quick Launch toolbar, you can create an icon by dragging the Outlook Express icon from the Start menu to the Quick Launch toolbar.

✔ In Internet Explorer, choose Tools⇨Mail and News⇨Read Mail.

✔ In Internet Explorer, click the Mail button and then choose Read Mail from the pop-up menu that appears.

However you open it, Outlook Express springs to life, displaying the window shown in Figure 10-1.

Each time you start Outlook Express, the program automatically checks to see whether you have any new mail. As long as you leave Outlook Express open (you can minimize it if you want), Outlook Express periodically checks to see whether new mail has arrived. Any new messages that you haven't yet read appear in boldface in the Inbox pane.

Hotmail: The poor man's e-mail

Hotmail is a free e-mail service offered by the Microsoft Network (also known as *MSN*). Hotmail is also a Web-based e-mail service, which means that you can access it from any web browser (including Internet Explorer) by going to www.Hotmail.com. The Hotmail Web site includes Web pages that allow you to see e-mail messages that have been sent to you and to send e-mail to other Internet users.

You can find complete information for using Hotmail in Chapter 12.

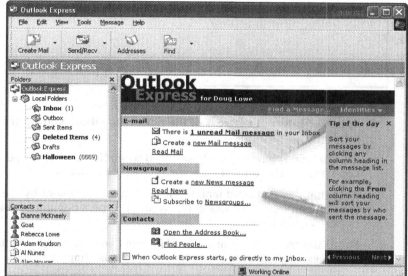

Figure 10-1:
Outlook
Express.

Sending E-Mail

To send e-mail, all you have to do is follow these steps:

Create Mail

1. **Click the Create Mail button on the left side of the toolbar.**

   Or, choose Message➪New Message or use the keyboard shortcut Ctrl+N. Whichever option you choose, a new, blank message appears, as shown in Figure 10-2.

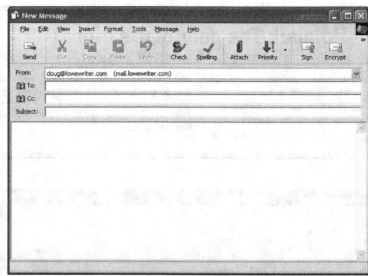

Figure 10-2:
A new
message.

2. **Type the Internet address of the person to whom you want to send the message.**

   The To field is automatically selected when the New Message dialog box appears, so you can just type the recipient's address.

   Note that you can send mail to more than one recipient by typing more than one name or address in the To field. Type a comma or semicolon between each name.

   For examples of different kinds of Internet addresses, check out the "Addressing your e-mail" sidebar, later in this chapter.

   If you frequently send e-mail to a particular person, you can add that person's e-mail address to your Address Book. Then, you can easily retrieve that person's e-mail address from your Address Book whenever you send her a message without having to retype the entire address each time. For more information about using the Address Book, see the section "Using the Address Book," later in this chapter.

3. **If you want to send a copy of the message to another user, type that person's address in the Cc field.**

   Click in the Cc field and then type the address or addresses of anyone to whom you want to send a copy of the message.

   If you want to send a copy of a message to someone else but you don't want the other recipients to know about it, use the Bcc field rather than the Cc field. A copy of the message is sent to each person listed in the Bcc field, but the people listed in the To and Cc fields aren't notified of the Bcc recipients. (If the Bcc field doesn't appear in the New Message window, choose the View⇨All Headers command to enable this optional field.)

4. **Type a succinct but clear title for the message in the Subject field.**

Click in the Subject field and then type the subject of your message. For example, type **Let's Do Lunch** or **Jetson, You're Fired!**

5. **Type your message in the message area of the New Message dialog box.**

Figure 10-3 shows what a message looks like with all this information typed and ready to go.

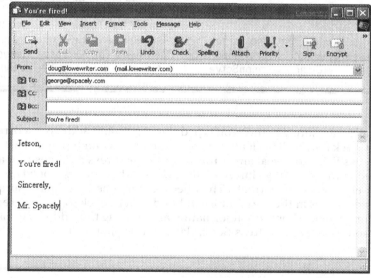

Figure 10-3:
A message all ready to be sent.

Send/Recv

6. **When you finish typing your message, click the Send/Recv button.**

Outlook Express dismisses the New Message dialog box and sends the message to the intended recipients.

If you're working in Internet Explorer and you want to send some quick e-mail without starting up Outlook Express, just click the Mail button on the toolbar and choose New Message from the pop-up menu that appears. The New Message command takes you straight to a New Document window, where you can compose and deliver your message without starting Outlook Express.

Rather than type a full Internet address, you can simply type the person's name if you already created an entry for that person in your Address Book. For more information, see the section "Using the Address Book."

Addressing your e-mail

Before you send e-mail, you need to know the address of the person to whom the message is intended (just like that pesky post office expects with paper mail). The easiest way to find out someone's e-mail address is to ask for it.

To send e-mail to a user of one of the major online services, compose the user's e-mail address as follows:

- For America Online users, type the user-name followed by @aol.com. For example, Lurch@aol.com.

- For CompuServe users, type the screen name followed by ¢.com. For example, Gomez¢.com. (Older CompuServe accounts, known as *CompuServe Classic accounts,* have numeric account numbers, such as 12345.6789. To send mail to a CompuServe Classic account, use the numeric user ID followed by @compuserve.com, but use a period rather than a comma to separate the two parts of the numeric user IDL: for example: 12345.6789@compuserve.com.

- For users of The Microsoft Network, type the username followed by @msn.com; for example, BillG@msn.com. (No, that's not really Bill Gates's e-mail address. Please don't flood The Microsoft Network with hate mail — or love mail — for Bill!)

Check

If you're not sure whether you typed the names and addresses correctly, click the Check button. This feature checks the names you typed against the Address Book to reveal any errors. (Outlook Express assumes that any name typed in the form of an Internet address — rather than bounced off the Address Book — is correct.) The Check feature checks to make sure that the address is in the correct format but doesn't check to make sure that the address exists. (For more information about using the Address Book, see the section "Using the Address Book," later in this chapter.)

Checking Your Message for Spelling Errors

If you have Microsoft Office or any of its programs (Word, Excel, or PowerPoint), Outlook Express includes a bonus feature: a spelling checker capable of catching those embarrassing spelling errors before they go out to the Internet. The spelling checker checks the spelling of every word in your message, looking up the words in its massive dictionary. Any misspelling is brought to your attention, and the spelling checker is under strict orders from Bill Gates himself not to giggle or snicker at any of your misspellings, even if you insist on putting an *e* at the end of *potato.* The spelling checker even gives you the opportunity to tell it that you are right and it is wrong — and that it should learn how to spell the way you do.

To spell-check your messages, follow these steps:

Spelling

1. **In the New Message window, click the Spelling button.**

   Or, if you prefer, choose the Tools⇨Spelling command or press F7. Whichever way you choose, the spelling checker comes to life, looking up your words in hopes of finding a mistake.

2. **Try not to be annoyed if the spelling checker finds a spelling error.**

   Hey, you're the one who told it to look for spelling mistakes; don't get mad if it finds some. If the spelling checker finds an error, it highlights the offending word and displays the misspelled word along with a suggested correction, as shown in Figure 10-4.

Figure 10-4:
The spelling
checker
does its
thing.

3. **Choose the correct spelling and then click either Change or Ignore to skip to the next word the spelling checker doesn't recognize.**

   • If you agree that the word is misspelled, scan the list of suggested corrections and click the one you like. Then click Change.

   • If, on the other hand, you prefer your own spelling, click Ignore. To prevent the spelling checker from asking you over and over again about a particular word that it doesn't recognize (such as someone's name), click Ignore All.

   • If you spelled the word correctly and think that you'll use the word often, click Add to add the word to the spell checker's dictionary.

   If the correct spelling doesn't appear on the list, type the correct spelling for the word in the Change To box. Then click Change.

4. **Repeat Steps 2 and 3 until the spelling checker gives up.**

   When you see the message `The spelling check is complete,` **your work is done.**

Sending Attachments

An *attachment* is a file you send along with your message. Sending an attachment is kind of like paper-clipping a separate document to a letter. In fact, Outlook Express uses a paper clip icon to indicate that a message has an attachment, and the button you click to add an attachment sports a paper clip design as well.

Here is the procedure for adding an attachment to an outgoing message:

Attach

1. Click the Attach button.

The Insert Attachment dialog box, as shown in Figure 10-5, appears.

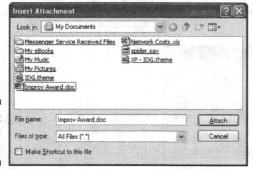

Figure 10-5:
Inserting an
attachment.

2. Rummage through the folders on your hard drive until you find the file you want to insert.

When you find the file you want to attach, click the filename to select it.

3. Click Attach.

The file is inserted into the message as an attachment. An icon for the attachment appears on a special Attach line that is inserted beneath the Subject field in the message header, as shown in Figure 10-6.

4. Finish the message and then click the Send button.

Finish typing the message you want to send and then click Send to send the message on its way.

Here are some things to consider when you send attachments:

✔ Be aware that sending large attachments can sometimes cause e-mail troubles, especially for attachments that approach a megabyte or more in size. If possible, you should mail several smaller attachments rather than one large one.

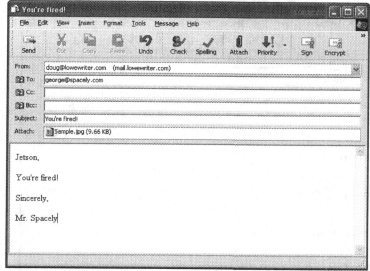

Figure 10-6:
E-mail attachments are shown on a separate Attach line in the heading portion of the message.

✔ If the attachment is large, consider shrinking it with a file compression program, such as WinZip, before you attach it. (You can download WinZip from www.winzip.com.)

✔ If you attach a file and then change your mind before you have sent the message, you can remove the attachment by right-clicking the attachment's name on the Attach line and then choosing Remove from the pop-up menu that appears.

Using HTML Formatting

Outlook Express has a nifty feature that enables you to add formatting to your e-mail messages. For example, you can change the font, size, or color of your message text, and you can insert pictures to liven things up. Figure 10-7 shows how you can make even the rudest of messages seem friendly by using Outlook Express formatting.

To accomplish its formatting virtuosity, Outlook Express employs the same HTML formatting codes used to create pages on the World Wide Web. Of course, when you send an HTML-formatted message to another Internet user, that user must have a mail program that's capable of reading messages formatted with HTML. Otherwise, your beautiful formats will be for naught. (Also, messages formatted with HTML take a little longer to send and receive than unformatted messages.)

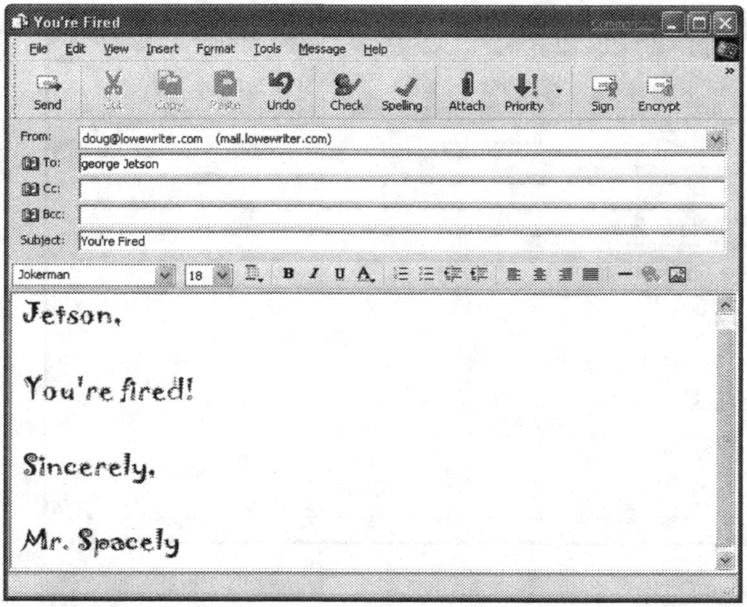

Figure 10-7:
A message
that uses
HTML
formatting.

To apply HTML formatting, you use the special HTML formatting toolbar that appears in the New Message window. If your New Message window doesn't have this toolbar, summon the Format➪Rich Text (HTML) command.

Table 10-1 shows how you can use the various buttons and controls on the HTML formatting toolbar to enhance the text in your e-mail messages.

Table 10-1	Controls on the HTML Formatting Toolbar
Control	*Format*
 Jokerman ⌄	Changes the font
 18 ⌄	Sets the size of the text font
 🔽	Selects a heading style or other style for the text
 **B**	Makes the text bold
 *I*	Makes the text italic

Control	Format
U	Underlines the text
A	Changes the text color
	Creates a numbered list
	Creates a bulleted list
	Decreases the indentation
	Increases the indentation
	Left-aligns the text
	Centers the text
	Right-aligns the text
	Aligns the text on left and right
	Inserts a horizontal line
	Creates a hyperlink
	Inserts a picture

Receiving E-Mail

E-mail wouldn't be much good if it worked like a send-only set, sending out messages but not receiving them. (I once had an aunt who worked that way.) Fortunately, you can receive e-mail as well as send it — assuming, of course, that you have friends who write.

To read e-mail that other users have sent you, follow these steps:

1. **Start Outlook Express.**

   Refer to the section "Starting Outlook Express," at the beginning of this chapter, if you're not sure how.

2. **Go to the Inbox by clicking the Inbox icon.**

   The Inbox icon appears on the list of folders on the left side of the Outlook Express window. When you go to the Inbox, Outlook Express displays a list of all the messages you've received, as shown in Figure 10-8. Any new messages you haven't read are displayed in boldface type

3. **Double-click a new message to read it.**

   The message is displayed in its own window.

   If the message is small, you can skip this step. Instead, just read the message in the preview pane that appears in the main Outlook Express window.

4. **Read the message.**

5. **After you read the message, dispense with it in one of the following ways:**

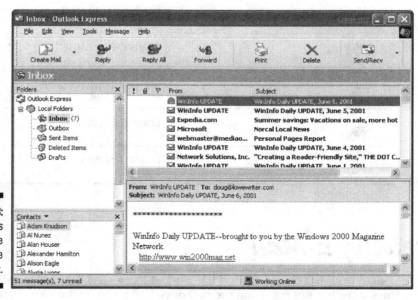

Figure 10-8: Messages wait to be read in the Inbox.

Reply

- If the message is worthy of reply, click the Reply button. A new message window appears, allowing you to compose a reply. The To field is automatically set to the user who sent you the message, the subject is automatically set to RE: (whatever the original subject was), and the complete text of the original message is inserted at the bottom of the new message. Compose your reply and then click the Send button.

Reply All

- If the message was originally sent to several people, you can click the Reply All button to send a reply to all the original recipients.

Forward

- If the message was intended for someone else, or if you think that someone else should see it (maybe it contains a juicy bit of gossip!), click the Forward button. A new message window appears, enabling you to select the user or users to whom you want to forward the message. The original message is inserted at the bottom of the new message, with space left at the top for you to type an explanation of why you think the message qualifies for more audience (Hey Mr. Spacely, get a load of this!).

- To print the message, click the Print button.

Delete

- If the message is unworthy even of filing, click the Delete button. Poof!

When you first install Outlook Express, you automatically receive two messages in your Inbox: one welcoming you to Outlook Express and the other describing the security features available in Outlook Express. Be sure to read both these messages.

Saving an Attachment As a File

If someone is kind enough to send you a message that includes an attached file, you can save the attachment as a separate file by following these steps:

1. **Open the message that has the attachment.**

   You can tell which messages have attachments by looking for the paper clip icon (as shown in the margin) next to the message on the message list.

2. **Right-click the attachment icon and then choose the Save As command from the pop-up menu.**

   A Save As dialog box appears.

3. **Choose the location where you want to save the file.**

   You can use the controls in the standard Save As dialog box to navigate to a different drive or folder.

4. **Type a filename for the file.**

   Outlook Express, always trying to help out, proposes a filename. You need to type a new filename only if you don't like the filename that Outlook Express suggests.

5. **Click Save.**

   The attachment is saved as a file.

If the attachment is a graphic image, Outlook Express displays the image directly in the message when you open the message. As a result, you don't have to do anything special to view images your friends send to you via e-mail.

Beware of attachments from unfamiliar sources: They may contain a virus that could infect your computer. Unfortunately, Outlook Express doesn't have any built-in virus protection. If you're concerned about viruses (and you should be), purchase and install separate virus-protection software, such as Norton AntiVirus (www.norton.com) or McAfee VirusScan (www.mcafee.com).

Using the Address Book

Most Internet users have a relatively small number of people with whom they exchange e-mail on a regular basis. Rather than retype their addresses every time you send e-mail to these people, you can store your most commonly used addresses in the Outlook Express Address Book. As an added benefit, the Address Book enables you to refer to your e-mail friends by name (for example, George Jetson) rather than by address (george@spacely.com).

Adding a name to the Address Book

Before you can use the Address Book, you must add the names of your e-mail correspondents to it. The best time to add someone to the Address Book is after you receive e-mail from that person. Here's the procedure:

1. **Open an e-mail message from someone whose e-mail address you want to add to the Address Book.**

   Outlook Express displays the message.

2. **Right-click the user's name and then choose Add to Address Book.**

   A dialog box similar to the one shown in Figure 10-9 appears, describing the person's e-mail address information.

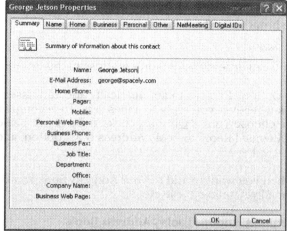

Figure 10-9:
The
Summary
tab lists
contact
information.

3. **If the summary information is incorrect, click the Name tab. Then type the correct address information in the appropriate fields.**

   Figure 10-10 shows the dialog box that appears after you click the Name tab. In some cases, these fields may already correctly contain the person's name. More often, however, the First field contains the person's e-mail address and the Middle and Last fields are blank.

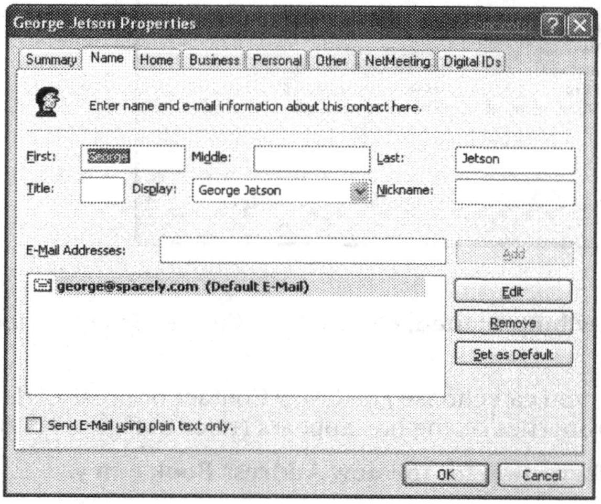

Figure 10-10:
Adding an
address to
the Address
book.

As you type the first, middle, and last names, Outlook Express automatically fills in the complete name in the Display field. For example, if you type **George** in the First field and **Jetson** in the Last field, the Display field is automatically set to George Jetson.

4. Click OK.

The address shows up in the Address Book.

5. Close the message.

Thereafter, you can access the person's address in the Address Book.

TIP

You can configure Outlook Express to automatically add addresses to your Address Book whenever you reply to a message. To accomplish this feat of automation, choose Tools➪Options, click the Send tab, select the Automatically Put People I Reply to in My Address Book option, and then click OK.

For those times when you want to add to your Address Book someone who hasn't sent you e-mail yet, follow these steps:

1. In Outlook Express, choose Tools➪Address Book.

Addresses

Or, click the Addresses button or press Ctrl+Shift+B. One way or the other, the Address Book window appears, as shown in Figure 10-11.

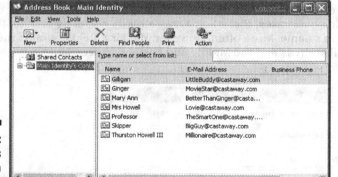

Figure 10-11:
The Address Book main window.

2. Click the New button; then, choose New Contact from the menu that appears.

New

If you prefer, you can choose File➪New Contact or press Ctrl+N. In any event, the Properties dialog box appears (refer to Figure 10-10).

3. Type the information for the new Address Book entry.

Type, at a minimum, the person's first and last name and e-mail address. If you want, you can include additional information, such as phone numbers and addresses under the Home, Business, Personal, and Other tabs.

4. Click OK.

The Address Book adds your new entry.

Sending a message to someone in the Address Book

To send a message to a user who's already in the Address Book, follow these steps:

  1. **In the New Message window, click the little Address Book icon next to the To field.**

The Select Recipients dialog box appears, as shown in Figure 10-12.

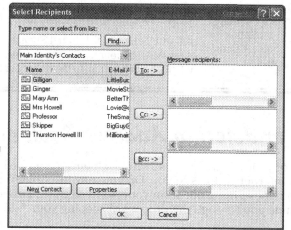

Figure 10-12:
The Select
Recipients
dialog box.

2. **Double-click the name of the person to whom you want to send e-mail.**

The person's name appears on the To list, on the right side of the dialog box. If double-clicking is against your religion, just click once on the person's name and then click the To button.

You can add more than one name to the To list. You can also add names to the Cc or Bcc lists by clicking the Cc or Bcc buttons, respectively. (Bcc stands for *b*lind *c*arbon *c*opy; names you add to the Bcc list receive a copy of the message, but other recipients of the message don't know that a copy was sent to the Bcc recipient.)

3. **After you have selected all the names you want, click OK.**

Poof! You're back at the New Message dialog box, and the names you selected appear in the To, Cc, and Bcc fields.

Synchronizing mail accounts

Most e-mail accounts provided by Internet Service Providers automatically delete your e-mail messages from the mail server when you receive the mail to your Inbox. If you use only one computer to access your e-mail, this arrangement works fine. But what if you want to access your e-mail from two or more computers? Suppose that you want to access e-mail from your computer at work and your computer at home. If you do, some of your messages may wind up in the Inbox on your office computer while other messages may be in the Inbox on your home computer. Neither computer contains all the messages you've received.

If you access mail from two or more computers, you may want to consider setting up a special type of e-mail account called an IMAP account. IMAP mail accounts don't automatically delete messages from the server whenever you download mail to your Inbox. Instead, IMAP accounts keep copies of downloaded messages and enable you to synchronize the Inbox on each computer you use to access your e-mail. To synchronize your e-mail account, choose the Tools⇨Synchronize All command.

Unfortunately, not all Internet Service Providers offer IMAP accounts. You have to ask your ISP whether it can set up an IMAP account for you.

Changing or deleting Address Book entries

On occasion, one of your e-mail buddies switches Internet Service Providers and gives his new Internet address to you. Or, you may lose touch with someone and decide to remove her name from your Address Book. Either way, the following steps guide you through the process of keeping your Address Book up to date:

Addresses

1. **From Outlook Express, click the Addresses button or choose Tools⇨Address Book.**

   The Address Book dialog box appears (refer to Figure 10-11).

2. **Click the address you want to change or delete.**

3. **To delete the address, click the Delete button.**

   Or, if you prefer, you can right-click the name and then choose Delete from the shortcut menu.

4. **To change the address, click the Properties button.**

   After the Properties dialog box appears, make any necessary changes and then click OK.

5. **Click OK when you're finished.**

Working with Address Book folders

With Outlook Express, you can organize your Address Book contacts into folders, much like you can organize your files into folders in Windows Explorer. By default, Outlook Express dumps all your Address Book contacts into a single folder named Contacts. This method is okay if you have just a few dozen contacts. But if you have more contacts than you can easily keep track of in a single folder, you should consider creating additional folders to help you categorize your contacts. For example, you can create folders with names, such as Business or Friends and Relatives or Washed-Out '60s Sitcom Stars.

The following procedure shows you how to create an Address Book folder and move one or more existing contacts from the Contacts folder to the new folder:

New

1. **In the Address Book window, click the New button; then, choose New Folder from the menu that appears.**

   If you prefer, you can choose File⇨New Folder or press Ctrl+R. Outlook Express then asks for a name for the new folder, using the dialog box shown in Figure 10-13.

Figure 10-13: Creating a new Address Book folder.

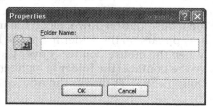

2. **Type a name for the new folder; then, click OK.**

   Outlook Express returns you to the Address Book window. Your newly created folder appears on the list of folders at the left side of the Address Book window, as shown in Figure 10-14.

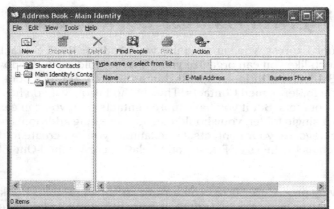

Figure 10-14:
A folder is
born.

3. **Click the Contacts folder on the folder list at the left side of the
   Address Book window.**

   This step opens the Contacts folder.

4. **Drag to the folder you created in Step 2 each contact you want to
   move from the Contacts folder.**

   To *drag* a contact, start by positioning the cursor over the contact name,
   clicking the left mouse button, and holding the button on the contact
   name. Next, while holding the mouse button down, move the mouse
   pointer to the new folder that appears on the folder list at the left side of
   the Address Book window. When the mouse pointer is over the folder
   into which you want to move the contact (the folder is highlighted),
   release the mouse button. Outlook Express moves the Address Book
   entry to the new folder.

5. **That's all!**

Here are a few additional details you should know about:

- If you can't see the folder list at the left side of the Address Book
  window, you can display the list by choosing View➪Folders and Groups.

- If you want to change the name of a folder, right-click the folder and
  select the Properties command from the shortcut menu. Doing this summons the Folder Properties dialog box, where you can type a new name
  for the folder. Click OK and you're done.

- To send mail to a recipient you've placed in a folder, call up the Select
  Recipients dialog box as usual (by clicking the To button while composing a new message). The Select Recipients dialog box contains a drop-
  down list that lists your folders. Use this drop-down list to select the
  folder that contains the address of the person you want to send mail to.

Chapter 11

More E-Mail Shortcuts and Tricks

* *

* *

*I*f you send or receive more than a few e-mail messages each week, you'll want to check out the timesaving shortcuts and tricks in this chapter. Here, you can find out how to save time by setting up folders to sort your e-mail messages, filter out messages you don't want to read, set up Outlook Express for more than one user, and more.

You can also find out about Outlook Express features that let you dress up your e-mail. Stationery lets you change text fonts and add colorful backgrounds, and signatures let you automatically add your name, address, phone number, and perhaps a catchy phrase to the end of all your messages.

Have fun!

Using Outlook Express Folders

When you first install Outlook Express, five message folders are set up to store and organize messages you have sent and received. These folders are displayed as icons on the left side of the main Outlook Express window. You spend most of your time working in the Inbox folder, which contains messages you have received. But you can display the contents of other folders by clicking the icon for the folder you want to view.

The five message folders initially set up for Outlook Express are

- ✔ **Inbox:** Where Outlook Express stores your incoming messages.

- ✔ **Outbox:** Where Outlook Express stores your outgoing messages until they're sent to their intended recipients.

- ✔ **Sent Items:** Where Outlook Express places copies of messages you have sent.

- ✔ **Deleted Items:** Where Outlook Express stores deleted messages. (Much like the Windows Recycle Bin, the Deleted Items folder enables you to undelete a deleted message if you later decide that you want the message back.)

- ✔ **Drafts:** Where Outlook Express stores messages you have not yet finished. Suppose that your favorite episode of *Gilligan's Island* comes on while you're in the middle of composing a long message. Just click the Close button (the little X in the upper-right corner of the New Message window) and then choose Yes when Outlook Express asks whether you want to save the message. Outlook Express saves your message in the Drafts folder so that you can return to it after Gilligan spoils the rescue attempt.

Outlook Express also enables you to create your own message folders. For example, you may want to create separate folders for different categories of messages, such as work-related, friends and family, and so on. Or you may want to create date-related folders for storing older messages. For example, you can create a 2001 folder to save all the messages you receive in 2001.

This section explains how to work with message folders.

Don't confuse the mail folders I describe in this section with Address Book folders, which I describe in Chapter 10. Address Book folders let you organize contacts in your Address Book. In contrast, Outlook Express folders let you organize mail messages you have sent or received.

Creating a new folder

Before you start saving important messages, you would be wise to create one or more folders in which to save the messages. I use just a single folder, named Saved Items, but you may want to create several folders for saving messages according to their content. For example, you can create a Personal Items folder for personal messages and a Business Items folder for business messages. You can come up with your own scheme for organizing saved messages, but my advice is to keep your method simple. If you create 40 folders for storing saved messages, you run the risk of forgetting which message is in which folder.

To create a new folder, follow these steps:

1. **Click Local Folders on the Outlook Express folders list.**

2. **Choose File⇨Folder⇨New Folder.**

   The Create Folder dialog box appears, as shown in Figure 11-1.

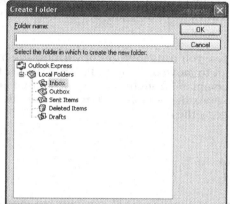

Figure 11-1:
The Create
Folder
dialog box.

3. **Type a name for the new folder.**

   For example, type **Work Items**.

4. **Click OK.**

The new folder is visible in the folder tree on the left side of the Outlook Express window. If you click on the new folder, the message There are no items in this view appears in the folder view area, indicating that the folder you have just created is empty.

Moving messages to another folder

After you create a folder for your messages, moving a message to the folder is easy. Just follow these steps:

1. **In the Inbox, position the mouse pointer over the message you want to move.**

2. **Click and hold the left mouse button. While holding the left button, drag the message to the folder in which you want it stored.**

   The folder is located in the folder tree on the left side of the Outlook Express window.

3. **Release the mouse button when the mouse pointer is over the folder to which you want to move the message.**

   The folder is highlighted when you move the mouse pointer over it. When you release the mouse button, Outlook Express moves the message to the folder you selected and deletes the message from the Inbox folder.

If you prefer, you can make a copy of the message rather than move the message. Just hold down the Ctrl key before dragging the message to the new folder.

If dragging isn't your cup of tea, you can move or copy a message by right-clicking the message you want to move or copy and then choosing the Move to Folder or Copy to Folder command from the pop-up menu that appears. This action brings up a dialog box that enables you to designate the folder to which you want to move or copy the message.

Filtering Your Mail

A common complaint of frequent e-mail users is receiving too much unsolicited mail. Outlook Express has several features that let you deal with this problem, as I describe in this section.

Using message rules

One way to deal with the problem of unwanted mail is to create message rules. *Message rules* let you set up Outlook Express so that it automatically takes a specific action whenever a certain type of message arrives. For example, you can set up a message rule to automatically delete any message sent to you from a specific e-mail address. Or, you can have Outlook Express automatically move to a folder you've created any message that contains specific text in the subject line.

A message rule consists of two parts. The first part is a called a condition. The *condition* identifies which specific e-mail messages the rule applies to. Outlook Express lets you use conditions to filter these types of messages:

✔ Messages that contain specific names or words on the From, To, or Cc lines.

✔ Messages that contain specific words on the Subject line.

✔ Messages that are larger than a size you specify.

✔ Messages that are marked as high priority.

- Messages that are encrypted.

- Messages that have attachments.

- Messages that are sent to a specific mail account you specify. (This option is particularly useful when you have subscribed to more than one e-mail service and want to route incoming messages into different folders based on the account the messages were sent to.)

- All other messages. (This option is useful if you want to perform some special action for messages that aren't handled by other filters you set up.)

You can specify more than one condition for a message rule. For example, you can set up a rule to handle all messages that contain the word *Picture* on the Subject line and are larger than 10K.

The second part of a message rule is the *action,* which indicates what you want Outlook Express to do with messages that meet the criteria for the rule's condition. You can choose any of these actions for each of your message rules:

- Move the message to a specific folder.

- Copy the message to a specific folder, leaving the original in your Inbox.

- Delete the message.

- Forward the message to another person.

- Reply to the message.

- Highlight the message with a color of your choosing.

- Flag the message.

- Mark the message as having already been read.

- Do not download the message from the server.

- Delete the message from the server. (Some servers keep a copy of messages that have been sent to you.)

As with conditions, you can specify more than one action for each message rule. For example, you can create a rule that automatically deletes messages you don't want to read and sends a reply message that says something like "Stop sending me mail!" (Of course, that probably doesn't work. Many automated spam systems pretend that they never receive this type of message.)

To illustrate how to set up a message rule, suppose that you want to create a rule that automatically moves to a folder all messages that have a specific word on the Subject line. Here's how to do it:

1. **Choose Tools➪Message Rules➪Mail from the main Outlook Express window.**

   This action summons the New Mail Rule dialog box, as shown in Figure 11-2.

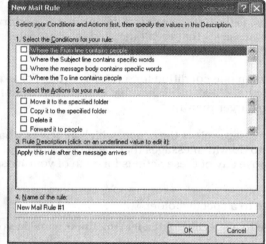

Figure 11-2:
The New
Mail Rule
dialog box.

If you have previously created a message rule, the Message Rules dialog box appears rather than the New Mail Rule dialog box. The Message Rules dialog box is shown later in this section, in Figure 11-4. To summon the New Mail Rule dialog box, click the New button in the Message Rules dialog box.

2. **Choose Where the Subject Line Contains Specific Words for the condition.**

   When you do, the following line is added to the Rule Description text box:

   ```
   Where the Subject line contains specific words
   ```

3. **Click the Contains Specific Words option in the Rule Description text box.**

   The Type Specific Words dialog box appears, as shown in Figure 11-3.

4. **Type a word or phrase in the text box and then click Add.**

   The word or phrase you typed appears in the bottom of the Type Specific Words dialog box. For example, if you type **SARAH:** in the text box, the following appears at the bottom of the Type Specific Words dialog box:

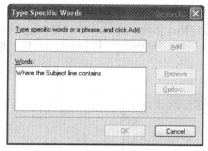

Figure 11-3:
The Type
Specific
Words
dialog box.

```
Where the Subject line contains
SARAH:
```

Note that capitalization doesn't matter in message rules. If you type **SARAH:** in the text box, the rule applies to messages that have **SARAH:**, **Sarah:**, or **sarah:** in the Subject field.

You can type additional words or phrases in the text box. Each time you type a word or phrase, click the Add button to add the words to the Words list at the bottom of the dialog box.

5. **Click OK.**

   You return to the New Message Rule dialog box. The condition line in the Rule Description text box now shows the message rule you have created — for example:

   ```
   Where the Subject line contains 'SARAH:'
   ```

6. **Choose Move It to the Specified Folder for the rule action.**

   When you do, the following line is added to the Description text box:

   ```
   Move it to the specified folder
   ```

7. **Click Specified in the Rule Description text box.**

   A dialog box showing all your Outlook Express folders appears.

8. **Click the folder you want the messages moved to; then click OK.**

   When you return to the New Mail Rule dialog box, the message rule description is adjusted to indicate the folder you selected. For example, if you select Sarah's Mail for the folder, the Rule Description box contains this line:

   ```
   Move it to the Sarah's Mail folder
   ```

9. **Type a meaningful name for the rule in the Name of the Rule text box.**

   For example: **Sarah's Messages**.

10. Click OK.

The New Message Rule dialog box gives way to the Message Rules dialog box, as shown in Figure 11-4. This dialog box lists all the message rules you have created.

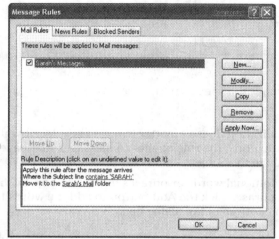

Figure 11-4:
The
Message
Rules
dialog box.

11. Click OK.

From now on, any message you receive with the word you specified on the Subject line (in this case, SARAH:) is automatically moved to the folder you specified (in this case, Sarah's Mail).

If you create more than one message rule, the rules are applied to your incoming mail in the order in which they're listed in the Message Rules dialog box. Suppose that you create a rule to move all messages with the word *SARAH:* in the subject line to the Sarah's Mail folder and then create a second rule to delete any message from george@spacely.com. If george@spacelysprockets.com sends you a message with SARAH: on the subject line, that message is moved to the Sarah's Mail folder because of the first message rule. However, if you reverse the order of the rules so that the Delete-messages-from-george@spacelysprockets.com rule appears first, the message would be deleted.

You can change the order in which rules are listed in the Message Rules dialog box by using the Move Up and Move Down buttons.

To delete a rule, click the rule to select it and then click Remove.

Blocking senders

Another way to deal with unwanted mail is to create a Block Senders list, which is simply a list of e-mail addresses from which Outlook Express refuses to accept mail. Any mail received from a sender on the Blocked Senders list is automatically moved to the Deleted Items folder.

If you receive a piece of obnoxious mail from someone, you can quickly add that person to your Blocked Senders list by clicking the message in your Inbox and then choosing the Message⇨Block Sender command. A dialog box appears and informs you that the person has been added to your Blocked Senders list.

To review the list of e-mail senders you have blocked, choose Tools⇨ Message Rules⇨Block Senders List. This command summons the dialog box shown in Figure 11-5, which shows all the e-mail senders you have blocked. The buttons on this dialog box enable you to add, remove, or modify any of these blocked senders.

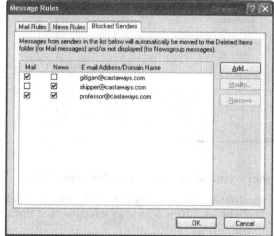

Figure 11-5:
Managing
your
Blocked
Senders list.

Using Stationery

Outlook Express lets you attractively format your e-mail messages using what it calls stationery. *Stationery* lets you create fancy messages with background images, alternative text fonts, and even boilerplate text. This section shows you how to create messages that use stationery and how to set the default stationery that will be used for all new messages.

For stationery to work, you must activate HTML formatting. To do so, choose the Format➪Rich Text (HTML) command when you create the message.

Because stationery requires HTML formatting, messages that use stationery may take longer to download than unformatted messages.

Creating a message with stationery

Outlook Express comes with 14 different stationery selections for you to choose from. To create an e-mail message using one of these 14 stationery options, follow these steps:

1. **In Outlook Express, choose the Message➪New Message Using➪Select Stationery command.**

   The Select Stationery dialog box appears, as shown in Figure 11-6.

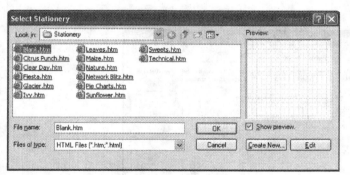

Figure 11-6:
The Select
Stationery
dialog box.

2. **Select the stationery you want to use and then click OK.**

   A New Message window appears, using the stationery you selected. For example, Figure 11-7 shows a New Message window that uses the Ivy stationery.

3. **Compose and send your message.**

   Note that some stationery selections include sample text for your message. For example, several stationery choices have the text Your message here in the stationery. To compose your message, you should delete the Your message here text and then type your own text in its place.

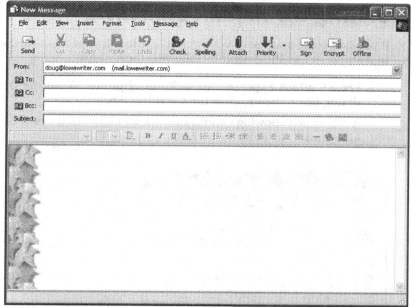

Figure 11-7:
A new message that uses the Ivy stationery.

Here are a few other tidbits of useful stationery information:

- Outlook Express keeps track of up to ten of your most recent stationery choices. The ten most recently used stationery selections appear as menu choices when you choose the Message⇨New Message Using command.

- In Outlook Express, you can click the arrow that appears next to the New Message button to reveal a menu that includes the ten most recent stationery selections.

- If you want to change the stationery of a message while you're in the New Message window, choose Format⇨Apply Stationery and select the stationery you want to use.

- To remove stationery, choose Format⇨Apply Stationery⇨No Stationery.

- If the Format⇨Apply Stationery command is not available, use the Format⇨Rich Text (HTML) command to enable stationery. You can then use the Format⇨Apply Stationery command.

Setting the default stationery

If you find some stationery you want to use for all your messages, you can set that stationery as the default by following these steps:

1. **From Outlook Express, choose Tools⇨Options. When the Options dialog box appears, click the Compose tab.**

   A dialog box showing various options for composing new messages appears, as shown in Figure 11-8.

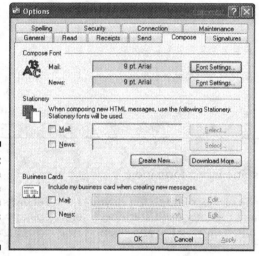

Figure 11-8:
The Compose tab in the Options dialog box.

2. **Click in the Mail check box to activate stationery for new mail messages.**

3. **Click the Select button.**

   This step summons the Select Stationery dialog box (refer to Figure 11-6).

4. **Select the stationery you want to use and then click OK.**

   You return to the Options dialog box. The stationery you selected is listed next to the Mail check box.

5. **Click OK again.**

   The Options dialog box disappears. From now on, all your e-mail messages use the stationery you just selected.

Creating new stationery

If you aren't satisfied with any of the stationery selections that come with Outlook Express, you can easily create your own stationery. Outlook Express includes the Stationery Setup Wizard to simplify the process of creating stationery.

To access the Stationery Setup Wizard, follow these steps:

1. **Choose the Tools⇨Options command and then click the Compose tab.**

   This step summons a dialog box that lists the options used for composing new messages, as shown in Figure 11-8, earlier in this section.

2. **Click the Create New button.**

   The Stationery Setup Wizard appears, as shown in Figure 11-9.

Figure 11-9: The Stationery Setup Wizard comes to life.

3. **Click Next.**

   The Stationery Setup Wizard displays options for the message background, as shown in Figure 11-10.

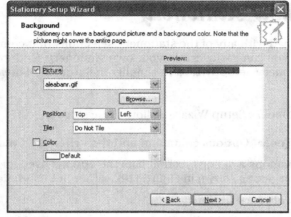

Figure 11-10:
The
Stationery
Setup
Wizard lets
you choose
a back-
ground.

4. **Set the background options and then click Next.**

You can set the background of your stationery to a picture or to a solid
color. To use a picture, click Picture and then select one of the pictures
listed in the drop-down box or click the Browse button to select any
image file you want to use. You can also set the picture's position, and
you can specify how you want the picture to be tiled: horizontally, verti-
cally, filling the entire page, or not tiled.

To use a solid color for the background, click Color and then choose the
color you want to use from the drop-down list.

After you select the background you want, click Next. The Stationery
Setup Wizard displays the font options that will be used for your message, as shown in Figure 11-11.

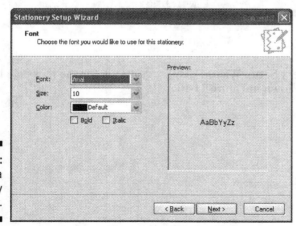

Figure 11-11:
Pick a
font — any
font.

5. Choose the font options you want to use and click Next.

The Stationery Setup Wizard lets you choose the font, size, and color from drop-down lists. In addition, you can use the Bold and Italic check boxes to use bold or italic text.

When you click Next, the Stationery Setup Wizard displays the margin options, as shown in Figure 11-12.

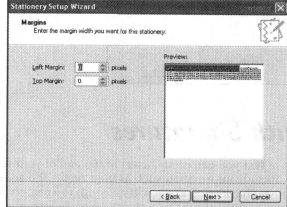

Figure 11-12:
The
Stationery
Wizard
issues a
margin call.

6. Adjust the margin settings and then click Next.

The margins are measured in *pixels,* the tiny dots that make up your screen display. Clicking the arrows next to the margin fields increases or decreases the margins in units of 25 pixels.

When you click Next, the Stationery Setup Wizard next asks for a name for your new stationery, as shown in Figure 11-13.

7. Type a name for your new stationery and click Finish.

After you click Finish, Outlook Express creates the new stationery and returns you to the Options dialog box (refer to Figure 11-8).

8. Click OK to dismiss the Options dialog box.

You're done! You can now use your new stationery.

Another way to get more stationery is to click the Download More button in the Compose tab of the Options dialog box. This action fires up Internet Explorer and takes you to a page at the Microsoft Web site from which you can download additional stationery files.

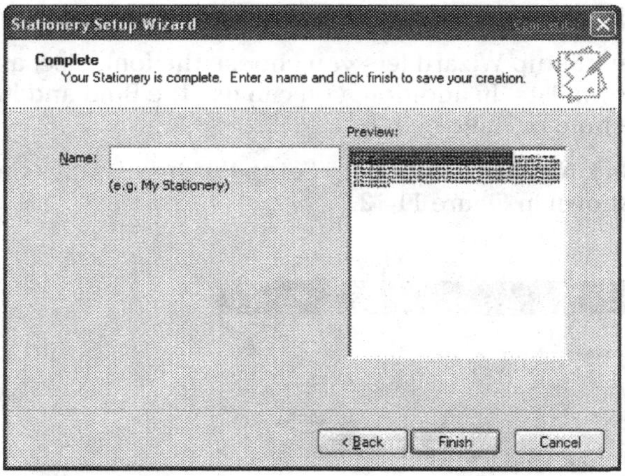

Stationery Setup Wizard

Complete
Your Stationery is complete. Enter a name and click finish to save your creation.

Name:

(e.g. My Stationery)

Preview:

< Back   Finish   Cancel

Figure 11-13:
Time to
name your
stationery.

Signing Off with Signatures

A *signature* is a bit of text you can easily insert at the end of your messages. Signatures usually include information such as your name, the address of your home page (if you have one), and a witty saying. You can configure Outlook Express to automatically insert a signature at the end of every message, or you can insert a signature manually whenever you want to use one.

To create a signature, follow these steps:

1. **In Outlook Express, choose Tools⇨Options.**

   Doing so summons the Options dialog box.

2. **Click the Signatures tab.**

   By doing so, you summon the Signatures options, as shown in Figure 11-14.

3. **Click the New button.**

   A signature named Signature #1 is created.

4. **Click in the text box that appears in the Edit Signature portion of the dialog box and then type the text you want to use for your signature.**

   To create a signature that consists of more than one line, just hit the Enter key when you want to create a new line.

5. **If you want the signature to be automatically attached to every message you send, choose the Add Signatures to All Outgoing Messages option.**

   If you don't select this option, you have to manually insert the signature. I list the steps to do so later in this section.

6. Click OK.

The Options dialog box is dismissed.

You can create more than one signature by clicking the New button. A new signature (named Signature #2) appears in the Signatures list box. You can change the text for any signature by first selecting the signature from the Signatures list box and then editing the signature text in the Edit Signature text box.

Figure 11-14:
Creating a
signature.

If you want to change the name of a signature, select the signature in the Signatures list box, click the Rename button, and then type a new name for the signature.

To manually insert a signature into a new message, choose Insert⇨Signature when you create the new message. If you have created more than one signature, the Insert⇨Signature command leads you to a menu that lists all your signatures.

Looking Up an E-Mail Address

Outlook Express includes a built-in link to several Internet search services that can help you find an e-mail address for an individual or business. To use this feature, choose Edit⇨Find⇨People. The Find People dialog box, as shown in Figure 11-15, appears.

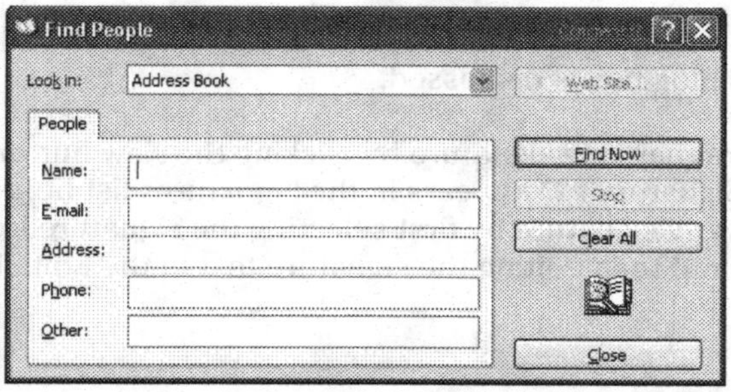

Figure 11-15:
The Find
People
dialog box.

This dialog box enables you to access the following address databases and services:

✔ Your very own Address Book

✔ Yahoo! People Search

✔ Bigfoot

✔ InfoSpace

✔ InfoSpace Business

✔ SwitchBoard

✔ Verisign

✔ WhoWhere?

To search for a person's e-mail address, first select the search service you want to use from the drop-down list. Then type the person's name and click the Find Now button. After a brief delay, the Find People dialog box expands to show a list of all those who match the name you typed, as shown in Figure 11-16.

If the name you're looking for doesn't appear on the list, you can try again with a different search service. If the name does appear, select it and then click the Add to Address Book command.

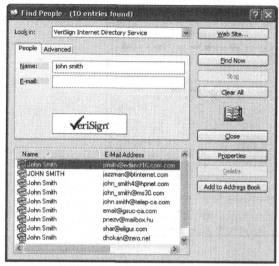

Figure 11-16:
Check out
all the John
Smiths.

Creating and Using Mailing Groups

If you find that you frequently send mail to a particular group of people, you can create a special type of Address Book entry known as a mailing group. A *mailing group* is simply a list of people selected from your Address Book. When you send a message to the group, Outlook Express automatically sends a copy of the message to each person in the group.

To create a mailing group, follow these steps:

Addresses

1. **Click the Addresses button on the Outlook Express toolbar.**

   The Address Book appears. (If you forgot what it looks like, refer to Figure 10-11 in Chapter 10.)

2. **Create an Address Book entry for each person you want to include in the group.**

   If all the people in the group are already in your Address Book, you can skip this step.

New

3. **Click the New button and then choose New Group from the menu that appears.**

   Or choose File➪New Group. Either way, a Properties dialog box for a new mailing group appears, as shown in Figure 11-17.

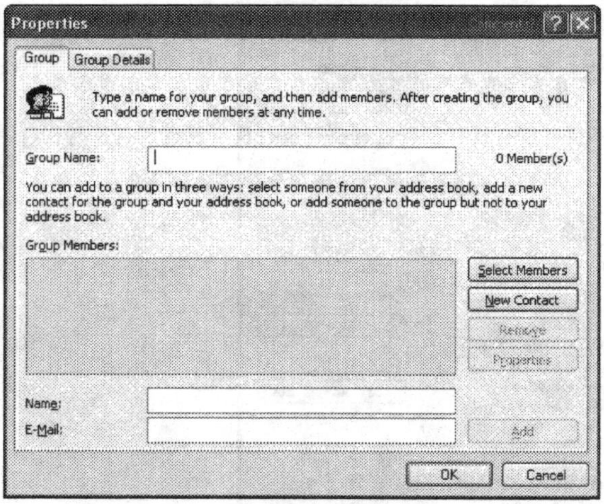

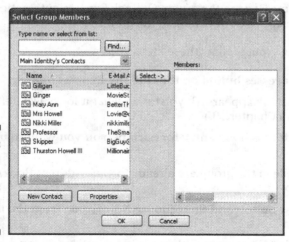

Figure 11-17:
Creating a
new mailing
group.

4. **Type a name for the new group in the Group Name text box.**

   For example, to create a group that consists of your friends who are stranded on a desert isle, type something like **castaways**.

5. **Click the Select Members button.**

   The Select Group Members dialog box appears, as shown in Figure 11-18.

Figure 11-18:
Selecting
group
members
for a mailing
group.

6. To add a member to the group, click the member from the list on the left side of the dialog box and then click the Select button.

Alternatively, you can simply double-click the name on the list on the left. Either way, Outlook Express adds the name to the Members list box on the right side of the Select Group Members dialog box.

7. Repeat Step 6 for each person you want to add to the group.

If you accidentally add the wrong person to the group, you can remove that person by selecting his or her name in the Members list box and pressing the Delete key.

8. After you finish adding names to the group, click OK.

You're returned to the Properties dialog box for the group. The names you selected for the group appear in the Members list box.

9. Click OK.

The Address Book reappears, as shown in Figure 11-19. The name of the group you created appears on the list at the left side of the Address Book window. If you select the group, the names of the group members appear in the window as well.

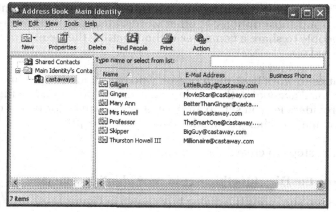

Figure 11-19: No phone, no lights, no motor cars. Not a single luxury.

10. Click the Close button (the X in the upper-right corner of the window) to dismiss the Address Book.

You're done!

After you create a group, sending mail to the group is easy. When you're composing a new message, click the To button to summon the Select Recipients dialog box. The groups you created are highlighted in the Select Recipients dialog box by a special icon.

Here are a few additional points to keep in mind when you work with groups:

- ✔ A person's e-mail address can appear in more than one group. This feature lets you include Thurston Howell III in not only the Castaways group, but also another group named Eccentric Millionaires (along with Bill Gates and Ross Perot).

- ✔ You can easily add names to an existing group by clicking the group name in an Address Book window and then clicking the Properties button. When the Group Properties dialog box appears, click Select Members and add your new member to the group.

- ✔ To remove a person from the group, call up the Group Properties dialog box. Then, click the member you want to remove and click the Remove button.

Changing Identities

If more than one person uses your computer to access e-mail or Internet newsgroups, you may want to consider creating a separate Outlook Express *identity* for each person. Each identity can have its own Inbox and other Outlook Express folders, separate contacts in the Address Book, and separate newsgroup subscriptions. In other words, identities make it easy for two or more people to share a computer without getting their e-mail and newsgroups mixed up.

For identities to work best, each person who has an identity should have a separate e-mail account with your Internet service provider. Most Internet service providers let you set up additional e-mail names for family members, though you may be charged an additional fee for the privilege.

Here are the steps to create a new identity:

1. Choose the File⇨Identities⇨Add New Identity command.

This step summons the dialog box shown in Figure 11-20.

Figure 11-20:
Establishing
your
identities.

2. **Type a name for the new identity in the text box.**

3. **If you want to create a password for the identity, check the Require a Password check box.**

4. **Click OK to create the identity.**

   When Outlook Express offers to switch to the new identity, click Yes. Outlook Express then starts the Internet Connection Wizard, which asks you for important information, such as your full name, e-mail address, and the Internet address for your mail server. Type all this information dutifully, and Outlook Express creates the new identity for you.

After you have created an identity, you can switch to that identity at any time by choosing the File⇨Switch Identity command. This action brings up the dialog box shown in Figure 11-21, which lists the identities you have created. Click the identity you want to switch to and then click OK.

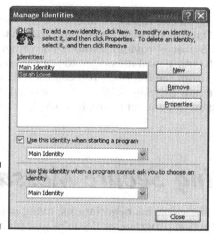

Figure 11-21:
Switching
identities.

If you have created more than one identity for Outlook Express, an Exit and Log Off Identity command appears on the File menu. You should use this command whenever you exit Outlook Express. That way, the Switch Identities dialog box (refer to Figure 11-21) appears the next time you start Outlook Express so that you can choose the identity you want to work with.

Reading Mail Offline

Outlook Express includes an offline reading feature that lets you dial in to the Internet, download your mail, and then disconnect from the Internet so that you can read your mail offline. This feature is useful if

- ✔ Your Internet service provider charges by the hour.
- ✔ You want to download your e-mail to a laptop computer and then take your computer to the park and read your mail.
- ✔ You want to free up your phone line so that your teenager can use it while you read your e-mail.

To set up Outlook Express to work offline, choose the Tools➪Options command and click the Connection tab. Select the Hang Up After Sending and Receiving option and then click OK.

To download your e-mail so that you can read it offline, click the Send and Receive button on the toolbar. Outlook Express uses your modem to connect your computer to your Internet Service Provider, establish a connection with your e-mail server, download all your e-mail messages to your Inbox, and then disconnect your computer from the Internet. You can then read your mail, compose replies, or create new messages. When you're finished, click the Send and Receive button again to connect to the Internet and send your replies and new messages.

Sending and Receiving Secure Messages

If you're involved in top-secret nuclear arms negotiations, living in Fryburg under the Federal Witness Protection program, or if you're just plain paranoid, you may want to use the Outlook Express security features to send and receive messages. Outlook Express has two methods for securing your e-mail: *encryption,* which scrambles the text of your message so that no one other than the intended recipient can read the message, and *digital signing,* which guarantees the sender's identity.

Before you can use either encryption or digital signing, you must obtain a *digital ID,* which is sort of the online equivalent of a driver's license. You can get digital IDs from several certification authorities on the Internet for a modest fee (about $15 per year).

To get a digital ID, go to the Microsoft Outlook Express Digital ID page, at `www.microsoft.com/windows/oe/certpage.htm`. Then, follow one of the links to one of the certification authorities to obtain a digital ID.

After you have obtained your digital ID, sending a secure message is easy:

- ✔ To encrypt a message, choose the Tools➪Encrypt command when you compose the message.
- ✔ To sign the message, choose Tools➪Digitally Sign.

When you receive a message that has been encrypted, Outlook Express automatically decodes the message for you. If the message has been signed, Outlook Express verifies the sender's digital ID and displays a warning message if a problem occurs with the ID — for example, if the ID has expired.

Chapter 12

Hotmail: E-Mail for Free!

* * *

In This Chapter

▶ Signing up for a new Hotmail account

▶ Configuring Outlook Express to work with an existing Hotmail account

▶ Using your Hotmail account in Outlook Express

▶ Accessing your Hotmail account from a web browser

* * *

Hotmail is a free e-mail service that doesn't require you to use a special e-mail program, such as Outlook Express. Instead, Hotmail works through the World Wide Web, so you can access your Hotmail e-mail account using Internet Explorer or any other web browser.

The best part about Hotmail is that it's free. Microsoft makes money from Hotmail by selling advertising for the Hotmail Web site — not by charging membership fees. Unfortunately, this means that you have to put up with sometimes obnoxious advertisements when you check your mail, but at least you don't have to pay for your Hotmail account.

Why Bother with Hotmail?

Because you must have an Internet account to access Hotmail and most Internet accounts come with an e-mail account, why would you bother setting up a Hotmail account? You have several reasons:

✔ You can access your Hotmail account from any computer connected to the Internet, as long as the computer has a fairly current version of Internet Explorer or Netscape Navigator. This feature is a great plus if you need to access your e-mail account while you're traveling.

✔ With your ISP e-mail account, your e-mail address changes if you decide to switch to a different ISP. In contrast, Hotmail lets you set up a permanent e-mail address that doesn't change even if you decide to switch to a different ISP.

✔ If several members of your family use the Internet through a single ISP account, each person can create her own Hotmail e-mail account. Although some ISPs let you have more than one e-mail account, many give you only one, requiring that all your family members share a common e-mail account. And providers that do allow you to create more than one e-mail account usually charge you for the privilege.

✔ If you have an e-mail account at the company where you work, you can use Hotmail to set up a private e-mail account for personal mail. You don't have to worry about your boss's snooping through your personal e-mail.

Signing Up for a Hotmail Account

Before you can use Hotmail, you must sign up for a Hotmail account. Fortunately, Hotmail accounts are free and the procedure for setting one up is pretty simple. Just follow these steps:

1. Fire up Internet Explorer and go to the Hotmail home page.

The address is www.hotmail.com. Figure 12-1 shows the Hotmail home page.

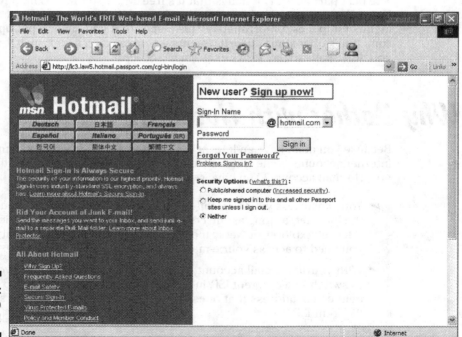

Figure 12-1:
Welcome to Hotmail!

2. **Click the link labeled Sign Up Now.**

   This step takes you to the Hotmail Registration page, as shown in Figure 12-2.

3. **Fill in the identification information requested by the Hotmail Registration Page.**

   Hotmail wants to know your first and last names, the country, state, zip code, and time zone where you live, your gender, and the year you were born.

4. **Type in the Sign-In Name field the name you want to use for your e-mail address.**

   Your sign-in name is combined with @hotmail.com to form your complete e-mail address. For example, if your sign-in name is George, your e-mail address is George@hotmail.com.

   Don't fret too much over the sign-in name at this point. Because Hotmail already has a few million users, odds are good that the name you want to use has already been taken. You see what to do in that case a few steps later in this procedure.

5. **Type twice the password you want to use for your e-mail account: once in the Password field and again in the Re-Enter Password field.**

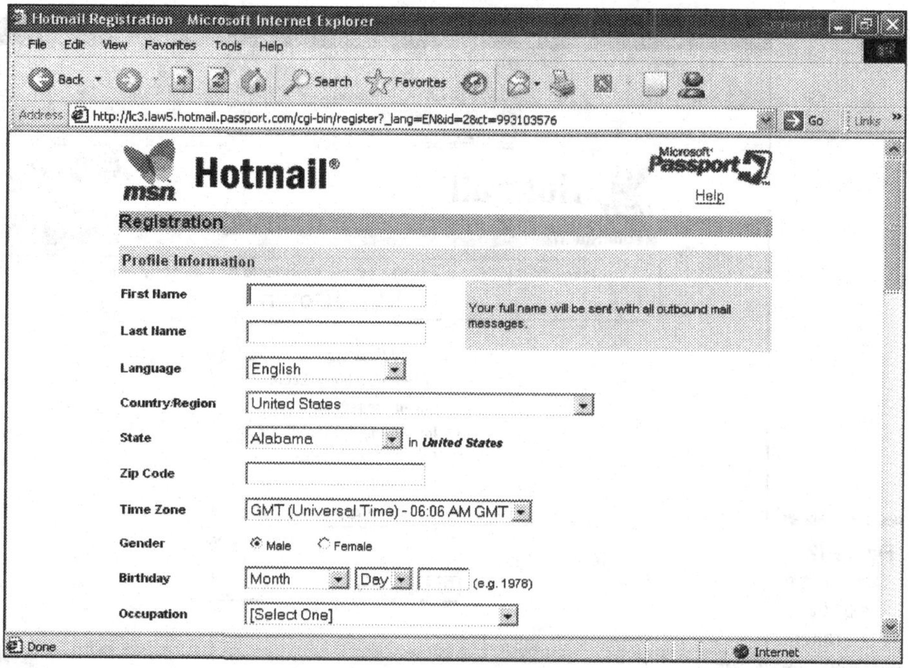

Figure 12-2:
The Hotmail registration page.

For security reasons, your password isn't displayed on the screen as you type it. As a result, Hotmail asks you to type the password twice to make sure that you didn't type it incorrectly.

You can use any word you want for your password, but the password must be at least eight characters long.

6. Type a secret question and the question's answer in the appropriate fields.

The secret question is used to verify your identity in case you forget your password.

Make sure that the answer to your question is truly secret. Otherwise, anyone can break into your Hotmail account by answering the question. For example, don't use a question like "Who wrote the Monroe Doctrine?" or "Who's buried in Grant's Tomb?" Questions such as "What is my mother's maiden name?" and "What year did I graduate from high school?" are also pretty easy to figure out.

7. Click the Submit Registration button.

Hotmail processes your registration information. Ninety-nine percent of the time, Hotmail next informs you that the sign-in name you chose has already been taken. For example, Figure 12-3 shows the screen I saw when I requested *LoweDown* as my sign-in name. As you can see, Hotmail suggests a few alternatives to the name you requested.

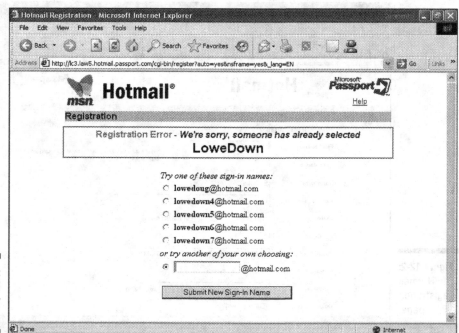

Figure 12-3: That name is already taken.

8. Pick one of the alternatives suggested by Hotmail or type a new login name in the text box.

If you type a new login name, you may again pick a name that is already in use. In other words, you may have to repeat this step several times before you get a name you like.

Most of the good names are already taken. You can keep trying to get a cool name, such as Mulder, Darth Maul, or Mini-Me, but, trust me, the good names are already taken. You may as well just pick one of the alternatives suggested by Hotmail. If you want a cool name, you probably have to attach a number to the end of it, such as jetson67 or minime38994.

9. Click Submit New Login Name.

If the new name you picked is also one that is already in use, return to Step 8.

When you finally settle on a unique login name, you see a page similar to the one shown in Figure 12-4.

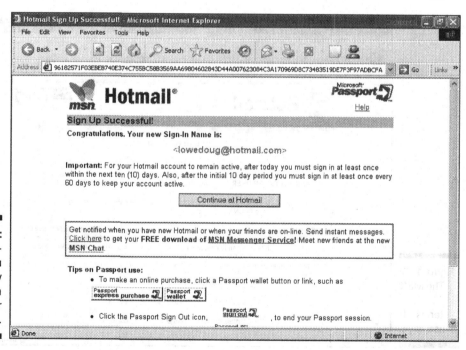

Figure 12-4: Congratulations — you have finally made a name for yourself.

10. **Click Continue at Hotmail to access your Hotmail account.**

    This step takes you to the MSN Web Site Terms of Use page, as shown in Figure 12-5.

11. **Read the terms of use.**

    Yeah, right. The terms-of-use page contains 7,330 words carefully composed by the Microsoft legal department to describe the rules you must follow if you want to use Hotmail or any other part of the Microsoft MSN Web site.

    To quote Inigo from *The Princess Bride:* "Let me explain — no, there is too much. Let me sum up." The rules basically say that you must behave yourself. You can't use Hotmail to send junk mail, chain letters, or obscene materials.

    If you haven't seen *The Princess Bride,* put this book down now, go to the nearest video store, and rent it. A couple of hours spent watching *The Princess Bride* is far more enjoyable than two hours spent reading the MSN Web Site terms of use.

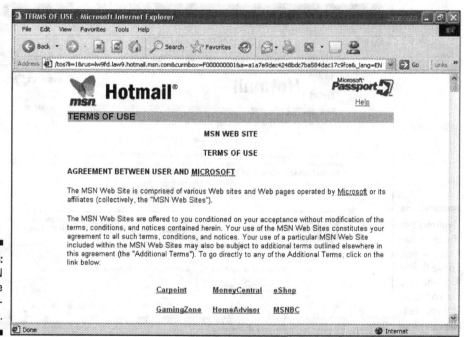

Figure 12-5:
The MSN Web site terms-of-use page.

12. **Scroll down to the bottom of the Terms of Use page and click I Accept.**

You're taken to a page that lists various services you can subscribe to that automatically send you e-mail about topics you may be interested in. Sign up for one or more of these services if any of the topics strike you as interesting or if you don't have any friends to send you real e-mail.

13. **Click Continue.**

Another page of subscription offers appears.

14. **Click Continue again.**

Finally! You're now taken to your Hotmail inbox, from which you can send and receive mail using your new Hotmail account.

Configuring Outlook Express to Use a Hotmail Account

After you have created a Hotmail account, you can configure Outlook Express to use it if you want. Or, you can skip this section altogether and access your Hotmail account from Internet Explorer.

To configure Outlook Express for a Hotmail account, follow these steps:

1. **In Outlook Express, choose the Tools➪Accounts command.**

The dialog box shown in Figure 12-6 appears. This dialog box lists all the Internet accounts Outlook Express is configured to work with.

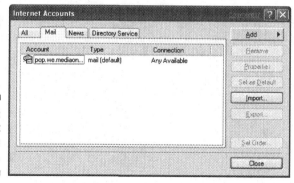

Figure 12-6:
The Internet Accounts dialog box.

2. **Click the <u>A</u>dd button and then choose <u>M</u>ail from the menu that appears.**

   The Internet Connection Wizard appears, ready to set up a mail account for you, as shown in Figure 12-7.

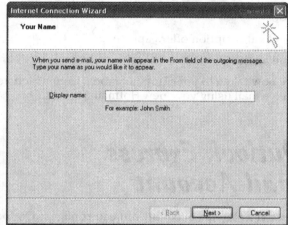

3. **Type the name you want to use as your display name and then click <u>N</u>ext.**

   The *display name* is the name that Outlook Express puts in the From field when you send a message to someone. Usually, you should just type your real name here.

   When you click Next, the Internet E-Mail Address page appears, as shown in Figure 12-8.

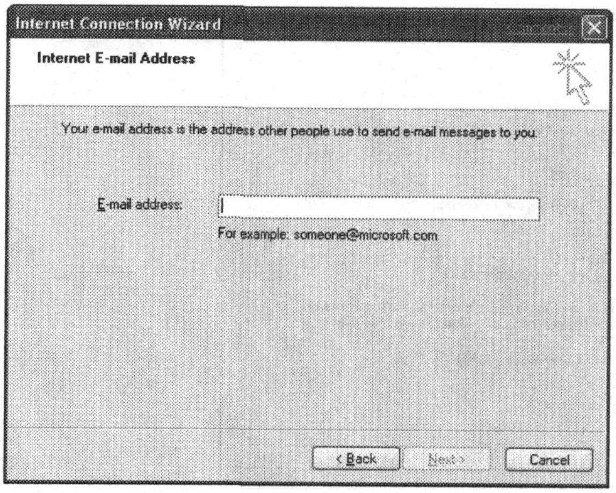

Figure 12-8:
Type your
Hotmail
address.

4. **Type your complete Hotmail e-mail address in the E-Mail Address field and then click Next.**

   For example, if your Hotmail account name is Gilligan, type gilligan@Hotmail.com in the E-Mail Address field. When you click Next, the E-Mail Server Names page appears, as shown in Figure 12-9.

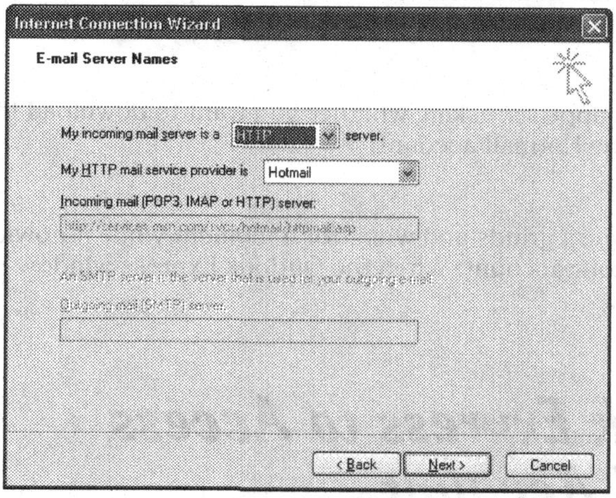

Figure 12-9:
Type the
Hotmail
server
address.

5. **Choose HTTP for the incoming mail server type and Hotmail for the HTTP Service Provider field, and then click Next.**

   When you click Next, the Internet Mail Logon page appears, as shown in Figure 12-10.

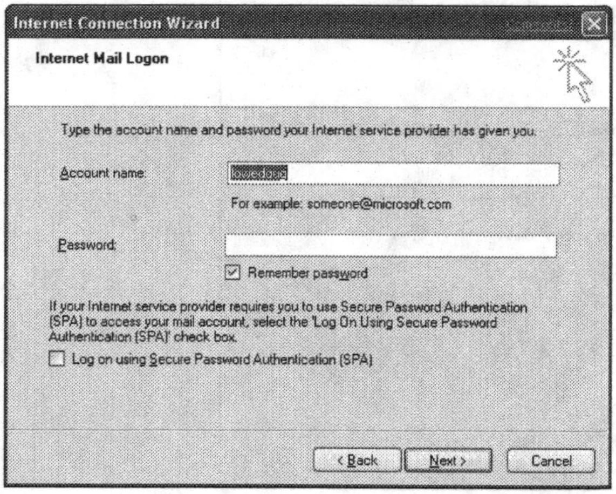

Figure 12-10:
The Internet
Mail Logon
page.

6. **Type your Hotmail password in the Password field and then click Next.**

   The last page of the Internet Connection Wizard appears, congratulating you for successfully setting up Outlook Express for your Hotmail account. Aren't you proud?

7. **Click Finish.**

   You're returned to the Internet Accounts dialog box, which now includes the Hotmail account you just added.

8. **Click Close.**

   A dialog box appears, asking whether you want to download the message folders for the Hotmail account.

9. **Click Yes.**

   Outlook Express grinds and whirs for a moment while it downloads the folders for your account. When the Outlook Express window reappears, you're done.

Using Outlook Express to Access Your Hotmail Account

After you have set up your Hotmail account, you can access it from Outlook Express to send and receive mail. Although using a Hotmail account from Outlook Express is similar to using your regular e-mail account, they have a few differences:

✔ To read your incoming mail, scroll down the Folders list to the Hotmail folders and click on the Inbox. You can read messages and send replies the same as you do with your regular e-mail account.

✔ Unlike regular e-mail accounts, Hotmail keeps a copy of all your e-mail messages on its servers. That way, you can access your Hotmail inbox from another computer and still read your mail. However, Hotmail limits the total size of all your e-mail messages to 2MB. When your stored messages exceed the 2MB limit, Hotmail sends you mail to let you know that you should delete some messages. If you don't delete messages within a few days, Hotmail automatically deletes some of your messages. For that reason, you should make a point of regularly deleting old messages.

✔ To send a message via your Hotmail account, you must first tell Outlook Express that you want to send the message using Hotmail rather than your regular e-mail account. You can do that by clicking the Hotmail icon in the folder list before you click the New Mail button. Or, you can click the New Mail button and then choose your Hotmail account from the drop-down list that appears in the From header of the New Message dialog box.

Using Hotmail from the Web

One of the benefits of using Hotmail is that you can access it from any computer that has a connection to the Internet and a web browser. All you have to do is connect to the Internet, go to the Hotmail home page at www.Hotmail.com, and sign in using your Hotmail sign-in name and password. Figure 12-11 shows the page that appears when you access your Hotmail account.

Across the top of the Hotmail page is a horizontal menu that lets you access several basic Hotmail functions:

✔ **Inbox:** Lets you read mail that has been sent to you. Incoming messages are listed in the middle of the page.

In Figure 12-11, you can see that I've received one message: a welcome message from the Hotmail staff. You, too, will receive this friendly welcome when you join Hotmail.

To read a message in your Inbox, just click the underlined name of the message in the From column.

You can delete one or more messages by clicking the check boxes for the messages you want to delete and then clicking the Delete button near the top of the Inbox message list.

✔ **Compose:** Lets you create an e-mail message to send to someone else. A separate Compose page appears, with fields you can fill in for the To address, Subject, and message text. You can also spell-check your message, attach pictures or other files, and use stationery.

✔ **Addresses:** Lets you keep track of e-mail addresses of the people you frequently send mail to. Note that your Hotmail Address Book is separate from your Outlook Express Address Book. The first time you click Addresses, you're taken to an empty Hotmail address book — even if you have dozens or hundreds of names stored in your Outlook Express Address Book.

✔ **Folders:** Lets you organize your e-mail by storing messages in folders. Hotmail has several built-in folders:

  • **Inbox:** Holds incoming e-mail messages.

  • **Sent Messages:** Holds messages you've already sent.

  • **Drafts:** Holds drafts of messages until you're ready to send them.

  • **Trash Can:** Holds messages you have deleted.

  • **Bulk Mail:** A repository for your junk mail.

You can also create your own folders to help you organize messages you have received.

✔ **Options:** Lets you set options that affect how Hotmail works. You can use the Options page to change your display name, password, and other account information. You can also set up message filters and a blocked-senders list. And, you can access a Hotmail feature, called the Inbox Protector, that's designed to limit the amount of junk mail that reaches your inbox. You can also use the Options page to set up a signature that is automatically attached to messages you send.

✔ **Calendar:** Calls up MSN Calendar, a Web site that lets you keep track of your schedule, create to-do lists, and compose other notes. You can also use MSN Calendar to schedule appointments with other MSN Calendar users.

✔ **Help:** Provides information about using Hotmail.

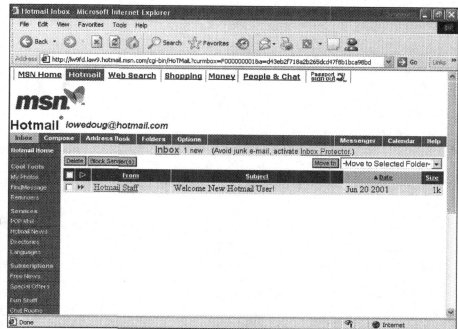

Figure 12-11:
Accessing
your Hotmail
account
from the
Web.

Chapter 13

The Instant Message Connection

*T*his chapter shows you how to use two Internet Explorer programs that are designed to let you chat online with other Internet users: MSN Messenger Service and NetMeeting.

The MSN Messenger Service — which I call MSN Messenger, for short — is a basic instant-message program that lets you find out whether your friends are connected to the Internet and exchange instant messages with them. MSN Messenger is similar to the popular America Online program AOL Instant Messenger (also known as AIM) and other Internet chatting services, such as ICQ and IRC.

NetMeeting is a much more complicated program that enables you to communicate with other Internet users — not just with instant messages, but also with voice and video if your computer is equipped with a microphone or videocamera.

Using MSN Messenger

To use MSN Messenger to chat online with your friends, you must first set up MSN Messenger to identify your friends. In addition, the friends you want to communicate with through MSN Messenger must have the service installed on their computers. After everything is set up, whenever your friends log on to the Internet, you're alerted. When MSN Messenger informs you that one of your friends is online, you can easily send a message, which your friend receives almost immediately. MSN Messenger is a great way to stay in touch with your Internet friends.

Although MSN Messenger is similar to AOL Instant Messenger, MSN Messenger and AIM are competing services. Unfortunately, that means that MSN Messenger users and AIM users cannot talk to one another. To talk to one of your online buddies, you and your friend must both use the same service — either MSN Messenger or AIM.

Setting up MSN Messenger

MSN Messenger is available as part of Internet Explorer 6 and is also included in Windows Millennium Edition and Windows XP. To find out whether MSN Messenger has been installed on your computer, look for the MSN Messenger icon on your Windows taskbar.

If the MSN Messenger icon isn't present on your taskbar, you must install MSN Messenger before you can use it. To download and install the latest version of MSN Messenger, fire up Internet Explorer and visit the MSN Messenger Service Web site at messenger.msn.com, as shown in Figure 13-1.

Click the big Download Now! button to download and install MSN Messenger.

Figure 13-1:
The MSN Messenger Service Web site.

Running MSN Messenger

After you have installed MSN Messenger, MSN Messenger runs automatically each time you start your computer. If you have closed the MSN Messenger window or if you have turned off the option that automatically runs MSN Messenger, you can start MSN Messenger using one of these methods:

- ✓ Double-click the MSN Messenger icon on the Windows taskbar.
- ✓ Click the Start button on the Windows taskbar and then choose All Programs⇨MSN Messenger Service. (In previous versions of Windows, choose Programs⇨MSN Messenger Service.)

- ✓ From Internet Explorer, choose the Tools⇨MSN Messenger Service command or click the Messenger button on the toolbar.
- ✓ From Outlook Express, choose the Tools⇨MSN Messenger Service command.

Whichever method you use to start MSN Messenger, a window similar to the one shown in Figure 13-2 appears. In the center of the MSN Messenger window is a list of your online contacts, indicating which contacts are online and which are not. You can send instant messages to any of your contacts who are online. (As you can see, the MSN Messenger contact list is empty. For information about adding contacts, see the section "Adding contacts," later in this chapter.)

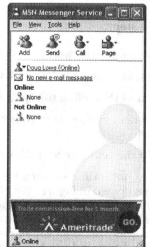

Figure 13-2:
MSN
Messenger.

Below the menu bar at the top of the MSN Messenger window is a toolbar that contains these icons:

- ✔ **Add:** Adds a person to your contact list
- ✔ **Send:** Sends an instant message to another MSN Messenger user
- ✔ **Call:** Initiates an Internet phone call
- ✔ **Page:** Pages a digital cell phone or mobile pager

Adding contacts

Before you can use MSN Messenger to send instant messages to your online friends, you must first create a list of your online contacts. The tricky part is that each of your online contacts must also have the MSN Messenger software and an account with a free Microsoft service known as *Passport*. If you try to add someone to your contact list who doesn't have the MSN Messenger software or a Passport account, MSN Messenger asks for your permission to send that person an e-mail message telling him how to download and install MSN Messenger and sign up with Passport.

Note that both Hotmail and the Microsoft MSN Internet Access service are automatically linked to Passport. So if your friend has a Hotmail account or uses MSN Internet Access to connect to the Internet, or she already has a Passport account.

To add someone to your MSN Messenger contact list, first find out that person's e-mail address. Then, follow these steps:

Add

1. **Click the Add button on the MSN Messenger toolbar.**

   The Add a Contact dialog box appears, as shown in Figure 13-3.

2. **Check the By E-Mail Address option and then click the <u>N</u>ext button.**

   This action summons the dialog box where you provide your contact's e-mail address, as shown in Figure 13-4.

3. **Type your contact's e-mail address in the text box and click <u>N</u>ext.**

   If MSN Messenger finds a Passport account for the e-mail address you entered, a dialog box similar to the one shown in Figure 13-5 is displayed. Otherwise, MSN Messenger informs you that you cannot add this person to your contact list until she sets up a Passport account. As a favor, MSN Messenger offers to send your friend an e-mail message explaining how she can sign up with Passport and use MSN Messenger.

Figure 13-3:
The Add a Contact dialog box.

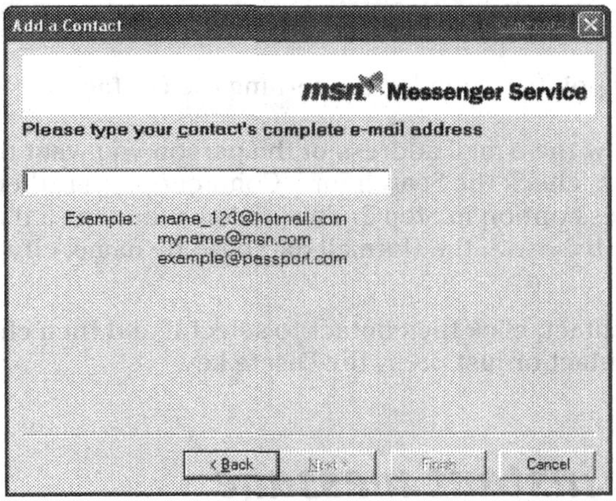

Figure 13-4:
Type your friend's e-mail address.

Figure 13-5:
Congratulations! You can now send messages to your friend.

4. **If you want to send e-mail to your friend instructing him how to download and install MSN Messenger, click the Yes option.**

   If you're sure that the person already has MSN Messenger installed, click the No button so that the e-mail message isn't sent.

   If you do choose to send an e-mail message, click the Preview E-Mail button to see a preview of the e-mail message that will be sent to your friend.

5. **Click the Next button.**

   Another dialog box appears, congratulating you again for successfully adding a contact to your contact list.

6. **To add another contact, click the Next button and repeat Steps 2 through 5.**

7. **When you're through adding contacts, click the Finish button.**

   You're returned to the MSN Messenger window, where the contact list shows the new contacts you added.

Here are a couple of points to ponder concerning the contact list:

✔ If you don't know the e-mail address of the person you want to add to your contact list, check the Search for a Contact option rather than the By E-Mail Address option in Step 2. This action summons a dialog box that allows you to search the Hotmail database by name, city, state, and country.

✔ To remove a contact, click the contact to select it and then choose File⇨Delete Contact or just press the Delete key.

Sending an instant message

Suppose that you're busy at work playing Solitaire on your computer one day, and it suddenly occurs to you that one of your friends is probably playing Solitaire too, and wouldn't it be nice to find out. MSN Messenger is designed to enable precisely this kind of important communication. Just follow these steps to send your friend an instant message:

1. **Double-click the contact to whom you want to send a message.**

Send

   Or, if you prefer, click the Send button and choose from the list of online contacts that appears the person to whom you want to send the message. Either way, an Instant Message dialog box appears, as shown in Figure 13-6.

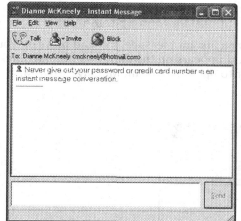

Figure 13-6:
Sending an
instant
message.

You can send instant messages only to contacts who appear on the Contacts Currently Online section of the MSN Messenger contact list. You cannot send messages to the contacts that appear in the Contacts Not Online section.

2. **Type in the text box at the bottom of the Instant Message dialog box the message you want to send.**

   For example, type **Hey, are you playing Solitaire too?**.

3. **Click the Send button.**

   Or, if you prefer, just press the Enter key.

That's all there is to it. Your message is sent over the Internet to your online friend. Your friend receives the message in a matter of seconds.

You can also send a message to someone who isn't on your contact list, as long as that person has an MSN Messenger account and you know the person's Hotmail address. To send a message to someone who isn't on your contact list, click the Send button and choose Other from the menu that appears. Type the person's MSN Messenger logon name (her Hotmail address minus the @Hotmail.com) and then click OK.

MSN Messenger conversations aren't limited to just two participants. As many as five people can join together in an instant conversation. To invite someone else to join a conversation, click the Invite button, choose To Join This Conversation from the menu that appears, and then choose another one of your online contacts from the list that appears.

Receiving an instant message

When someone sends you an instant message, a sound plays on your computer and a flashing window appears on the Windows taskbar. Click the flashing window on the taskbar to open the Instant Message window, as shown in Figure 13-7.

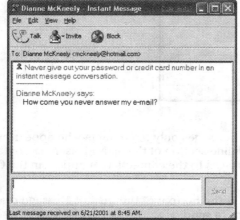

Figure 13-7:
Receiving
an instant
message.

You can reply to the message by composing a message of your own in the text box at the bottom of the Instant Message window and then clicking the Send button or pressing Enter.

You and your friend can talk back and forth like this for hours, if you want. When you're ready to leave the conversation, choose File➪Close or click the Close button (the X in the upper-right corner) of the Instant Message window.

Gone fishing: Letting your friends know that you're offline

If you're going to leave your computer or are unable to participate in instant-message conversations for some other reason, you can let MSN Messenger know so that other MSN Messenger users know that you aren't available. Actually, you can choose from several different status settings:

✔ **Online:** You're at your computer, able and willing to accept instant messages.

✔ **Busy:** You can't talk now because you're busy doing something else.

- **Be Right Back:** You can't talk now, but you'll be back soon.
- **Away:** You can't receive messages because you're not at your computer.
- **On the Phone:** You're engaged in a low-tech conversation.
- **Out to Lunch:** Either literally or figuratively.
- **Appear Offline:** You're at your computer, but appear to be offline to anyone who attempts to contact you via MSN Messenger. You can still send messages of your own, however.

To change your status, click the icon for yourself that appears just beneath the toolbar and then choose from the menu that appears the status option you want to use. If you prefer to use menus, you can choose File⇨My Status and then select your status.

Keep in mind that other MSN Messenger users who have added you to their contact list can see your status and can still send you messages. The only exception is if you change your status to Appear Offline. If you do, you appear to be offline to other MSN Messenger users.

If you change your status to Busy, Be Right Back, Away, On the Phone, or Out to Lunch, be sure to change your status back to Online when you return.

Smiley faces and such

MSN Messenger lets you spice up your conversation by including special symbols like smiley faces, thumbs-up signs, or broken hearts. These symbols are called *emoticons* because they're icons that represent emotions. You must type a certain combination of characters to send an emoticon. For example, type **:)** to send a smiley face or **(Y)** to send a thumbs-up sign. When you press the Enter key to send the message, the character combination is converted to the appropriate emoticon.

In all, you can send 31 different emoticons. Table 13-1 shows them and lists the character combinations you use to send each one.

Table 13-1	Smiley Faces and Other Symbols		
Emoticon	*Type This*	*Emoticon*	*Type This*
☺	: -) or :)	☺	: - > or : >
☺	: -0 or : o	☺	: -P or : p
☺	; -) or ;)	☹	: - (or : (

(continued)

Table 13-1 *(continued)*

Emoticon	Type This	Emoticon	Type This
☺	: - s or : s	☺	: - | or : |
👍	(Y) or (y)	👎	(N) or (n)
♥	(L) or (l)	💔	(U) or (u)
👄	(K) or (k)	🎁	(G) or (g)
🌹	(F) or (f)	🌹	(X) or (x)
🚶	(Z) or (z)	📷	(P) or (x)
📱	(B) or (x)	🍸	(D) or (x)
📞	(T) or (x)	🐱	(@)
☕	(C) or (c)	💡	(I) or (i)
👀	(H) or (h)	💤	(S) or (s)
☆	(*)	♪	(8)
✉	(E) or (e)	👤	(M) or (m)
🦇	(-[or ([		

Sending a file

You can easily send a file from your computer to a friend's computer using the MSN Messenger Send File feature. Here are the steps:

1. **Start up a conversation with one of your contacts.**

   Refer to the section "Sending an instant message," earlier in this chapter, for more information.

2. **Choose File➪Send a File.**

   This step summons the dialog box shown in Figure 13-8.

3. **Choose the file you want to send.**

   If the file doesn't initially appear in the Send a File dialog box, you need to navigate your way to the folder that contains the file.

4. **Click Open.**

   The recipient is notified that you're attempting to send a file. As soon as he accepts your offer, the file is sent.

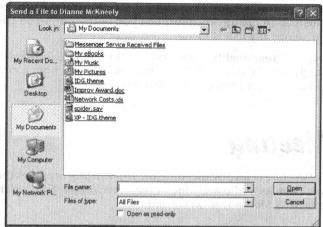

If someone tries to send you a file, a dialog box appears, informing you who is trying to send the file, the name of the file, and the file's size. You can accept the file by clicking Accept or refuse the file by clicking Decline.

Other MSN Messenger features

In addition to exchanging instant text messages and files, MSN Messenger has a few other nifty features you may want to explore:

- ✔ **Voice chatting:** While you're chatting with a friend, you can click the Talk button (as shown in the margin) to initiate a voice conversation, assuming that both you and your friend have microphones plugged in to your sound cards.

- ✔ **E-mail:** You can send e-mail to contacts who are offline by double-clicking the contact in the Not Online section of the MSN Messenger window.

- ✔ **Block:** If someone harasses you via MSN Messenger, you can prevent that person from contacting you again by clicking the Block button when you're in a conversation with that person. Or, you can right-click the contact in the main MSN Messenger window and choose Block from the menu that appears.

- ✔ **Profile:** You can set your personal profile, which lets other people know something about you, such as your hobbies and interests, by choosing Tools⇨Options.

- ✔ **Net2Phone:** You can place a phone call to a telephone anywhere in the world by clicking the Call button (as shown in the margin). This telephone service is provided by a company called Net2Phone. Unfortunately, the Net2Phone service isn't free, so you need to compare the cost of placing an Internet call with the cost of using your own phone instead. A dialog box informing you of the rate to be charged appears before any call is made.

Don't expect great quality when you use this service, however. Even with a high-speed cable or DSL connection, Internet phone calls usually sound like really bad cell phone connections.

Using NetMeeting

Microsoft *NetMeeting* is an advanced instant-messaging program that provides features such as audio and video communications. You can think of NetMeeting as MSN Messenger on steroids.

NetMeeting offers the following instant communication features:

- ✔ **Voice communication:** If you have a microphone plugged in to your computer's sound card, you can use NetMeeting like a telephone. You can talk to people all over the world without paying long distance phone charges. (Unfortunately, the quality of the connection leaves something to be desired, even with a cable or DSL connection. What do you expect for free?)

- ✔ **Video:** If your computer is equipped with a videocamera, you can send a video picture of yourself to someone else on the Net. Likewise, you can view video images when you connect with someone whose computer has a videocamera.

- ✔ **Whiteboard:** A drawing area is displayed in which all the participants in a conference can doodle.

- ✔ **Chat:** Similar to MSN Messenger, NetMeeting chat enables more than two users to join together in a conference and type messages to one another. (Only two users can use voice or video communications.)

- ✔ **File transfer:** You guessed it — you can send files to other NetMeeting users.

- ✔ **Program sharing:** Other NetMeeting users can see on their screens an application you're running on your computer. You can also share applications so that several NetMeeting users can work together on a single document over the Internet.

- ✔ **Remote desktop sharing:** A remote computer can access your desktop, which is great for accessing files and programs on another computer or troubleshooting problems.

NetMeeting is included with Windows XP, Windows 2000, and Windows Millennium Edition. If you use an earlier version of Windows and don't have NetMeeting, you can download and install it from the NetMeeting home page at www.microsoft.com/windows/netmeeting.

Placing a NetMeeting call

In NetMeeting, you place a *call* to establish a connection between you and another NetMeeting user. To call someone with NetMeeting, you must first connect to the Internet via your Internet Service Provider. After you're online, follow these steps:

NetMeeting

1. **Start NetMeeting by double-clicking the NetMeeting icon on your desktop.**

   Or, if you prefer, you can start NetMeeting by clicking the Start button on the Windows taskbar and then choosing Programs⇨Accessories⇨ Communications⇨NetMeeting. Either way, NetMeeting comes to life and displays the window shown in Figure 13-9.

Figure 13-9:
NetMeeting.

2. **Click the Find Someone in a Directory button.**

   This step brings up the Find Someone window, as shown in Figure 13-10. As you can see, the Find Someone window lists your MSN Messenger contacts.

   If your MSN Messenger contacts don't appear in the Find Someone window, choose Microsoft Internet Directory from the Select a Directory drop-down list, at the top of the Find Someone window.

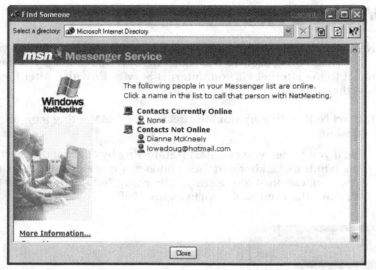

Figure 13-10:
The Find
Someone
window.

3. Click the name of the person you want to call.

NetMeeting attempts to contact the user you selected. This process may take a few moments, so be patient. Messages appear next to the name of the person you're attempting to call to let you know the status of your call.

If the person you're trying to call is already in another call, NetMeeting extends the offer to barge in on the conference. However, the members in that conference may decide not to let you in, so don't be surprised if your call goes unanswered. If they do let you in, you can exchange voice or video with only one of them at a time.

When the connection is finally established, you're returned to the NetMeeting main window, as shown in Figure 13-11.

4. Talk into your microphone.

NetMeeting works just like a telephone. You talk into the microphone, and you can hear the person on the other end of the line through your computer's speakers.

5. Watch the video screen.

If you have connected with someone who has a videocamera, crude images appear in the video window. Don't expect broadcast quality.

6. When you're done, say good-bye and click the End Call button.

That's all there is to it!

Figure 13-11:
NetMeeting
in a call.

You can also start a NetMeeting call directly from MSN Messenger. In MSN Messenger, choose Tools⇨Send an Invitation⇨To Start NetMeeting. This command brings up a menu of your contacts who are online; just choose from this menu the person you want to call. For example, to call Dianne, choose Tools⇨Send an Invitation⇨To Start NetMeeting⇨Dianne.

Using the NetMeeting chat feature

NetMeeting includes a text chat feature that is similar to MSN Messenger. To use NetMeeting Chat, follow these steps:

1. **Call up another NetMeeting user.**

   See the section "Placing a NetMeeting call," earlier in this chapter.

2. **Click the Chat button.**

   Or, if you're allergic to buttons, choose Tools⇨Chat or press Ctrl+T. Whichever method you use, up springs the Chat window, as shown in Figure 13-12.

3. **Type something in the text box at the bottom of the Chat window.**

4. **Press Enter to send your message.**

   Or, click the Send button. Messages that other NetMeeting users send are displayed automatically.

Figure 13-12:
The
NetMeeting
Chat
window.

5. **When you're finished chatting, choose File⇨Exit.**

   You can also close Chat by clicking the Close button in the upper-right corner of the Chat window.

Drawing on the Whiteboard

Another way to communicate in NetMeeting is with the Whiteboard, which is sort of like an Internet version of the venerable Paint accessory that comes with Windows. The difference between the two programs is that both you and your friend on the other end of the call can doodle on the Whiteboard, and you can instantly see each other's artistic endeavors.

To use Whiteboard, follow these steps:

1. **Establish a call to another NetMeeting user.**

   See the section "Placing a NetMeeting call," earlier in this chapter.

2. **Click the Whiteboard button.**

   If the use of buttons is against your religion, you can choose Tools⇨Whiteboard instead. Or, just press Ctrl+W. Whichever method you use, the Whiteboard appears, as shown in Figure 13-13.

3. **Draw something.**

   If you know how to use Microsoft Paint, you already know how to use Whiteboard. Just select one of the drawing tools from the toolbar on the left edge of the Whiteboard window and then doodle something in the drawing area. (You can find at the end of this section an explanation of each of the drawing tools.)

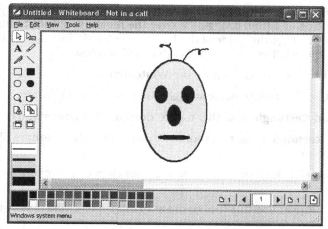

Figure 13-13:
Doodling
with the
whiteboard.

4. **Gasp in amazement when the Whiteboard appears to draw stuff all by itself.**

   Whiteboard isn't really drawing that stuff — your counterpart on the other end of the NetMeeting call is. The whole point of the Whiteboard is that any NetMeeting participants can draw on the Whiteboard at the same time. Anything one person draws on the NetMeeting Whiteboard automatically shows up on every participant's computer.

5. **If the drawing is worth hanging on to, choose File➪Save to save the drawing or File➪Print to print it.**

6. **When you're done, close the Whiteboard by clicking the Close button (you know, the one with the X on it that's in the upper-right corner of the window).**

   Alternatively, you can choose File➪Exit.

The following paragraphs describe the various drawing tools on the Whiteboard's toolbar:

   ✔ **Selector:** Use this tool to move objects around the drawing area or to delete objects. To move an object, click the Selector tool and then point to the object you want to move. Press and hold the left mouse button and drag the object to its new location. To delete an object, click the Selector tool, click the object you want to delete, and then press the Delete key.

   ✔ **Eraser:** Use this tool to delete an object from the drawing area. First click the Eraser tool and then click the object you want to delete.

   ✔ **Text:** Add text to the drawing by clicking the text tool and then clicking anywhere in the drawing area and typing your text. You can change the font, size, color, and other text formats by clicking the Font Options button at the bottom of the Whiteboard window.

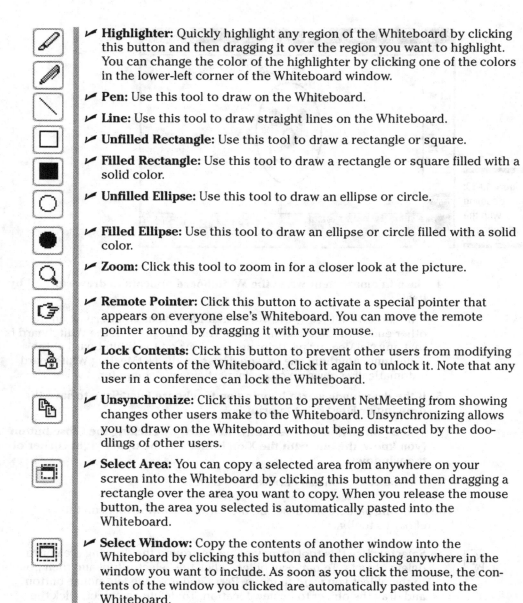

✓ **Highlighter:** Quickly highlight any region of the Whiteboard by clicking this button and then dragging it over the region you want to highlight. You can change the color of the highlighter by clicking one of the colors in the lower-left corner of the Whiteboard window.

✓ **Pen:** Use this tool to draw on the Whiteboard.

✓ **Line:** Use this tool to draw straight lines on the Whiteboard.

✓ **Unfilled Rectangle:** Use this tool to draw a rectangle or square.

✓ **Filled Rectangle:** Use this tool to draw a rectangle or square filled with a solid color.

✓ **Unfilled Ellipse:** Use this tool to draw an ellipse or circle.

✓ **Filled Ellipse:** Use this tool to draw an ellipse or circle filled with a solid color.

✓ **Zoom:** Click this tool to zoom in for a closer look at the picture.

✓ **Remote Pointer:** Click this button to activate a special pointer that appears on everyone else's Whiteboard. You can move the remote pointer around by dragging it with your mouse.

✓ **Lock Contents:** Click this button to prevent other users from modifying the contents of the Whiteboard. Click it again to unlock it. Note that any user in a conference can lock the Whiteboard.

✓ **Unsynchronize:** Click this button to prevent NetMeeting from showing changes other users make to the Whiteboard. Unsynchronizing allows you to draw on the Whiteboard without being distracted by the doodlings of other users.

✓ **Select Area:** You can copy a selected area from anywhere on your screen into the Whiteboard by clicking this button and then dragging a rectangle over the area you want to copy. When you release the mouse button, the area you selected is automatically pasted into the Whiteboard.

✓ **Select Window:** Copy the contents of another window into the Whiteboard by clicking this button and then clicking anywhere in the window you want to include. As soon as you click the mouse, the contents of the window you clicked are automatically pasted into the Whiteboard.

The Whiteboard can contain more than one drawing page. To display a different page, use the Next Page or Previous Page buttons, at the bottom of the Whiteboard window. To create a new page, click the Insert New Page button, in the lower-right corner of the window.

Sending a file

You can send a file to another NetMeeting user by following these steps:

1. **Call up another NetMeeting user.**

   See the section "Placing a NetMeeting call," earlier in this chapter.

2. **Click the Transfer Files button.**

   Or, if clicking buttons makes you belch, try using Tools➪File Transfer instead. Or, just press Ctrl+F. However you go about it, the File Transfer dialog box appears, as shown in Figure 13-14. You use this dialog box to first build a list of files you want to send and then to actually send the files.

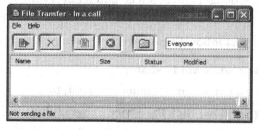

Figure 13-14:
Sending a
file with
NetMeeting.

3. **Click the Add Files button.**

   A dialog box appears that allows you to select the file you want to add to the list of files to be sent.

4. **Select the file you want to send and then click Add.**

   You may have to navigate through the folders on your hard drive to find the file you want to send. When you click Add, you're returned to the File Transfer dialog box. The file you selected appears on the list of files to send.

5. **Repeat Steps 3 and 4 for any other files you want to send.**

   You can send as many files as you want.

6. **If more than one person is in your NetMeeting call, choose from the drop-down list that appears in the upper-right portion of the File Transfer dialog box the person to whom you want to send the file or files.**

   By default, the file or files are sent to everyone in the call.

7. **Click the Send All button.**

   The files are sent.

8. **When the transfer is finished, close the File Transfer dialog box by clicking its Close button.**

   You're returned to the main NetMeeting window.

If someone sends you files, the File Transfer dialog box appears on your screen automatically. When the transfer is finished, you can retrieve the files that were sent to you by clicking the View Received Files button.

Sharing an application

One of the coolest NetMeeting features is that it enables you to share programs on the Internet with other NetMeeting users. For example, if you're discussing your marketing budget in a NetMeeting conference, you can call up Microsoft Excel, open the budget spreadsheet, and let everyone in the conference see and even edit the spreadsheet.

To share an application, just follow these steps:

1. **Start the application you want to share.**

   If you want to share a particular document, open it, too.

2. **In the NetMeeting window, click the Share Program button.**

   If your mouse button is broken, choose Tools➪Sharing instead. Or, press Ctrl+S. One way or another, a dialog box appears, listing the programs that are running on your computer.

3. **Select from the list of programs the application you want to share and then click Share.**

   The program appears on the screens of the other people in your NetMeeting call.

4. **Use the application as you normally would.**

   Anything you do in the application is visible to the other members of the NetMeeting conference. However, other conference participants cannot take over and use the application until you complete the next step.

5. **Click the Allow Control button.**

   This button enables other users to take over and use the program you have shared. When another user takes over your application, you see your mouse pointer move magically by itself, with the other user's initials tacked on to the bottom of the mouse pointer so that you can tell who's driving. You can wrest control away from the other user at any time by simply clicking the mouse.

Note that when you click the Allow Control button, the name of the button changes to Prevent Control. You can then click the Prevent Control button to prevent people from playing with your program. (The button then changes back to Allow Control.)

6. **To stop sharing the program, select the program in the Sharing dialog box and then click the Unshare button.**

Beware of security problems when you share a program — especially when you use the Allow Control button. When you give someone access to your application from across the Internet, that person can delete files, open sensitive documents, and even plant macro viruses on your computer. You should use the Allow Control feature only with users you trust. And never leave your computer unattended — even for a moment — with Allow Control enabled.

Chapter 14

Accessing Newsgroups with Outlook Express

*B*esides handling Internet e-mail, the Outlook Express program that comes with Internet Explorer can also access *newsgroups,* the Internet equivalent of a bulletin board. This chapter explains the ins and outs of using Outlook Express to access newsgroups.

Introducing Newsgroups

A *newsgroup* is a place where you can post messages (called *articles*) about a particular topic and read messages that others have posted about the same topic. People with similar interests visit a newsgroup to share news and information; find out what others are thinking; ask questions; get answers; exchange programs, pictures, music, and other types of files; and generally shoot the breeze.

The Internet has thousands of newsgroups — *tens* of thousands — on topics ranging from astronomy to barbershop quartets. You can find a newsgroup for virtually any subject that interests you.

Newsgroups come in two basic types:

- **Moderated newsgroup:** In a moderated newsgroup, one person is designated as a moderator and has complete control over what appears in the newsgroup. All new articles are submitted to the moderator for her review. Nothing is posted to the newsgroup until the moderator approves it.

  The moderator establishes the criteria for which articles get posted to the newsgroup. For some newsgroups, the criterion is simply that the article must be somehow related to the subject of the newsgroup. Other newsgroups use more stringent criteria, enabling the moderator to be more selective about what's posted. As a result, only the best postings make it into the newsgroup. This supervision may seem stifling, but in most cases, the monitoring dramatically improves the quality of the newsgroup articles.

- **Unmoderated newsgroup:** In an unmoderated newsgroup, anyone and everyone can post an article. Unmoderated newsgroups are free from censorship, but they're also often filled with blatant solicitations, chain letters, and all sorts of noise, such as articles that have nothing to do with the newsgroup topic.

Using Usenet

The term *Usenet* refers to a collection of newsgroups that are distributed together to computers that run special software called *news servers.* Each Internet Service Provider (ISP) provides its own news server so that you can access the newsgroups that are part of Usenet. For example, my ISP, MediaOne, has a news server named nntp.we.mediaone.net.

In theory, Usenet servers share their new postings with one another so that all the servers contain the most recent postings. In practice, Usenet servers are never really quite up-to-date, nor are they always in sync with one another. When you post an article to a newsgroup, a day or so may pass before your article propagates through Usenet and appears on all servers. Likewise, replies to your articles may take a while to show up on your server.

Each Usenet site decides which Usenet newsgroups to carry. As a result, you may find that a particular newsgroup isn't available from your Internet Service Provider.

Because the content of some newsgroups, particularly the renegade alt newsgroups, is sometimes a bit offensive, your Internet Service Provider may not automatically grant you access to all newsgroups. If you find yourself locked out of these groups, consult your ISP to find out how to gain access.

Understanding Usenet newsgroup names

Usenet has literally tens of thousands of newsgroups. Each newsgroup has a unique name that consists of one or more parts separated by periods. For example, the `soc.culture.assyrian` newsgroup discusses Assyrian culture, `sci.polymers` contains information on the scientific field of polymers, and `rec.food.drink.beer` is a place to discuss your favorite brew.

The first part of a newsgroup name identifies one of several broad categories of newsgroups, as I describe in the following list:

- `comp`: Newsgroups that start with `comp` contain discussions about computers. Many participants in the `comp` newsgroups wear pocket protectors and glasses held together by tape.

- `news`: These newsgroups contain discussions about Usenet itself, such as help for new Usenet users, announcements of new newsgroups, and statistics about which newsgroups are most popular.

- `rec`: Recreational topics such as sports, fishing, basket weaving, and model railroading are discussed in `rec` newsgroups.

- `sci`: Look to the `sci` newsgroups for discussions about science.

- `soc`: In the `soc` newsgroups, people gather to shoot the breeze or to discuss social issues.

- `talk`: These newsgroups favor long-winded discussions of topics such as politics and religion.

- `misc`: Topics that don't fit into any of the other categories fit here.

- `bit`: The Bitnet network supports Internet mailing lists. (A *mailing list* is like a newsgroup, except that all messages are exchanged via e-mail.) `bit` *newsgroups* are Bitnet mailing lists presented in newsgroup form.

- `biz`: This prefix denotes a business-related newsgroup.

- `bionet`: Newsgroups with this prefix discuss topics related to biology.

- `alt`: Hundreds of newsgroups using this prefix discuss topics that range from bizarre to X-rated to paranoid. These newsgroups aren't officially sanctioned by Usenet, but some of the more popular newsgroups fall into the `alt` category. The most visited of the `alt` newsgroups are those with an `alt.binaries` designation. These newsgroups contain binary files (such as pictures, sounds, and actual programs) that are specially encoded to be sent via the Usenet text-only messages. Fortunately, Internet Explorer can automatically decode these attachments, so you don't have to worry about using a separate program to do so.

- Regional newsgroups: Newsgroups that share regional interests are indicated by a short prefix (usually two or three letters), such as `aus` (Australia) or `can` (Canada). Most states have regional newsgroups designated by the state's 2-letter abbreviation (`CA` for California or `WA` for Washington, for example).

The Microsoft Public Newsgroups

Microsoft sponsors several dozen newsgroups that provide official online support for various Microsoft products. These newsgroups all have names that begin with the words `microsoft.public`, followed by the name of a Microsoft product (or an abbreviation of it). Here are a few of the Microsoft newsgroups dedicated to supporting users of Internet Explorer 6 and related products:

✔ `microsoft.public.inetexplorer.ie6.browser`

✔ `microsoft.public.inetexplorer.ie6.outlookexpress`

✔ `microsoft.public.inetexplorer.ie6.setup`

These newsgroups are available on most news servers. If you can't find them on your Internet Service Provider's list of newsgroups, you can access them via the Microsoft public news server, at `msnews.microsoft.com`.

You can launch Outlook Express as a newsreader from within Internet Explorer in the following ways:

✔ Click the Mail icon and select the Read News command from the pop-up menu that appears.

✔ Choose Tools➪Mail & News➪Read News.

✔ Click a link to a newsgroup.

Accessing Newsgroups

Outlook Express can handle Internet news just as easily as it can handle e-mail. To read Internet newsgroups, follow these steps:

1. **Start Outlook Express by clicking the Launch Outlook Express button that appears on the Windows taskbar.**

   Or, click the Start button and click E-mail: Outlook Express. Or, look for Outlook Express after you choose Start➪Programs.

2. **Click the Read News link, which appears near the center of the main Outlook Express window.**

   If you prefer, you can click on a news server account on the list of accounts on the left side of the Outlook Express window. Either way, assuming that you haven't previously subscribed to any newsgroups, Outlook Express responds by displaying the dialog box shown in Figure 14-1.

Figure 14-1:
You haven't
subscribed
to any
newsgroups.

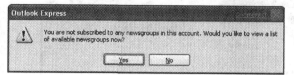

If you don't have a Read News link in your Outlook Express window,
click the Set Up a Newsgroups Account link instead. Then, follow the
instructions that appear in order to set up your news server.

3. Click Yes.

Outlook Express displays a list of all newsgroups available on your news
server, as shown in Figure 14-2.

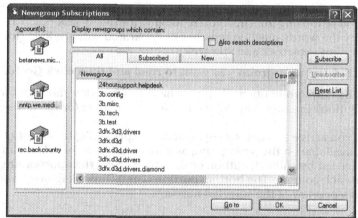

Figure 14-2:
Outlook
Express lists
the available
newsgroups.

You can scroll through this list to find the newsgroup you want to
access, but that will take a while: On most servers, the list contains
thousands of servers. (Mine lists more than 48,000. Figure 14-2 shows
only ten of them, but that's just the tip of the iceberg.)

**4. Type a word or phrase in the Display Newsgroups Which Contain text
box.**

For example, to find newsgroups that pertain to *Star Trek,* type **startrek**
in the text box. Outlook Express narrows the newsgroup listing to just
those newsgroups that contain the word or phrase you typed, as shown
in Figure 14-3. (It may take a few moments for Outlook Express to find
the newsgroups you requested. Be patient.)

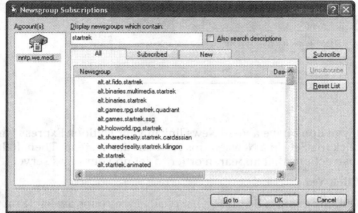

Figure 14-3:
A list of
Star Trek
newsgroups.

You may have to try several different spellings of the word or words you're looking for. Or, if you're looking for two words (such as *Star Trek*), try the words mushed together or separated with periods (for example, try both **startrek** and **star.trek**).

5. **Click the newsgroup you want to read and then click G̲o To.**

The newsgroup opens. You may have to wait a few moments while Outlook Express downloads the subject headers for the newsgroup.

When you arrive at a newsgroup, Outlook Express displays a list of the messages available on the newsgroup, as shown in Figure 14-4. You can sort the message list by subject, author, or date by clicking the appropriate header above each column. The bottom portion of the Outlook Express window shows a preview of the selected message.

Subscribing to a Newsgroup

If you find a newsgroup you want to visit frequently, you should subscribe to it. *Subscribing* to a newsgroup adds the newsgroup to a list of newsgroups that appears on the folders list on the left side of the Outlook Express window — so you can access the list quickly.

To subscribe to a newsgroup, find the newsgroup you want to subscribe to by following the procedure described in the section "Accessing Newsgroups," earlier in this chapter. Click the newsgroup on the list of newsgroups to select it and then click the Subscribe button. Or, just double-click the newsgroup to which you want to subscribe.

Click the Read News link in the Outlook Express main window to summon a list of all the newsgroups you have subscribed to, as shown in Figure 14-5.

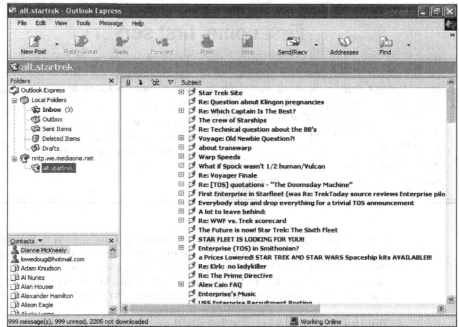

Figure 14-4:
A news-
group.

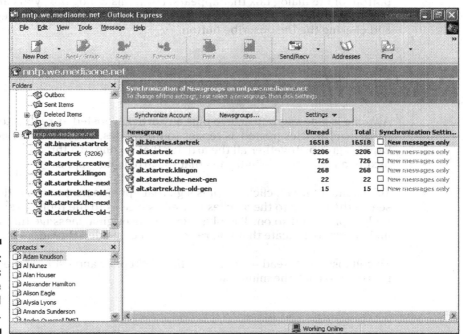

Figure 14-5:
Newsgroups
you have
subscribed
to.

First come, first server

If you use more than one news server, the servers appear on the folders list on the left side of the Outlook Express window. To switch to another news server, just click its icon. Each news server has a different set of newsgroups, so some newsgroups may not be available on every server.

If you need to configure Outlook Express to work with a different news server, choose Tools⇨Accounts and click the News tab. You can find buttons that enable you to add a new server, delete a server, or change the properties of a server.

You can find a list of free and commercial news servers by searching Yahoo! or another search service for Usenet Servers.

You can call up the list of newsgroup subscriptions shown in Figure 14-5 at any time by clicking the name of the news server that appears in the folder tree on the left side of the Outlook Express window. Each newsgroup you've subscribed to is listed in the folder tree beneath the news server. Just double-click a newsgroup in the folder tree to go directly to that newsgroup.

You can also view a list of subscribed newsgroups by clicking the Newsgroups button and then clicking the Subscribed tab that appears at the bottom of the dialog box that appears. From this dialog box, you can then remove a newsgroup from your subscription list by selecting the newsgroup and clicking the Unsubscribe button.

Reading Threads

A *thread* is a newsgroup article plus any articles posted as replies to the original article, articles posted as replies to the replies, and so on. Outlook Express groups together all the articles that belong to a thread. A plus sign next to a message title indicates that the article has replies.

To expand a thread, click the plus sign that appears next to the article. You see all the replies to the articles as well as replies to the replies, replies to the reply replies, and so on. The plus sign on the original message turns into a minus sign to indicate that you're seeing an expanded thread.

To collapse the thread — that is, to hide all replies and list only the original message — click the minus sign.

Reading an Article

To read an article, double-click the article's title. The article appears in a separate window, as shown in Figure 14-6. After you finish reading the article, click the article window's Close button to close the window.

To save an article to your computer, choose File⇔Save As or click the Save button. Then, select the folder you want to save the article in and the format (you can save it as a newsgroup message or as a plain text file) and click Save.

Print

To print an article, choose File⇔Print or click the Print button.

You can go to the next or previous articles by clicking the following buttons:

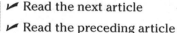

Next

▶ Read the next article

▶ Read the preceding article

Previous

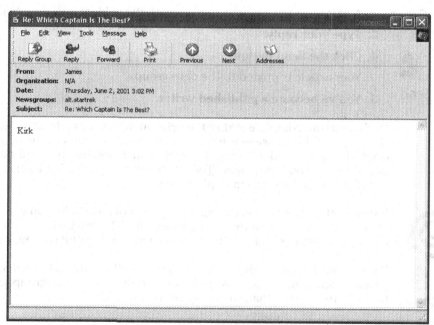

Figure 14-6:
A news-
group
article.

Replying to an Article

To reply to a newsgroup posting, follow these steps:

1. **Count to ten and then reconsider your reply.**

   Keep in mind that replying to a newsgroup isn't like replying to e-mail. Only the intended recipient can read an e-mail reply. Anyone on the planet can read your newsgroup postings. If you don't really have anything to add to the discussion, why waste your time?

   To make matters worse, after you post a message to a newsgroup, your inbox is soon filled with a flood of spam from e-mail bulk mailers who continually scan newsgroups, looking for new e-mail addresses. For this reason, many Usenet users don't list their real e-mail address when they create a news account. (To change your news account e-mail address, choose Tools⇨Accounts, click the News tab, select the news account, and click Properties.)

Reply Group

2. **After reading the article you want to reply to, click the Reply Group button on the toolbar.**

   A new message window appears with the subject line already filled in.

3. **Type your reply.**

4. **Click the Send button.**

Send

   Your article is posted to the newsgroup.

5. **You've become a published writer.**

By default, the complete text of the original message is added to the end of your reply. If the message is long, you may want to delete some or all of the original text. If you don't want the original message text to be automatically added to your replies, choose Tools⇨Options, click the Send tab, and deselect the Include Message in Reply option.

If you want to reply to several specific points of an article, you can intermingle your responses with the original message. The original message appears after greater-than signs, setting it off from your insightful responses.

Reply

If you want to send a private e-mail reply directly to the author of a newsgroup article rather than post your reply to the entire newsgroup, click the Reply button rather than the Reply Group button.

Déjà vu all over again

If you hang around newsgroups long enough, sooner or later you're going to want to find a newsgroup post that you remember seeing way back when. Or maybe one of your friends will tell you that he saw a really great post on a newsgroup last year that you should check out. Unfortunately, because news servers don't have unlimited amounts of disk storage, they periodically delete older newsgroup posts. So that old message you want to retrieve may not be available on your news server.

The good news is that you can find a huge archive of old newsgroup postings at Deja.com.

At the time I wrote this chapter, the Deja.com archive held more than 300 million posts from more than 45,000 newsgroups, dating back to March 1995. The only thing Deja.com doesn't archive is binary attachments. So you can't use Deja.com to retrieve pictures, videos, and other binary posts.

To use Deja.com, just point Internet Explorer to www.deja.com/usenet. You can then search the Deja.com archives for newsgroup messages by keywords in the message subject, newsgroup name, author of the message, and date the message was posted.

Writing a New Article

A *lurker* is someone who reads newsgroup postings but never leaves his own postings. When you have finally mustered the courage to step out of the shadows and post an article of your own to a newsgroup, follow these steps:

1. **Open the newsgroup in which you want to post a new article.**

New Post

2. **Click the New Post button.**

   A new message window appears.

3. **Type a subject for the article in the Subject box.**

   Make sure that the subject you type reflects accurately the topic of the article — or prepare to get flamed. (Being *flamed* doesn't mean that your computer screen actually emits a ball of fire in your direction, singeing the hair off your forearm. It refers to getting an angry — even vitriolic — response from a reader.) If your subject line is misleading, at least one Internet user is sure to chew you out for it.

4. **Type your message in the message area.**

Spelling

5. **If you're worried about your vice-presidential prospects, click the Spelling button.**

   If clicking buttons makes you dizzy, choose Tools⇨Spelling instead. Either way, the spelling checker dutifully examines each and every word in your message to find any potentially embarrassing misspellings, giving you the opportunity to correct your boo-boos. (For more information about spell-checking in Outlook Express, refer to Chapter 10.)

Send

6. **Click the Send button when you're satisfied with your response.**

Using Stationery and HTML Formatting

Just as it does with e-mail, Outlook Express allows you to create fancy stationery and HTML formatting options for your newsgroup postings. Stationery and HTML formatting let you create messages with fancy background designs, use fonts for your text, and add emphasis with bold, italic, or colored text, and more.

The procedure for creating stationery for newsgroup articles is the same as the procedure for e-mail messages, so I humbly refer you to Chapter 11 for the steps required to do so.

Be warned, however. For every post you create with stationery, you will probably receive a bucketful of flame posts deriding you for using stationery.

Dealing with Attachments

Originally, Internet newsgroups didn't allow you to include binary files (such as programs, pictures, and sound files) in newsgroup postings. Internet users are very resourceful, however, and they long ago figured out a way to get around this dilemma. They invented a technique, called *encoding,* that converts a nontext file into a series of text codes you can post as a newsgroup article. This type of article looks completely scrambled when you see it. However, you can save the article to a file on your hard drive and then run the saved file through a special decoding program that converts it back to its original form — whether it's a program, picture, or sound file.

With Outlook Express, the decoding routine is built in, so you don't need a separate program. All you have to do is open the message. If the message contains an image attachment, the image is decoded and displayed right in the body of the message. Other types of attachments (such as sounds) display an icon on the Attach line above the message body. Double-click the icon to play the attachment.

To save a binary file that has been attached to a newsgroup article, right-click the icon on the Attach line that appears above the message body and then choose the Save As command that appears on the pop-up menu. A Save As dialog box appears. Choose the folder where you want to save the file and then click Save.

Some attachments are too large to be posted in a single message. Instead, the binary attachment is broken apart and posted to several messages. Outlook Express lets you combine and decode such messages to re-create the attachment. Just follow these steps:

1. **Hold down the Shift key and click each of the messages that contains a part of the attachment.**

   You can usually tell which messages contain a split-up attachment by looking at the message subjects. For example, if you see a series of messages with subjects such as monkey.mpg [01/04] or monkey.mpg [02/04], each of the messages contains one part of a 4-part attachment. Hold down the Shift key and select all four messages.

2. **Choose Message⇨Combine and Decode.**

   A dialog box similar to the one shown in Figure 14-7 appears.

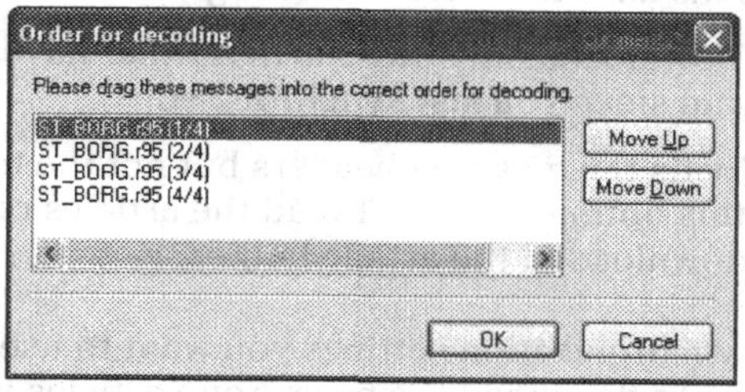

Figure 14-7:
Combining a multi-message attachment.

3. **If necessary, adjust the order in which the messages are listed.**

   To move a message on the list, select the message you want to move and then click the Move Up or Move Down button.

4. **Click OK.**

   The messages are downloaded and combined. A dialog box is displayed to show the progress of the download.

5. **Get a cup of coffee.**

   The download may take a while.

6. **Save the attachment if you want.**

   Outlook Express displays the combined message when the download is complete. You can then save the attachment by right-clicking the icon on the Attach line above the message body and choosing Save As from the menu that appears.

Working Offline

Outlook Express lets you access newsgroups you have subscribed to even when you're not connected to the Internet. To work offline, you should first set the synchronization settings for each of your subscribed newsgroups. To do so, click your news server on the Folders pane to display the newsgroups you have subscribed to (refer to Figure 14-5).

To set the synchronization setting for a newsgroup, first click the newsgroup to select it. Then, click the Settings button and choose one of the four options that appear:

- ✔ **Don't Synchronize:** Doesn't download messages for offline reading. Select this option if you don't want to synchronize the newsgroups for offline reading.

- ✔ **All Messages:** Downloads all articles for the newsgroup.

- ✔ **New Messages Only:** Downloads only those articles that have been posted to the newsgroup since you last synchronized.

- ✔ **Headers Only:** Downloads the message headers but not the text of the articles. If you select this option, you can't read the articles offline because you haven't downloaded the article bodies.

After you've selected the synchronization settings you want to use, click the Synchronize Account button to download the newsgroup articles from your news server. You can then disconnect from the Internet and read the articles offline.

If you decide to reply to any articles or post new articles, click the Synchronize Account button again. Outlook Express connects to the Internet and posts your articles.

Part IV
Customizing Your Explorations

The 5th Wave   By Rich Tennant

"This is amazing. You can stop looking for Derek. According to an MSN search I did, he's hiding behind the dryer in the basement."

In this part . . .

Turn to this part when you're tired of working with Internet Explorer the way it runs out of the box and you want to customize it to more closely suit your working style. These chapters show you how to customize the Internet Explorer toolbars, start page, and other options; set up parental controls to ensure that your kids have a safe and sane Internet experience; use the Internet Explorer security options; create a login script so that you don't have to type your user ID and password every time you connect to the Internet; and create your own home page on the Internet.

Chapter 15

Doing It Your Way: Personalizing Internet Explorer

In This Chapter
▶ Customizing the toolbars
▶ Fiddling with options
▶ Personalizing your home page

*I*nternet Explorer has a bushel of configuration options that affect the way you browse the World Wide Web. Of course, Internet Explorer can't help you with your *real* preferences, such as playing golf instead of toiling with your computer. But you can do stuff that's almost as much fun, such as rearrange the buttons on the toolbar, change the colors used to display links you already visited, or personalize your default start page.

Read this chapter after you become comfortable with the out-of-the-box version of Internet Explorer and you're ready to find out what all those options really do. This chapter describes the most useful options, but it tells you, more importantly, which options you can safely ignore so that you (unlike some people I know — me, for example) can catch up on your golf.

Note: I am aware, of course, that for some people golf is a more frustrating pastime than using your computer. And, for some, golf is more boring than reading the online help feature of Internet Explorer. If you're one of those poor, unenlightened souls, feel free to substitute your favorite nongolf pastime — and may I recommend *Golf For Dummies,* 2nd Edition, by Gary McCord (published by Hungry Minds, Inc.)?

Toiling with the Toolbars

Internet Explorer includes three built-in toolbars, which contain helpful buttons that let you perform common tasks. The three toolbars are

- **Standard Buttons:** Displays buttons for navigating the Internet, stopping long downloads, going back to your home page, and more

- **Address:** Includes a field in which you can type a Web address and has a Go button you click to go to a Web page

- **Links:** Contains buttons you can click to quickly call up your favorite Web pages

The following sections show you how to show or hide any of these toolbars in Internet Explorer and how to change the buttons that appear on the Standard Buttons toolbar.

Playing hide-and-seek with the toolbars

Normally, Internet Explorer displays the Standard Buttons, Address, and Links toolbars on separate lines at the top of the screen. This default arrangement of toolbars takes up lots of screen space. Fortunately, Internet Explorer lets you hide the toolbars you don't use or rearrange the toolbars into a less intrusive arrangement. For example, if you never use the Links toolbar, you can hide it, leaving more room on your screen to view Web pages.

To show or hide a toolbar, follow these steps:

1. **Choose the View⇨Toolbars command.**

   The Toolbars menu appears, as shown in Figure 15-1. A check mark appears next to the toolbars that are visible.

Figure 15-1:
The
Toolbars
menu.

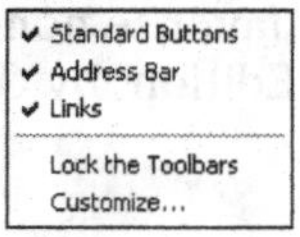

| ✓ Standard Buttons |
| ✓ Address Bar |
| ✓ Links |
| Lock the Toolbars |
| Customize... |

2. **Click the menu option for the toolbar you want to show or hide.**

   If the toolbar is visible, clicking the menu option makes it disappear. Likewise, if the toolbar is hidden, clicking the menu option makes it reappear.

Here are a few points to ponder when you play hide-and-seek with toolbars:

✔ If you don't like the position of the toolbars at the top of the Internet Explorer window, you can rearrange them by dragging the *move handle,* the vertical bar that appears near the left edge of each toolbar.

✔ You can arrange toolbars so that they're side-by-side rather than on top of each other. Just grab the move handle of one of the toolbars and then drag that toolbar on top of one of the other toolbars. You can also drag the move handle left or right to adjust how much of each toolbar is visible in a side-by-side arrangement.

Figure 15-2 shows how I like to arrange the toolbars when I use Internet Explorer. As you can see, I've placed all three toolbars side-by-side to free up more room to view Web pages. The Standard toolbar buttons I use most are visible on the left, the Address toolbar is in the middle, and the Links toolbar is squeezed in on the right. (I've also customized the toolbars to use smaller icons without text, as described in the next section, "Customizing the Standard Buttons toolbar.")

✔ Another way to summon the Toolbars menu is to right-click on any visible toolbar.

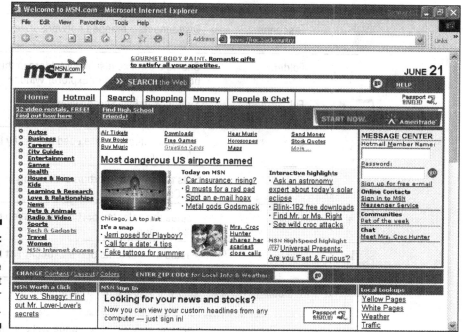

Figure 15-2: One way to arrange the Internet Explorer toolbars.

Customizing the Standard Buttons toolbar

The good people at Microsoft who created Internet Explorer did their best to anticipate which buttons you would use most, putting those buttons in plain view on the Standard Buttons toolbar. However, after stuffing the Standard Button toolbar to the gills with buttons, they had a few buttons left over that they didn't know what to do with. So the Microsoft folks decided to throw them into a Customize Toolbar dialog box, which you can use to add extra buttons to your Standard toolbar, if you want.

Table 15-1 lists the extra buttons you can add to the Standard Buttons toolbar. Note that the first three buttons — Map Drive, Disconnect, and Folders — are useful when you use Internet Explorer to browse folders on your hard drive or a network server.

Table 15-1		Extra Buttons You Can Add to the Standard Buttons Toolbar
Button	*Name*	*What It Does*
	Map Drive	Lets you assign a drive letter to a folder on a network file server
	Disconnect	Disconnects a mapped network drive
	Folders	Shows a treelike display of folders in the left portion of the Internet Explorer window
	Full Screen	Switches to Full-Screen view
	Size	Lets you select the size used to display text on Web pages
	Cut	Cuts the selected portion of the Web page to the Clipboard
	Copy	Copies the selected portion of the Web page to the Clipboard
	Paste	Pastes the contents of the Clipboard at the current cursor position
	Encoding	Lets you select a different language
	Print Preview	Lets you preview how a page will appear when printed before sending it to the printer
	Related	Automatically searches for Web pages on related topics

To add one or more of these buttons to your Standard Buttons toolbar, follow these steps:

1. **Summon the View⇨Toolbars⇨Customize command.**

   The Customize Toolbar dialog box appears, as shown in Figure 15-3. The right side of this dialog box shows the buttons that are already on your Standard Buttons toolbar. The left side of the dialog box lists the extra buttons you can add.

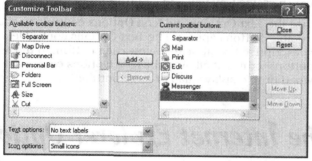

Figure 15-3:
The
Customize
Toolbar
dialog box.

2. **From the Available Toolbar Buttons list on the left side of the Customize Toolbar dialog box, click the button you want to add to the toolbar.**

3. **Click Add.**

   The button you selected in Step 2 is moved from the Available Toolbar Buttons list to Current Toolbar Buttons.

4. **If you want, use the Move Up or Move Down buttons to change the new button's location on the toolbar.**

   Each time you click Move Up or Move Down, the button you added in Step 3 changes position. Keep clicking Move Up or Move Down until the button lands where you want it.

5. **Repeat Steps 2 through 4 to add more buttons.**

   Add all the buttons, if you want.

6. **After you finish, click Close.**

   The Customize Toolbar dialog box is dismissed.

Here are a few additional thoughts about the Customize Toolbar dialog box:

✔ You can remove buttons from the Standard Buttons toolbar by selecting from the Current Toolbar Buttons list the button you want to remove and then clicking Remove. The button is removed from the Current Toolbar Buttons list and added to the Available Toolbar Buttons list.

✔ If you get your toolbar all jumbled up, you can restore it to its original, pristine condition by clicking Reset.

✔ You can use the Move Up and Move Down buttons to rearrange the order in which the toolbar buttons appear. Just select from the Current Toolbar Buttons list the button you want to move and then click Move Up or Move Down to change the button's position.

✔ If you have lots of buttons on your toolbar, you can insert one or more separator lines to visually divide the buttons into groups. The separator is listed at the top of the Available Toolbar Buttons list. You can add it to the toolbar the same way you add a button.

✔ You can use the Text Options and Icon Options controls to change the way the toolbar buttons appear. The Text Options control lets you select whether descriptive text appears below each button, to the right of just certain buttons, or not at all. And the Icon Options control lets you choose whether to display small or large buttons.

Tweaking the Internet Explorer Options

Internet Explorer has about a gazillion options that let you customize everything from the color of hyperlinks to whether you want to allow Java programs to run on your computer. You access all these options by selecting the Tools⇨Internet Options command. Be prepared, however: The Tools⇨Internet Options command summons a killer dialog box that has tabs out the wazoo (whatever a *wazoo* is). Each of the tabs has a set of controls. To switch from one tab to another, just click the tab label at the top of the dialog box.

Here's the lowdown on the seven tabs that appear in the Internet Options dialog box:

✔ **General:** Contains options that affect the general operation of Internet Explorer

✔ **Security:** Enables you to indicate whether you want to be warned before doing something that may jeopardize your security (see Chapter 17)

✔ **Privacy:** Enables you to indicate whether you want to allow cookies that may invade your privacy (see Chapter 17)

✔ **Content:** Enables you to filter out pages with questionable content (see Chapter 16)

✔ **Connections:** Indicates which dial-up connection to use to establish a connection to the Internet

✔ **Programs:** Enables you to indicate which programs to use to read Internet mail and newsgroups and do other necessary chores

✔ **Advanced:** Holds a number of options that just don't fit anywhere else

To set any of the preceding options, follow this general procedure:

1. **Choose Tools➪Internet Options.**

   The Internet Options dialog box appears.

2. **Click the tab that contains the option you want to set.**

   If you're not sure which tab to click, just cycle through all the tabs until you find what you're looking for.

3. **Set the options however you want.**

   Most options are simple check boxes you click to select or deselect. Some require that you select a choice from a drop-down list, and some have the audacity to require that you type something as proof of your keyboard proficiency.

4. **Repeat Step 3 until you've exhausted your options (or yourself).**

   You can set more than one option with a single use of the Tools➪Internet Options command.

5. **Click OK.**

   You're done!

The following sections explain the options that appear on each of the tabs in the Options dialog box.

Saluting the General options

Back in the days of Internet Explorer 1.0, the options on the General tab were lowly Private options. But they reenlisted for Version 2.0 and eventually decided to become Career options. Now, with Internet Explorer 6, they boast the rank of General. I suggest that you snap-to whenever you call up these options, which are shown in Figure 15-4.

The General options comprise the following three categories:

✔ **Home Page:** Enables you to set the location of the page that's displayed when you first start Internet Explorer or click the Home button. For example, if the only Internet site you're really interested in is David Letterman's Top Ten List, you can set the Top Ten List site to be your home page.

The easiest way to set your home page is to first navigate your way to the page you want to use as your home page. Then, call up Tools➪ Internet Options and click the Use Current button. For more information about changing your home page, see the section "Changing Your Home Page," later in this chapter.

Figure 15-4:
The General
options.

✔ .**Temporary Internet Files:** Lets you manage the temporary files that Internet Explorer downloads to your hard drive. Whenever you visit a Web page, Internet Explorer keeps in a special folder on your hard drive a copy of the page and any graphics that appear on the page. That way, if you revisit the same page, Internet Explorer can quickly retrieve the information from your hard drive rather than from the Internet.

You can click the Settings button to bring up the dialog box shown in Figure 15-5. This dialog box lets you change how often Internet Explorer should check for newer versions of pages stored in the temporary folder, how much space Internet Explorer is allowed to use for temporary files, and the location of the folder used to store temporary files.

Figure 15-5:
Setting your
options for
temporary
Internet
files.

You can empty the Temporary Internet Files folder by clicking the Delete Files button. Be warned that deleting these files causes delays because Internet Explorer must then download files that were previously stored on your hard drive.

You can also delete any cookie files that Web sites have left behind on your computer by clicking the Delete Cookies button. For more information about cookies, see Chapter 17.

✔ **History:** Enables you to specify how many days of history information you want to retain. Also, you can click the Clear History button to remove all files from the History folder.

The four buttons at the bottom of the General tab bring up dialog boxes that let you change several other aspects of how Internet Explorer works:

✔ **Colors:** Change the colors used to display text and hyperlinks.

✔ **Fonts:** Change the default font used to display text.

✔ **Language:** Specify which language to use for Web pages that display information in two or more languages.

✔ **Accessibility:** Force Internet Explorer to use the colors and font selections you made via the Color and Fonts buttons.

Serenading the Security options

Figure 15-6 shows the Security options, which are designed to protect you from Internet sites that contain offensive content, to protect your privacy, and to warn you about potential security problems. To bring up these options, you can click the Security tab at the top of the Internet Options dialog box.

For complete information about how to use these options, see Chapter 17.

Primping the Privacy options

Figure 15-7 shows the Privacy options, which deal with how you want to deal with cookies. *Cookies* are small files that Web sites leave on your computer and access again later, such as when you revisit a site. Cookies are a privacy matter because they can be used to track your Internet activities.

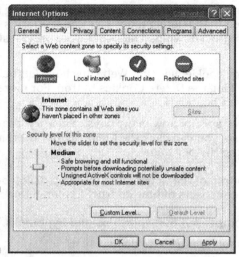

Figure 15-6:
The Security
options.

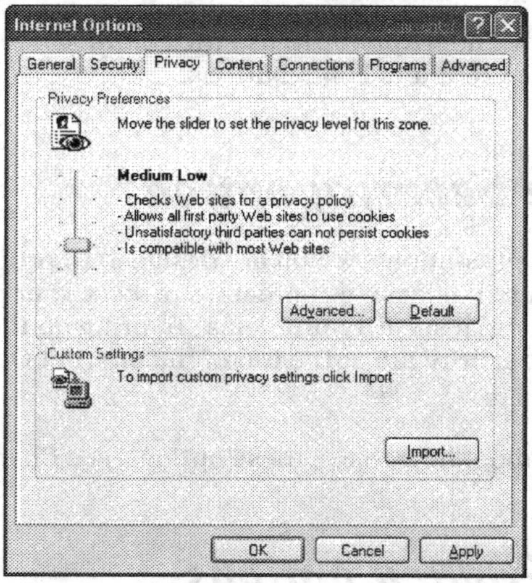

Figure 15-7:
The Privacy
options.

For more information about setting your privacy options, see Chapter 17.

Cruising with the Content options

The Content tab lets you fiddle with the Internet Explorer Content Advisor, which is designed to block access to offensive Web sites. Figure 15-8 shows the Content options.

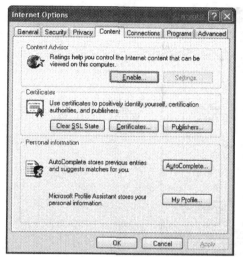

Figure 15-8:
The Content
options.

You can find a complete rundown on the Content Advisor in Chapter 16, so I don't discuss it further here.

Cajoling the Connections options

The Connections options, as shown in Figure 15-9, enable you to specify which dial-up connection you use to connect to the Internet. You may find yourself turning to this tab frequently if you have more than one Internet Service Provider and you often switch from one to another. You should also visit this tab if you decide to change providers.

If you have yet to create a dial-up connection for your Internet provider, click the Add button. The Make a New Connection Wizard comes to life to create a connection for you after you answer basic questions, such as the phone number you dial and your user ID. Your ISP should supply this information for you.

If more than one connection is listed in the Connections options, choose the connection you want to use when you access the Internet. You can use the buttons beneath this list box to create an additional connection (Add), delete an existing connection (Remove), or modify an existing connection (Settings).

Figure 15-9:
The
Connections
options.

Perusing the Programs options

The Programs tab, as shown in Figure 15-10, contains options that enable you to tell Internet Explorer which programs you want to use to read your e-mail, access newsgroups, and handle Internet calls. The default settings are Outlook Express for e-mail and news and Microsoft NetMeeting for Internet calls.

Figure 15-10:
The
Programs
options.

The other settings on the Programs tab enable you to choose the program to use for Internet phone calls, your Calendar, and your Address Book. You should leave these settings alone.

Achieving Advanced options

The Advanced options, as shown in Figure 15-11, enable you to set several features that govern Internet Explorer operation. Wow, lots of options are in this dialog box! It has so many, in fact, that Microsoft uses an unusual method of enabling you to set them. Rather than spew a bunch of check boxes into the Advanced options dialog box, all the options are shown in a big, scrollable list box. To set any of the options, scroll down the list until you find the option you want to set and then click the option.

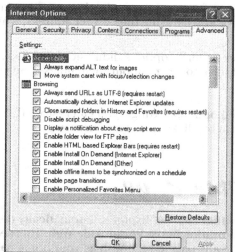

Figure 15-11: The Advanced options.

The Advanced options fall into the following categories:

- **Accessibility:** These options make Internet Explorer easier to use for users with disabilities.

- **Browsing:** These options control basic aspects of how the Internet Explorer browser works, such as whether it uses the AutoComplete feature to finish typing Web addresses for you and whether it uses fancy smooth scrolling. (If you have a slower computer, you may want to disable smooth scrolling.)

- **HTTP 1.1 settings:** Steer clear of these options unless you know what HTTP 1.1 is and know that you want to use it.

✔ **Microsoft VM:** If you're a Java guru, you may want to look at these options. Otherwise, try not to step in them.

✔ **Multimedia:** You can indicate whether graphics, sounds, and video are downloaded automatically whenever you go to a Web page. Disabling any or all of these options improves Internet Explorer performance over phone-line connections.

✔ **Printing:** Enables you to include background colors and textures when you print a Web page. If you have a color printer, this option can be nice. Otherwise, you should leave it off. (In fact, you should probably leave it off even if you have a color printer unless you want each page to be filled with the background color. Expect to go through lots of ink cartridges if you turn this option on.)

✔ **Search from the Address bar:** Configure Internet Explorer so that if you type an Internet address that doesn't exist, Internet Explorer can look for other, similar addresses using different domain suffixes. For example, if you type www.whitehouse.com, Internet Explorer can automatically find the White House for you by using the correct address, which is www.whitehouse.gov.

✔ **Security:** Yep, still more security options didn't fit on the Security tab. Fortunately, you don't have to worry about them unless you work for the CIA.

If you mess up the Advanced options settings, you can restore them all to their original factory settings by clicking Restore Defaults.

Changing Your Home Page

Your *home page* is the page that Internet Explorer automatically displays each time you begin an exploration of the World Wide Web. This section shows you how to designate any page on the Web as your home page.

Note: Your Internet Explorer home page isn't the same as a home page you can set up for other Web users to see. When you designate a page as your Internet Explorer home page or if you customize your home page, only *you* can see the home page and the custom options you select. If you want to create a home page that other Web users can see, you must make arrangements with your Internet Service Provider to place your home page on its web server.

Normally, Internet Explorer defaults to MSN.com (www.MSN.com) as its home page. If you obtain your copy of Internet Explorer from a company other than Microsoft, Internet Explorer may be configured with a different home page. Whatever your home page is now, Internet Explorer enables you to designate *any* page on the Web as the first one you see.

The home page is also the page that pops up when you click the Home button on the Standard toolbar.

To change your home page, follow these steps:

1. **Navigate your way to the page you want to use as your new home page.**

   See Chapter 3 for details about getting around on the Web.

2. **Choose View⇨Internet Options.**

   The Internet Options dialog box appears (refer to Figure 15-4).

3. **Click the Use Current button.**

   The home page is now set to the current page.

4. **Click OK to dismiss the Internet Options dialog box.**

   You're done!

You can change back to the default home page by choosing View⇨Internet Options and clicking the Use Default button. If you prefer to have no home page, click Use Blank. That way, Internet Explorer simply displays a blank page when you start it.

 If you can't find a Web page you want to use as your home page, you can always create your own home page. Just use any Web page editor, such as Microsoft FrontPage, or a program, such as Word, that can save documents in HTML format, to create a Web page that contains links to the pages you visit most often along with any other information you want to appear on your home page. Save this page to your computer's hard drive. Then, choose the View⇨Internet Options command to set the home page to the page you created.

Customizing MSN.com

One of the great things about the MSN.com (www.MSN.com) home page is that you can customize it to include information you're interested in seeing every time you access the Internet. For example, you can add or delete sports scores, daily news, weather reports, hyperlinks to your favorite Internet locations, and other useful information.

This section shows you how to customize MSN.com to include just the information you want to see. If you choose to use some page other than MSN.com as your home page, you can skip the rest of this chapter.

Information you can add

Microsoft designed the MSN.com home page to be the ideal jumping-off point to other information on the Internet. The MSN.com home page is filled with links to other useful MSN.com pages as well as a search box that lets you find Web pages on any subject imaginable.

However, the MSN.com home page is more than a search service and a collection of links: The MSN.com home page is filled with useful content, such as the major news headlines of the day, current stock quotes, sports scores, and more.

You can customize your MSN.com home page by changing the content items that appear. In all, you have about 70 content items to choose from when creating your own personalized MSN.com home page. The following list describes some of the content you can include when you personalize your MSN.com home page:

- ✔ **Business & Careers:** For the latest business news from the likes of *Forbes* and *The Wall Street Journal.*

- ✔ **Computing & Web:** Get the latest technology news from sources such as Computing Central, Microsoft TechNet, *Wired,* and more.

- ✔ **Daily Diversions:** Put fun things on your page, such as a quote of the day and a daily horoscope.

- ✔ **Entertainment:** For fun and games, you can include MSNBC Entertainment, MTV, and other entertainment features.

- ✔ **Games:** What fun would the Internet be without links to the latest information about computer games?

- ✔ **Health:** For health information, include MSNBC Health, MSN's WomenCentral, and *Prevention* magazine, among others.

- ✔ **HighSpeed:** Get access to real-time video news from MSNBC.

- ✔ **Home and Family:** Include information for home and family.

- ✔ **Local News and Weather:** If you provide your zip code, your home page can display local information, such as a local weather forecast and local news headlines. You can also include the MSN City Guide for your favorite city.

- ✔ **News:** You can display news headlines from MSNBC News as well as other sources.

- ✔ **People & Chat:** Get links to live chat events, Webcams, and more.

- ✔ **Personal Finance:** You can display quotes for specific stocks or stock indexes as well as financial information from the likes of Charles Schwab, Forbes, and Merrill Lynch.

✔ **Reference:** Get the information you need from reference sources, such as the Discovery Channel and Encarta.

✔ **Shopping:** Keep tabs on daily specials from various online merchants.

✔ **Sports:** Find out sports news and scores from MSNBC Sports.

✔ **Travel:** Include travel information from Expedia.

✔ **Your links:** Add links of your own to your home page.

Customizing your home page

Now that you know what clips are available, you're ready to create your own, customized MSN.com home page to add the information you're interested in. To do so, follow these steps:

1. **Go to the MSN.com home page.**

   The address is www.MSN.com. Just click the Home button.

2. **Click Change Content on the navigation bar.**

   The page illustrated in Figure 15-12 appears. You can do your home page customization from this page.

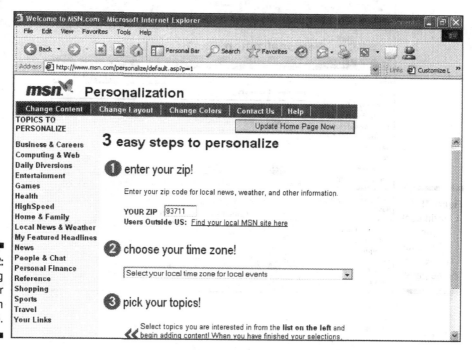

Figure 15-12: Customizing your MSN.com home page.

3. **Type your zip code in the YOUR ZIP text box and select your time zone from the drop-down list.**

   Typing your zip code enables MSN.com to display local information, such as movie times and weather forecasts, on your home page.

4. **To add a content item to your home page, click one of the categories that appears on the left side of the page and then click the check box for the item you want to include.**

   When you select a category, one or more content items is displayed. For example, Figure 15-13 shows the content items available under the Business & Careers category. To add one or more of these items to your MSN.com home page, just click the appropriate check boxes.

5. **To change the order in which your items appear onscreen, click Change Layout on the navigation bar, near the top of the screen.**

   The page shown in Figure 15-14 appears.

6. **Select one of the items listed in the Content column. Then, click the up or down arrow in the Position column to change the position of the item on your home page.**

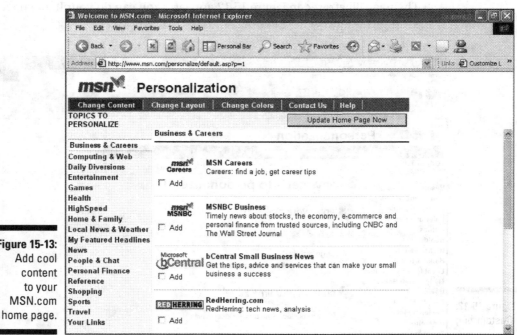

Figure 15-13:
Add cool content to your MSN.com home page.

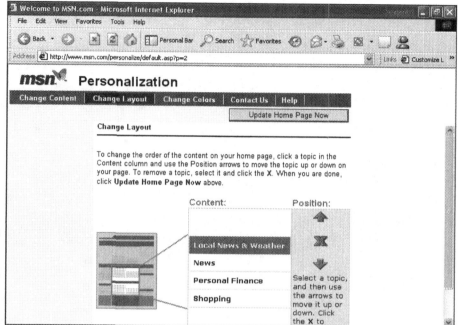

Figure 15-14:
Changing
the layout of
your home
page.

7. **When you're finished making changes, click the Update Home Page Now button.**

   Your custom MSN.com home page is built for you with the features you selected.

Here are some topics to wonder about while you lie awake at night, thinking about customizing your MSN.com home page:

✔ When you customize your MSN.com home page, the content items you select are displayed only when you sign to Microsoft Passport. If you don't have a Passport account, go to www.passport.com to get one. (You automatically get enrolled in Passport when you create a Hotmail e-mail account, so if you've signed up with Hotmail, you already have a Passport account.)

✔ Another way to customize the MSN.com home page is to scroll through your MSN.com home page to a section you want to customize and then click the Edit button that appears in the heading for that section. This action takes you directly to the part of the Personalize page that lets you customize that section.

Chapter 16

Using the Content Advisor to Make Sure That Your Kids Surf Safely

* * *

In This Chapter

▶ Determining your blush threshold

▶ Activating the Content Advisor feature of Internet Explorer

▶ Picking a secret password

▶ Requiring password access to restricted sites

▶ Using other rating services

* * *

*A*lthough the Internet can be a great resource for kids, it's also a notoriously unsafe place for kids to hang out unsupervised. For every museum, library, and government agency that springs up on the Internet, a dozen adult bookstores or sex shops seems to appear. What's a parent to do?

Fortunately, Internet Explorer has a built-in feature called the *Content Advisor,* which enables you to restrict access to many off-color Internet sites. The Content Advisor uses a system of ratings similar to the ratings system used for motion pictures. Although this system isn't perfect, it goes a long way toward preventing your kids from stumbling into something that they shouldn't.

About Internet Ratings

Internet ratings work much like motion picture ratings: They let you know what kind of content you can expect at a given Internet site. The ratings are assigned voluntarily by the publisher of each individual Internet site.

Although motion picture ratings give you an overall rating for a movie (G, PG, PG-13, R, or NC-17), the ratings system doesn't give you a clue about *why* a movie receives a particular rating. For example, does a PG-13 rating mean that a movie is filled with foul language, almost-explicit sex, or excessive violence? It could be any of these — or all of them.

By contrast, Internet ratings give specific information about several categories of potentially offensive material. Internet Explorer uses a ratings system that was created by a nonprofit organization called the Recreational Software Advisory Council, or RSAC, and was originally designed for rating computer games.

When used to rate Internet sites, the RSAC rating system is sometimes referred to as RSAC*i* (the *i* stands for *Internet*). The RSAC*i* rating system is managed by a nonprofit organization known as the Internet Content Rating Association (also known as ICRA).

RSACi assigns a rating of 0 to 4 for each of the following four categories:

✔ Violence

✔ Nudity

✔ Sex

✔ Language

Table 16-1 shows the specific meaning for each rating number in an RSAC rating.

Table 16-1		What the RSAC Ratings Mean		
Rating	*Violence*	*Nudity*	*Sex*	*Language*
4	Wanton and gratuitous violence	Provocative frontal nudity	Explicit sexual activity crimes	Explicit or crude language
3	Killing with blood and gore	Frontal nudity	Nonexplicit sexual activity	Obscene gestures
2	Killing	Partial nudity	Clothed sexual touching	Moderate expletives
1	Fighting	Revealing attire	Passionate kissing	Mild expletives
0	No violence	None	None	Inoffensive slang

With Internet Explorer, you can set a threshold value for each of the four categories. If any attempt is made to access a Web site that has a rating higher than the threshold value, Internet Explorer blocks the user from viewing the Web site.

For more information about RSAC*i* ratings, check out the ICRA Web site at www.icra.org. Figure 16-1 shows the ICRA Web page, where you can learn more about RSAC; if you're a Web publisher, you can find out how to provide a rating for your site.

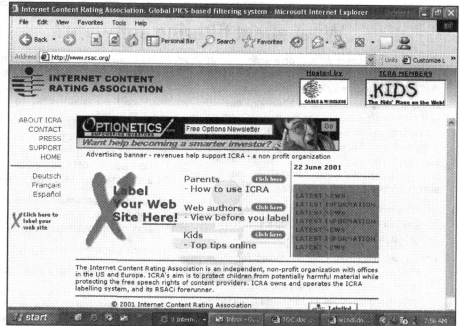

Figure 16-1:
The ICRA
Web site.

At this Web site, you can also learn about another, more detailed rating system offered by ICRA, known as the ICRA labeling system. For information about how to use other ratings systems, including ICRA, see the section "Using Other Rating Systems," later in this chapter.

Limitations of Internet Ratings

Before I show you how to activate and configure the Internet Explorer Content Advisor, I want to be sure that I don't lull you into a false sense of security, thinking that after you activate the Ratings feature, you don't have to worry about your kids getting into trouble on the Internet. Just to be sure, here are a few limitations of the RSAC rating system:

- ✔ Ratings are voluntary. Many sites are not rated at all. And for those sites that are rated, you have no guarantee that the Web site publisher has rated his site accurately.

- ✔ The Internet Explorer Ratings feature applies to only the World Wide Web. However, some of the nastiest Internet content is found not on the Web, but rather in Usenet newsgroups.

What about filtering software?

If the Content Advisor doesn't do a good enough job of protecting your kids from evils lurking on the Internet, you may want to consider purchasing a separate Internet filtering program. This type of program runs in the background on your computer and constantly watches everything that is sent to or from the Internet, filtering out anything that might be objectionable. Filtering programs have several advantages over the Internet Explorer Content Advisor:

✔ Filters watch *everything* that comes from or goes to the Internet, including e-mail, newsgroup postings, and chat rooms.

✔ Some filters can be configured for more than one user. Thus, you can place heavier restrictions on younger children, allow a little more freedom for teenagers, and give yourself unfiltered access.

✔ Filters come preloaded with lists of banned and accepted sites. Although new sites are cropping up all the time, at least you get a head start on which sites to allow and which to forbid.

✔ Filters can make judgments about unrated pages by scanning for offensive keywords. This method is not foolproof, of course, but it's better than banning all unrated pages.

You can purchase parental filtering software at most computer stores for about $50. For more information, check out these Web sites:

✔ NetNanny, at www.netnanny.com.

✔ Norton Internet Security, at www. symantec.com.

✔ Internet GuardDog, at www.mcafee.com.

✔ CyberPatrol, at www.cyberpatrol.com.

✔ Not all Web sites are rated. In fact, most are *not* rated. Internet Explorer enables you to either ban all unrated sites or allow full access to unrated sites. Neither option is good: If you ban unrated sites, you ban most of the Web. If you allow access to unrated sites, you let some garbage in. Sigh.

✔ Another area where kids get into trouble on the Internet is in chat rooms. Unfortunately, ratings don't apply to chat rooms.

✔ Kids are clever, and you can rest assured that some kids figure out a way to bypass the ratings feature altogether. No security system is totally secure.

Activating the Content Advisor

When you first install it, Internet Explorer doesn't check for Web site ratings. To screen out offensive Web sites, you must first activate the Content Advisor. Just follow these steps:

1. **Choose <u>V</u>iew⇨Internet <u>O</u>ptions.**

   The Internet Options dialog box appears.

2. Click the Content tab.

The Content options dialog box appears, as shown in Figure 16-2.

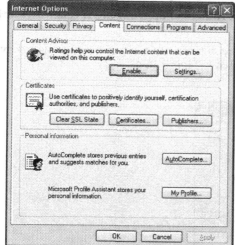

Figure 16-2:
Setting the
Content
options.

3. Click the Enable button in the Content Advisor area of the dialog box.

The Content Advisor dialog box appears, as shown in Figure 16-3.

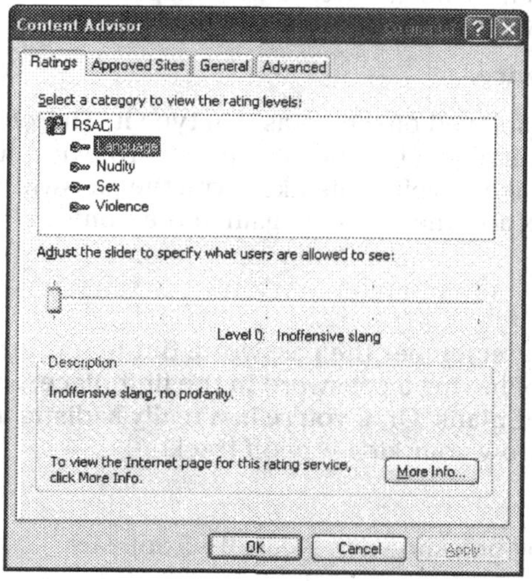

Figure 16-3:
The Content
Advisor
dialog box.

4. **Set the rating for each category by clicking the category and then adjusting the slider bar for the rating you want to use.**

   Notice that a description of each rating level appears beneath the slider bar; this description changes as you move the slider bar.

5. **After you have set the ratings to appropriate levels for your kids, click OK.**

   Internet Explorer asks you to create a supervisor password by displaying the dialog box shown in Figure 16-4.

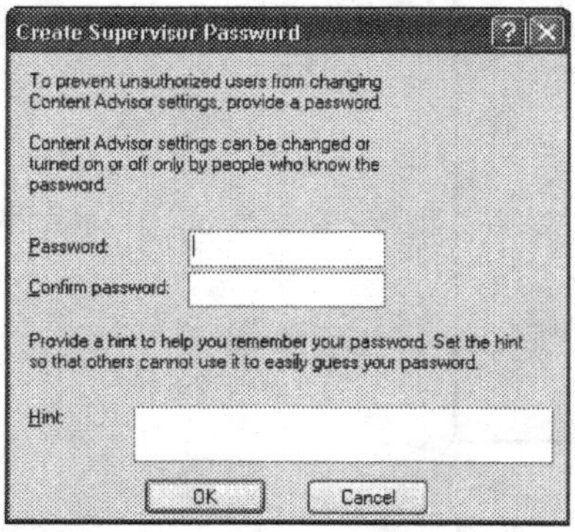

Figure 16-4:
The Create
Password
dialog box.

6. **Think up a good password.**

   Read the sidebar "Open sesame," later in this chapter, for guidelines on creating a good password.

7. **Type the password twice.**

   The password isn't displayed onscreen as you type it. Therefore, Internet Explorer requires you to type your password twice, just to make sure that you don't make a typing mistake. Type the password once in the Password text box and then type it again in the Confirm Password text box.

8. **Leave the hint blank.**

   The hint can help you remember the password. But that pretty much defeats the purpose of having a password in the first place. So I suggest that you leave the hint blank. Or, if you're in a really sadistic mood, type a bad hint that will throw your kids way off track.

9. **Click OK.**

   The informative dialog box shown in Figure 16-5 appears.

Figure 16-5:
Content
Advisor
has been
enabled.

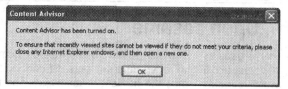

Figure 16-5:
Content
Advisor
has been
enabled.

10. **Click OK to return to the Internet Options dialog box; then, click OK again to dismiss the dialog box.**

    Finally! You're finished!

After the Content Advisor is in place, the dialog box shown in Figure 16-6 appears whenever someone attempts to access a site that your ratings don't allow.

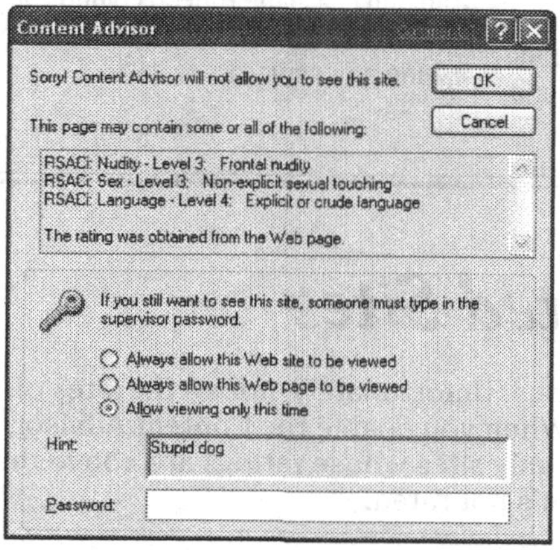

Figure 16-6:
Caught in
the act!

You can deactivate the Content Advisor at any time by calling up the Content options (choose View⇨Internet Options and then click the Content tab) and clicking the Disable Ratings button. You are, of course, required to enter your password in the process.

If you turn off the Content Advisor so that you (a consenting adult) can use Internet Explorer without restriction, don't forget to turn it back on after you're finished!

Open sesame

The Internet Ratings feature is only as good as the password you pick. Thus, you must make sure that you don't pick a password your kids can easily figure out. Here are some passwords to avoid:

✔ Your name or your kids' names

✔ The names of your pets

✔ The name of your boat

✔ Your birthday or anniversary

✔ Your car license plate number

✔ The password you use to access the Internet

✔ Any other word or number that's important to you and that your clever kids could come up with on their own

The best passwords are random combinations of letters and numbers. Of course, these are also the hardest to memorize. The next best passwords are a combination of two or three randomly chosen words. Just flip open the dictionary to a random page, pick a short word on the page, and flip to another random page and pick another short word. Jam the words together to create your password.

Above all, do *not* write the password down on a stick-on note attached to the computer monitor! If you must write the password down, put it in a secure place where only *you* can find it.

And don't fill in the Hint box when you create the password. That defeats the whole purpose of having a password.

Dealing with Unrated Sites

Internet ratings are a great idea. Unfortunately, not all the sites on the Net have yet rated themselves. When you enable the Content Advisor, Internet Explorer bans access to not only sites whose ratings are above the threshold you set, but also any site that's not rated.

Fortunately, Internet Explorer enables you to ease the ban on unrated sites. Here's the procedure:

1. **Choose <u>V</u>iew⇨Internet <u>O</u>ptions and click the Content tab.**

   The Content options appear (refer to Figure 16-2).

2. **Click the S<u>e</u>ttings button.**

   You're asked for your password. Type the password and then click OK. The Content Advisor dialog box appears.

3. **Click the General tab.**

   You see the General Content Advisor options, as shown in Figure 16-7.

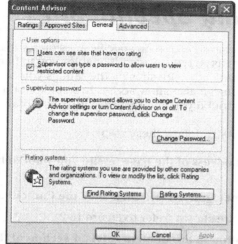

Figure 16-7:
The General
Content
Advisor
settings.

4. **Check the Users Can See Sites That Have No Rating check box.**

5. **Click OK to dismiss the Content Advisor dialog box.**

   You return to the Internet Options dialog box.

6. **Click OK to dismiss the Internet Options dialog box.**

Now you can view unrated sites without the constant message `Sorry! Your ratings do not allow you to see this site.`

To restrict access to unrated sites once again, repeat the procedure, but check (rather than uncheck) the Users Can See Sites That Have No Rating check box in Step 4.

Note that the General tab of the Content Advisor dialog box also enables you to change the supervisor password. Simply click the Change Password button. A dialog box in which you can type a new password appears. (As before, you must type the password twice to make sure that you don't make any typing errors.)

By entering the supervisor password, you can disable the dialog box that allows a user to type the supervisor password to view a site the Content Advisor has restricted. Just uncheck the Supervisor Can Type a Password to Allow Users to View Restricted Content option.

Banning or Allowing Specific Sites

Internet Explorer lets you control access to specific sites on a site-by-site basis using a feature known as *Approved Sites.* It enables you to ban access to a site you find offensive, even if the site slips by the ratings you have chosen for the Content Advisor. You can also allow access to a site that the Content Advisor may otherwise restrict if you find that the site is acceptable.

To ban or allow access to a site, follow these steps:

1. **Determine the Web address of the page or site you want to ban or approve.**

2. **Choose Tools⇨Internet Options and then click the Content tab.**

   The Content options are shown (refer to Figure 16-2).

3. **Click the Settings button in the Content Advisor section of the Options dialog box.**

   A dialog box appears, asking you to enter the Supervisor password.

4. **Type the password in the text box and then click OK.**

   The Content Advisor dialog box comes to life (refer to Figure 16-7).

5. **Click the Approved Sites tab.**

   This action takes you to the Approved Sites options, as shown in Figure 16-8.

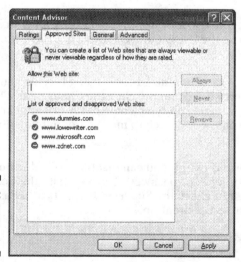

Figure 16-8: Banned and approved sites.

6. **Type in the Allow This Web Site text box the address of the site you want to ban or approve.**

7. **Click the Always button to approve access to the site or click the Never button to ban access to the site.**

   The Web site is added to the list of banned or approved sites.

8. **Repeat Steps 6 and 7 for any other Web sites you want to ban or approve.**

   You can also remove a Web site from the list of banned or approved sites by clicking the site you want to remove and then clicking the Remove button.

9. **Click OK to dismiss the Content Advisor dialog box.**

   You return to the Options dialog box.

10. **Click OK again to dismiss the Options dialog box.**

    You're done!

 When Content Advisor displays the Sorry! dialog box that prevents you from accessing a site, you have the option of typing the password to access the site anyway. If you choose the Always Allow This Web Site to be Viewed option when you type the password, the site is automatically added to your list of allowed sites.

Using Other Rating Systems

RASCi isn't the only rating system you can use to filter Web sites. The Content Advisor is designed to work with other rating systems as well. In fact, the Internet Content Rating Association (ICRA) publishes two types of ratings: RASCi ratings and ICRA ratings. ICRA ratings are more detailed and are designed to be more intelligent than RASCi ratings, by allowing such things as artistic considerations to apply. This feature allows you to view classic works of art — such as Botticelli's *Birth of Venus* — or sites about topics such as breast cancer even though they may contain nudity.

To use another rating system, you must first download for the rating system a special file, called a RAT file. You find instructions for downloading and installing this file on the Web site for the rating system you want to use.

 To locate other rating systems, call up the Content Advisor Settings dialog box, click the General tab, and then click the Find Rating Systems button. It takes you to a Web page that lists the rating systems you can use. Clicking the link for one of the rating systems listed on this page takes you to the home page for that rating system, where you can download the RAT file.

When you download the RAT file, you should save it to your \Windows\System or \WinNT\System32 folder. After you have downloaded the file, you can activate the new rating system by following these steps:

1. **Choose Tools⇨Options and click the Content tab.**

   This step brings up the Content Advisor options (shown back in Figure 16-2).

2. **Click Settings.**

   You're prompted for the supervisor password.

3. **Type the supervisor password and click OK.**

   The Content Advisor settings dialog box appears (refer to Figure 16-3).

4. **Click the General tab.**

   This step brings up the Content Advisor general settings, which was pictured in Figure 16-7.

5. **Click the Ratings Systems button.**

   The Rating Systems dialog box opens, as shown in Figure 16-9.

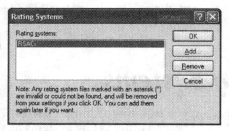

Figure 16-9:
The Rating
Systems
dialog box.

6. **Click Add.**

   This step brings up the Open Ratings System File dialog box, which looks like most other Open dialog boxes in Windows.

7. **Select the RAT file you downloaded for the ratings system and then click Open.**

   With luck, the Open Ratings System File dialog box opens to the folder that contains the RAT file you downloaded. If not, you have to navigate your way to the right folder.

   When you click Open, you're returned to the Rating Systems dialog box. The rating system you just added appears on the list of available rating systems.

8. Click OK.

You're returned to the Content Advisor Ratings tab. The rating options for the new rating service appear in this dialog box, as shown in Figure 16-10.

Figure 16-10:
New ratings!

9. Set the rating levels for each category for the new rating service you selected.

Each rating system has its own set of categories, so you need to examine them to determine how you want to set them up.

10. Click OK.

The Content Advisor dialog box vanishes and you're returned to the Internet Options dialog box.

11. Click OK again.

At last, you're done!

To remove a rating service, follow the procedure through Step 5. Then, select the rating service you want to delete and click Remove. Then, click OK to return to the Content Advisor, click OK again to return to the Internet options, and click OK a third time to return to Internet Explorer.

Chapter 17

Lowering the Cone of Silence: Using the Internet Explorer Security Features

* *

* *

*I*f Internet Explorer had been designed by Maxwell Smart, Secret Agent 86 from the popular 1960s television series *Get Smart,* it would have a Tools⇨Cone of Silence command you could use whenever you were about to send private information over the Internet. Of course, the computer you were trying to send your private information to wouldn't be able to see the information either, just as the Chief could never hear what Max was saying whenever Max insisted that they use the Cone of Silence.

The Cone of Silence from *Get Smart* illustrates well the dilemma of Internet security: balancing usability with security. The more usable the Internet is, the less secure it is. The more secure we try to make the Internet, the less usable it becomes. The trick to Internet security is to use enough security features to give users confidence that private information (such as a credit card number) won't be intercepted by criminals over the Internet, but not so much security that users have to jump through hoops to access a simple Web page.

This chapter lays out the security features of Internet Explorer, which attempt to manage this balancing act for you.

Security Issues to Worry About

The following sections summarize the basic security issues that all Internet users are exposed to and should therefore be concerned about.

Sending information over the Internet

Suppose that you want to purchase something over the Internet. When you type your name, address, and credit card information in the online order form, that information is sent over the Internet to the Web site. Without the right security measures, it isn't difficult at all for criminals to intercept that information and steal your credit card number.

You shouldn't be overly alarmed about the risk of using your credit card over the Internet. After all, your credit card number can also be stolen if you use it over the phone, through the mail, or in person at a retail store. However, your credit card numbers can be stolen if you send them over the Internet without using proper security, so you should think twice before using your credit card when ordering products online.

Before you send your credit card number or any other information to a Web site, make sure that the Web site you're sending information to uses a security measure known as *SSL*. If the site doesn't, get the 800 number and phone in your order instead. For more information about SSL (such as how to tell whether a Web site uses SSL), see the section "Scrambling: It's Not Just for Breakfast Any More," later in this chapter.

Downloading programs over the Internet

A common danger when downloading a program over the Internet is that the program you download may not do what it claims to do. For example, rather than play a game of chess, the program may instead erase everything on your hard disk. Or the program may plant a virus on your computer that can not only damage your computer but also infect other computers attached to a local area network or that you share disks with.

Internet Explorer uses a scheme known as *certification* to help prevent you from mistakenly downloading malicious programs. Check out the section "Certifying Your Security," later in this chapter, for more information about how certification works.

Although the Internet Explorer certification scheme helps, the best way to avoid malicious downloads is to use an antivirus program, such as Norton AntiVirus (www.norton.com) or McAfee VirusScan (www.mcafee.com).

Viewing Web pages that do more than meets the eye

In the early days of the World Wide Web, all a Web page could do was display information on your screen. Now, with programming tools such as Java and ActiveX and with scripting languages such as JavaScript and VBScript, a Web page can do more than display information: The page itself can act like a computer program. For the most part, this is good: It enables Web pages to come alive by displaying fancy animations and responding interactively to your mouse movements. But it also entails risk: An unscrupulous Web programmer can set up a Web page that displays a smiley face while it secretly erases files on your hard drive.

Preventing a Web page from doing damage is simple enough. The trick is to prevent a malicious Web page from doing damage without restricting a friendly Web page from doing good. Internet Explorer uses *security zones* to help manage the security restrictions that are placed on different Web sites. For more information, see the section "Zoning Out," later in this chapter.

Again, an antivirus program, such as Norton AntiVirus (www.norton.com) or McAfee VirusScan (www.mcafee.com), gives you extra protection against Web pages that contain malicious scripts.

Invading your privacy

What you do on the Web, what sites you visit, and how much time you spend there is your own business. But many Web sites have a nasty habit of leaving evidence behind on your computer in the form of cookies — little files that reside on your hard disk. Cookies serve a useful purpose: They allow a Web site to customize itself based on your preferences. In particular, *cookies* allow a Web site to know that you have visited the site before and are returning to see more. By examining cookies, a Web site can keep track of what pages of the site you have visited, what products you have ordered, and what files you have downloaded, for example.

Unfortunately, some Web operators have taken to cookie abuse: using cookies to find out more about you than they need to know or have a right to know. Fortunately, Internet Explorer has options that let you protect your privacy by controlling how cookies are used on your computer.

Scrambling: It's Not Just for Breakfast Any More

One of the most important methods of providing security on the Internet is to scramble information that is sent so that those who intercept the information cannot use it. Internet Explorer uses the latest scrambling technology, known as *Secure Sockets Layer,* or *SSL.* SSL effectively scrambles your information before sending it over the Internet and unscrambles it at the other end. The scrambling is done in such a way that other users who may intercept your message cannot unscramble it.

With SSL, sending credit card numbers and other personal information over the Internet is safe — provided that the party to whom you're sending the private information also uses SSL. Herein lies the rub: Not everyone on the Internet is using SSL. So, before you send any sensitive information over the Internet, make sure that the party you're sending the information to uses SSL to protect your data.

Most companies using SSL are happy to brag about the fact that they offer secure communications. For example, Figure 17-1 shows a page from the popular shopping site Amazon.com (www.amazon.com) assuring customers that they can safely place online orders without worrying about someone's stealing their credit card numbers. Most sites that use SSL include similar pronouncements. If you don't see this type of assurance, don't send sensitive information to the site.

 Of course, any Web site can claim to use a secure connection without actually being secure. Fortunately, Internet Explorer helps you verify a Web site's security claim by displaying the dialog box shown in Figure 17-2 whenever you enter a secured site. In addition, a Lock icon (as shown in the margin) is displayed on the status bar when you connect to a secure site. As long as the Lock icon is displayed, you can safely send credit card numbers and other private information over the Internet.

Whenever you leave the protection of a secure site, Internet Explorer displays a similar dialog box informing you that you are about to leave the secure connection.

 Do *not* send private information, such as credit card numbers, if the Lock icon doesn't appear on the status bar.

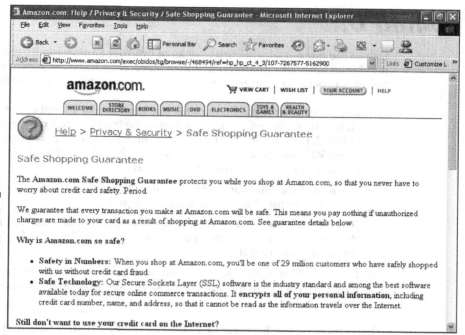

Figure 17-1:
Most Web
sites that
use SSL
security are
eager to let
you know
about it.

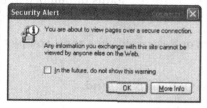

Figure 17-2:
Internet
Explorer lets
you know
when you're
entering a
secure site.

If you don't see the Security Alert dialog box when you enter and leave
secure sites and you want to, choose Tools⇨Internet Options, click the
Advanced tab, scroll down to the Security options section of the Advanced
option list, and check the Warn If Changing Between Secure and Not Secure
Mode option.

Zoning Out

One of the more useful security tricks of Internet Explorer is its ability to divide the Internet into different zones. Each zone enforces a different level of security procedures. Internet Explorer uses four basic security zones:

- **Local intranet:** If your computer is connected to a local area network (LAN), this zone encompasses files or Web pages that reside on the local network rather than on the Internet. Internet Explorer assumes that these Web pages are completely safe, so it imposes very few security precautions on pages that live in this zone.

- **Trusted sites:** This zone involves sites you have deemed fully trustworthy. Security for sites in this zone is relaxed.

- **Restricted sites:** This zone is composed of sites you think are not safe. Whenever you enter a site in the restricted zone, Internet Explorer insists on lowering the Cone of Silence.

- **Internet:** This zone is for sites that you don't know whether you should trust. Internet Explorer imposes modest security restrictions for sites in the Internet zone.

When you first install Internet Explorer, both the Trusted Sites and Restricted Sites zones are empty. That means that every Internet site you visit is placed in the Internet zone, where modest security measures are imposed. If you decide that a site can be elevated to Trusted status or dumped in the Restricted sites zone, you must do so yourself.

To add a site to the Trusted sites or Restricted sites zone, complete the following steps:

1. **Choose the Tools⇨Internet Options command.**

   The Internet Options dialog box appears.

2. **Click the Security tab.**

   This step displays the Security options, as shown in Figure 17-3.

3. **Click the icon for the zone you want to add a site to.**

4. **Click the Sites button.**

   This step summons a dialog box that allows you to add a Web site to the zone you selected in Step 3.

5. **Type the address of the page you want to add to the zone.**

   Unfortunately, you have to type the full Internet address of the Web site you want to add to the zone. It would be nice if Internet Explorer would fill in the address of the page you were viewing when you called up the Security options, but it doesn't.

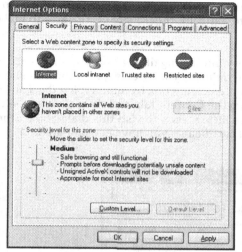

Figure 17-3:
Playing with
security
zones.

6. **Click the Add button.**

   The site you entered in Step 5 is added to the list of sites for the zone.

7. **Click OK.**

   This step returns you to the Internet Options dialog box.

8. **Click OK.**

You can also use the dialog box that appears in Step 4 to remove a page from a security zone if you decide that you misjudged the page.

Certifying Your Security

Another method Internet Explorer uses to ensure security is the use of certificates. A *certificate* is the computer equivalent of your driver's license. Certificates help guarantee that you are who you say you are and, more importantly, that the Web sites you send information to are what they say they are.

A complete explanation of how certificates work would span pages and require you to take a couple of Maalox before reading. But the basic concept is that an independent company, a *certification authority,* issues two different types of certificates:

✔ **Personal:** This certificate identifies you so that you can access Web sites that require positive identification (such as banks that allow online transactions).

✔ **Sites:** These certificates ensure that the site you're visiting isn't a fraud. Internet Explorer automatically checks site certificates to make sure that they're valid.

Internet Explorer has a very interesting dialog box that shows all the certificates you have accumulated during your Web explorations, as shown in Figure 17-4. You can get to this dialog box by summoning the Tools⇨Internet Options command, clicking the Content tab, and then clicking the Certificates button. However, you have little reason to visit this dialog box, other than to brag about the number of certificates you have accumulated.

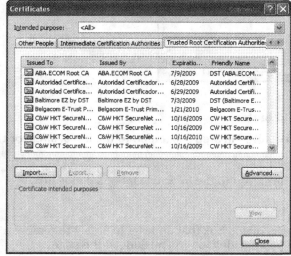

Figure 17-4: Internet Explorer loves to collect certificates.

Cooking Your Cookies

Cookies are little files that Web sites leave behind on your computer so that they can retrieve them when you return to the site. Most cookies serve useful purposes, such as keeping track of preferences you've set for a Web page and recording products you've purchased from a company. Cookies can also be used to store information about you that you supply to a Web site, such as your name, address, and phone number.

For security reasons, only the site that created a cookie can retrieve that cookie. Thus, if you visit a site that asks for your phone number and then stores that phone number in a cookie, other sites cannot peek at the cookie to find out your phone number. Only the site that created the cookie in the first place can retrieve it later.

However, in some cases, a Web site that you didn't realize you were accessing can create a cookie on your computer. This type of cookie, called a *third-party cookie,* usually comes from an advertising company that manages the advertising windows on a Web site. Whenever you view a page that has an advertisement, the advertising company has an opportunity to leave a cookie on your computer.

For example, some Internet ad agencies leave cookies on your computer that help them track what types of Web pages you're viewing. Then, they can tailor advertising to your preferences. In other words, the advertisement you see on one Web page may be determined by what other Web pages you've also visited.

Internet Explorer 6 has a new cookie privacy feature that lets you limit the use of third-party cookies. In addition, Internet Explorer 6 can ask Web sites that leave cookies on your computer to provide a privacy policy that states what kind of information is saved in cookies and how the information will be used.

To enable Internet Explorer privacy settings, choose Tools➪Internet Options and click the Privacy tab to summon the privacy options, as shown in Figure 17-5. Then, move the slider up or down to select the level of cookie privacy you want.

Depending on how you set the privacy option, Internet Explorer may reject all cookies, accept all cookies, or accept some and reject some depending on whether they're first- or third-party cookies. In some cases, a dialog box appears, informing you that a third cookie will be created and showing the privacy policy that accompanies the cookie. Then, you can decide whether to allow the cookie.

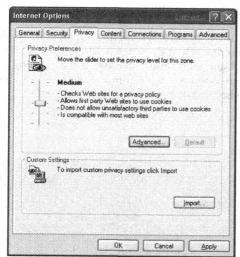

Figure 17-5:
Setting the
Privacy
options.

Security Options You Should Leave Alone

Thought you had had your fill of security options? But wait, there's more. Figure 17-6 shows some additional security options you can get to by choosing the Tools⇨Internet Options command, clicking the Advanced tab, and scrolling down to the Security options section.

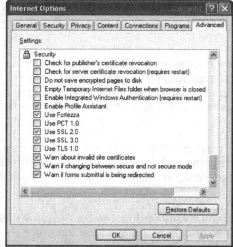

Figure 17-6:
Leave these
security
settings
alone!

You probably shouldn't mess with these security settings unless you have a Ph.D. in Advanced Computer Security and want to play. I show them here only so that you know that if you happen to stumble into this dialog box, you should click Cancel as quickly as possible.

You may find one of these security settings useful. The option labeled Empty Temporary Internet Files Folder When Browser Is Closed tells Internet Explorer to clean up after itself each time you close it by deleting temporary Internet files. That way, someone else can't come along later and easily find out what Web sites you've been visiting.

Chapter 18

Creating a Login Script

● ●

In This Chapter

▶ Getting to know scripts

▶ Planning your own Dial-up Networking script

▶ Creating a script file

▶ Using script commands

▶ Attaching a script to a connection

● ●

Scripting is a feature of Windows Dial-up Networking support that I hope you don't have to use. It's the type of feature that requires you to don a pocket protector and assume the role of a computer geek. But after you have it set up, a Dial-up Networking script can simplify your Internet sign-on procedures dramatically.

Scripting is designed for users whose Internet Service Providers require them to go through a complicated login sequence whenever they access the Internet. If, when you dial up your ISP, a terminal window pops up and greets you with a message such as User-ID: and a cold, blinking cursor, you should consider creating a Dial-up Networking script. If your Internet Service Provider launches you straight into Internet Explorer, you can fall down on your knees, give thanks, and skip this chapter.

What Is a Dial-Up Networking Script?

A *Dial-up Networking script* is a special file that contains text and commands that are automatically typed for you when you log in to a computer network. If the computer system you use to connect to the Internet requires you to manually enter information before it sends you to the Net, you can create a Dial-up Networking script to automate the process.

Some Internet Service Providers display a terminal window dialog box in which you're required to enter your user ID and password. In some cases, you may also be required to choose which of the provider's several systems you need to log in to before you're connected to the Internet.

By using a script, you can have the computer do the typing for you. The script can wait for your provider to ask for your user ID and then type the user ID. Then, it can wait for the password prompt and type your password. All you have to do is sit back and enjoy a sip of coffee while the script does all the work.

Unfortunately, you have to write the script yourself. The script is a simple text file that can be edited with ease, but it must contain certain commands, which I describe in the section "Working with Script Commands," later in this chapter. In addition, you have to attach the script to the Dial-Up Connection so that Windows knows to run your script when you dial in. I describe the procedure for attaching the script in the section "Attaching the Script to a Dial-Up Connection," later in this chapter.

Planning a Script

The first step in creating a script file is to plan the contents of the script. Get a piece of paper and label two columns Computer and Me. Then, sit down at your computer and log in to your Internet Service Provider. As you do, carefully write down in the Me column everything you must type. Make sure that you get the capitalization right and indicate when you must press the Enter key. In addition, enter in the Computers column the last thing you see displayed onscreen before anything you must type, such as `User id:` or `Password:`.

For example, here's what I wrote down to create the script for my provider:

Computer	Me
Username:	user ID (Enter)
Password:	*my password* (Enter)

The purpose of your script is to automatically type the information for you so that you don't have to type it yourself. The script includes special commands that wait for the computer to ask the questions you list in the Computer column and that automatically type the correct responses you list in the Me column.

Creating a Script

To create a script, you must use a text editor, such as Notepad. Here's the procedure for creating a script file:

1. **Click Start on the Windows taskbar and choose All Programs⇨ Accessories⇨Notepad.**

   Notepad appears in its own window.

2. **Type whichever commands you need to type to establish your Internet connection.**

   Use as a guide the information you gathered in the preceding section ("Planning a Script"). The commands vary depending on your service provider's requirements. Figure 18-1 shows the script I use for my provider. I describe each of the commands in this script in the following section, "Working with Script Commands."

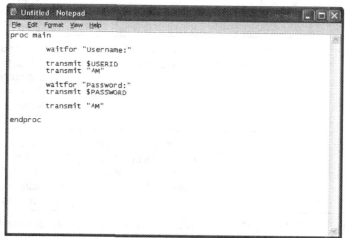

Figure 18-1:
A login
script.

3. **Choose File⇨Save As to save the file.**

   Choose a filename that ends in the .scp filename extension and save the file in your \Program Files\Accessories folder if you're using Windows 98 or Windows Millenium Edition or in the \WinNT\System32\RAS folder if you're using Windows XP, Windows 2000, or Windows NT.

4. **Choose File⇨Exit to quit Notepad.**

Your script filename must end in .scp, and your script must reside in the \Program Files\Accessories folder for Windows 98 or Millenium Edition or in \WinNT\System32\RAS for Windows XP, Windows 2000, or NT.

Working with Script Commands

The hard part of creating a script is knowing which commands to include in the script file. Table 18-1 lists the most commonly used scripting commands, and the sections that follow describe the commands I used for the script shown in Figure 18-1.

Table 18-1	Dial-Up Scripting Commands	
Command	*What It Does*	*Explanation*
`proc main`	Begins the script	The script begins running at the main procedure and stops at the end of the main procedure. (Every script must start with `proc main`.)
`endproc`	Marks the end of the script	When your computer reaches this command, Dial-up Networking starts PPP or SLIP.
`delay`	Pauses the script for n seconds before executing the next command	For example, `delay 4 <n seconds>` pauses for four seconds.
`waitfor "<string>"`	Waits until the computer you're connecting to has received the specified characters	*String* refers to the words your Internet Service Provider uses to prompt you for information (from the Computer Types column). Note that the string is not case sensitive.

Command	What It Does	Explanation
`transmit "<string>"`	Sends the specified characters to the computer to which you're connecting	*String* refers to the words you type as you log in to your Internet service (from the Me column).
`transmit $USERID`	Sends the user ID obtained from the Connect To dialog box	
`transmit $PASSWORD`	Sends the password obtained from the Connect To dialog box	
`set screen keyboard on	off`	Enables or disables keyboard input to the terminal window	
`getip <optional index>`	Reads an IP address and uses it as the workstation address	
`halt`	Causes Dial-up Networking to stop running the script but leaves the terminal window open so that you can enter additional information manually	
`;`	Indicates a comment	All text after the semicolon is ignored — comments are for your reference only.

Beginning and ending with proc main and endproc

Every script must begin with a line that says `proc main` and end with a line that says `endproc`. It's a programming thing, required probably because the programmers at Microsoft who created the Dial-up Networking Scripts tool were in a bad mood that day and figured, hey, because we have to type stuff like `proc main` and `endproc` all day, everyone should have the opportunity to enjoy the same wonderful experience.

So, the first thing you do when creating a script is add the following lines:

```
proc main

endproc
```

Notice that I left a blank space between `proc main` and `endproc`. This space is where the meat of the script goes.

Waiting for stuff: waitfor

Before your script can type anything to the computer, it must wait until the computer is ready to accept the information. To tell the script to wait, you must make note of the text that's displayed as a prompt and then use a `waitfor` command to tell the script to wait until that text appears on the screen.

For example, the following line tells the scripting tool to wait until the prompt `Username:` appears:

```
waitfor "Username:"
```

The only trick in using a `waitfor` command is to make sure that the text you specify is unique — it doesn't occur anywhere else during your login procedure.

The script in Figure 18-1 uses two `waitfor` commands. In both cases, I used the text I had written down in the Computer column when I planned the script.

Typing text: transmit

To send text to the computer, you use a `transmit` command. You may need to use several variations of this command:

- `transmit $USERID`: This command transmits the user ID you enter in the Connect To dialog box. By using this command in your script, you don't have to type your user ID into the script.

- `transmit $PASSWORD`: This command sends the password you enter in the Connect To dialog box. Again, typing your command this way enables you to send the password without having to type your top-secret password into the script.

- `transmit "^M"`: This cryptic command is equivalent to pressing the Enter key.

✔ `transmit "some text"`: This command transmits some text as though you had typed it at the keyboard. Note that if the text includes ^M, the Enter key is sent as well.

^M is but one example of several special characters you can send as part of a text string. Table 18-2 lists all the special characters you can include in strings.

Table 18-2	Special Characters for Strings
Character	*Description*
^M	Carriage return (Enter — same as `<cr>`)
`<cr>`	Carriage return (Enter — same as ^M)
`<lf>`	Line feed
\ "	Includes the quotation mark as part of the string
\ '	Includes the apostrophe as part of the string
\ ^	Includes the caret (^) as part of the string
\ <	Includes the less-than sign as part of the string
\ \	Includes the backslash as part of the string

Attaching the Script to a Dial-Up Connection

After you create your script, you must attach it to a dial-up connection so that the script plays automatically each time you start the connection. Here's the procedure for attaching a script in Windows XP:

1. **Click Start on the Windows taskbar and then choose Control Panel to summon the Control Panel. Then, click the Network Connections icon.**

   The Network Connections window appears, as shown in Figure 18-2.

2. **Select the connection to which you want to attach the script and then choose File⇨Properties.**

   Or, right-click the connection to which you want to attach the script and choose the Properties command from the pop-up menu that appears. Either way, a Properties dialog box similar to the one shown in Figure 18-3 appears.

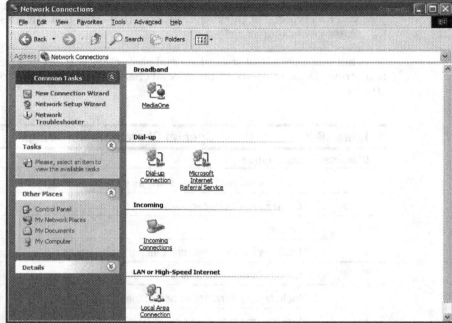

Figure 18-2:
The
Network
Connections
window.

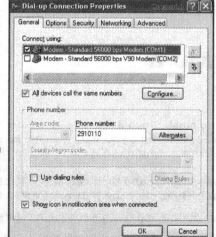

Figure 18-3:
The Dial-up
Connection
Properties
dialog box.

3. Click the Security tab to display the security settings.

Figure 18-4 shows the security settings that appear in the Properties
dialog box.

Figure 18-4:
The
Securities
tab, where
you find the
scripting
options.

4. **Click the Run Script check box and then click the Browse button.**

   An Open dialog box appears.

5. **Select the file you want to use as the script.**

   You may have to use the Open dialog box's navigation controls to find the correct drive and folder.

6. **Click the Open button.**

   You're returned to the Dial-up Connection Properties dialog box.

7. **If the Show Terminal Windows check box is checked, uncheck it.**

8. **Click OK.**

Now, you're ready to run the script. When you open the Dial-up Networking connection, the script should run automatically. As the script runs, watch it carefully to make sure that it appears to be running correctly. If it doesn't run properly, double-check the script to make sure that you're transmitting the correct information and, just as importantly, waiting for the correct text before transmitting information.

Chapter 19

Creating Your Own Web Site

S ooner or later, you grow weary of being an Internet spectator. After you've made the momentous decision to create your own Web site, you may need some help. This chapter can guide you through the steps involved in setting up your first Web site — deciding what to put on your site, finding a place to put your site, registering your own domain name, and obtaining the software programs you need to create a site.

As you would expect, Hungry Minds, Inc., offers plenty of books on creating Web sites. Considering that I have three teenage daughters who are going to college soon, I naturally recommend my own *Creating Web Pages For Dummies Quick Reference,* 3rd Edition, as a starting point. In addition, you can buy *Creating Web Pages For Dummies,* 4th Edition, by Bud Smith and Arthur Bebak; *HTML 4 For Dummies,* 2nd Edition, by Ed Tittel and Natanya Pitts; and *FrontPage 2002 For Dummies,* by Asha Dornfest.

Clarifying Some Familiar Terminology

Before I get far into this chapter, I want to clarify a few terms you're probably already familiar with. A *Web page* is a single page you can view with a web browser, such as Internet Explorer. A *Web site* is a collection of one or more pages linked together so that you can move from one page to another. A *home page* is the top page in a Web site — that is, the page that most users view first when they visit a Web site.

Many people (myself included) tend to use these three terms interchangeably. For example, if I tell you that I just set up a home page for my company, what I probably really mean is that I set up a company Web site with a home page and several other Web pages.

Deciding What to Put on Your Web Site

Before you even begin, you must decide what type of Web site you want to create and what information you want to put on the site. The following sections describe three of the most common types of Web sites: personal home pages, special-interest Web sites, and business Web sites.

Personal home pages

The Internet is stuffed to the gills with personal home pages. Personal home pages provide you with a place to put up pictures of your family vacation to the Grand Canyon; a list of your hobbies, your pet peeves, and your kid's soccer accomplishments; links to your favorite Web sites; and anything else that suits your fancy. Most personal home page sites consist of just one Web page.

Just about anyone with access to the Internet can create a home page. In fact, most Internet Service Providers offer a limited amount of space on their web servers for personal home pages. And if your ISP doesn't, you can choose from any of several free Web hosting services (which I describe later in this chapter, in the section "Getting a free site").

Here are some other ideas for what to put on your home page:

✔ A family photo album featuring pictures of you, your kids, and your pet turtle

✔ Your résumé

✔ The first chapter of your soon-to-be-published novel

✔ Voluminous tomes detailing your children's exploits in school and sports

✔ Your e-mail address so that people can send you comments about your Web page

✔ A discussion area so that people can leave comments that can be read by other visitors

Special-interest Web sites

Many of the most interesting Web sites are devoted to special interests. For example, if you're involved with a youth soccer league, you may want to create a Web page that includes team rosters, schedules, and standings. Or, if you're one of those annoying neighbors who decorates his house with

100,000 lights at Christmastime, you can create a Web page that focuses on Christmas decorating. The possible topics for a special interest Web site are limitless.

Business Web sites

By now, just about every major company has created an elaborate Web site, and many smaller companies ranging from custom cabinetmakers to mom-and-pop pizza parlors are putting up Web pages. The simplest corporate Web sites provide basic information about a company, such as a description of the company's products or services and phone numbers, for example.

A more elaborate corporate Web site can include any or all of the following:

- An online catalog that enables Internet users to see detailed information about products and services. If you want, the catalog can include pictures and prices

- Online ordering, which enables Internet users to place orders, pay for products, and arrange for shipment

- A customer survey so that you can find out whether customers are satisfied with your products and services

- Lists of frequently asked questions about the company's products and services

- Online support, where a customer can leave a question about a problem she is having with one of your products and receive an answer within a day or two

- Articles and reviews about your company's products and services

- Press releases

- Biographies of company employees

- Company policies, such as equal-opportunity statements and hiring practices

- Employment opportunities

Finding a Home for Your Web Site

To publish a Web site on the Internet, you must have access to a web server. A *web server* is a special computer that's connected to the Internet and runs special web server software that enables the computer to store Web page files that other Internet users can view on their computers.

A web server is also known as a *Web host*.

This section gives you some ideas for where to find web server space to host your Web site.

Internet Service Providers

If you access the Internet through an Internet Service Provider (ISP), you probably already have space set aside to set up a small Web site. Most ISPs give each of their users a small amount of disk space for Web pages included in their monthly service fee. The space may be limited to a few megabytes, but that should be enough to set up a modest Web site with several pages. You can probably get additional disk space, if you need it, for a small monthly fee. Some service providers also limit the amount of traffic your Web site receives. In other words, you can't host a wildly popular site that receives millions of visits per day on your ISP account.

Your ISP should be able to give you step-by-step instructions for copying your Web pages to the ISP's web server. Visit the help section of your ISP's home page for more information.

Web hosting services

A *Web hosting service* is a company that specializes in hosting Web sites on its own server computers. Unlike ISPs, which include limited Web hosting features as a part of their normal fee for Internet access, a Web hosting service charges you for hosting your Web site. However, Web hosting services offer much more than an ISP: your own domain name for your Web site, more disk space for your Web site and a larger traffic allowance, technical support for your web server, help designing and creating your Web site, and support for advanced web server features.

Of course, you have to pay for all this, and the cost varies from one service to the next. A typical Web hosting package includes

> ✓ Your own domain name so that you can pick the Web address users will use to access your site. The Web hosting service may register this name for you, or you can register it yourself. For more information, see the nearby sidebar, "Obtaining a domain name."

If you let the hosting service register the domain name for you, make sure that you're listed as the owner of the name so that you can take the name with you to another Web hosting service if you decide to switch later. The best way to make sure that you own the domain name is to register it yourself.

- ✔ A limited amount of disk storage on one of the hosting company's web server computers — typically from 15MB to 50MB for a basic package, with more space available at additional charge.

- ✔ A high-speed connection to the Internet for your Web site, with a relatively high limit on the amount of traffic, such as 1GB or 2GB per month. If your Web site becomes very popular, you may have to pay extra for the increased traffic. On the other hand, some Web host services provide unlimited traffic even with their basic packages.

A claim of unlimited traffic can be misleading — the Web host service may not have the equipment necessary to allow an unlimited amount of traffic for all their customers with acceptable speed. To find out, try accessing a few Web sites hosted by the Web host service you're considering to see how long it takes to access the Web pages.

- ✔ A web server that runs Windows NT, Windows 2000, or UNIX. Some Web hosting services let you choose the operating system and other software for the server.

- ✔ One or more e-mail accounts using your domain name. You can get additional e-mail accounts for a small fee, typically $1 per month per account.

Getting a free site

If you can't find a home for your Web site at your Internet Service Provider and you don't want to pay for a Web hosting service, you can opt for one of the many free web servers to host your Web site. You can't create a huge site on a free server, but most give you several megabytes of web server space free of charge — enough to set up a few pages at least.

What's the catch? Advertising. Users who visit your Web site have to put up with advertisements that pop up in their own windows or appear as banners on your pages. If you don't mind the advertisements, a free web server can be an easy way to get started creating Web pages.

If you don't want to mess with HTML or Web page editors, such as FrontPage, most free web servers include simple fill-in-the-blank tools that make it easy to create basic Web pages. For example, you can create a basic home page by selecting one of several templates, typing the page title and information you want on the page — such as your name and a description of your family, hobbies, or interests — and uploading pictures you want to appear on the page.

Obtaining a domain name

The best part about using a Web hosting service is that you get to register your own domain name. With an ISP-hosted Web page, your Web page address is based on a combination of your user ID and your ISP's domain name. For example, if your user ID is wilbur and your ISP's Web domain name is `www.myditzyprovider.com`, your Web page would have an address, such as `www.myditzyprovider.com/~wilbur`. But if you host your page with a Web hosting service, you can register your Web site under a name of your choosing, such as `www.myveryowncompany.com`.

Registering a domain name is inexpensive — $70 for the first two years and $35 each year after that to keep the name active. You can easily register a name yourself by going to the Network Solutions Web site at `www.networksolutions.com`. From there, you can search for a domain name that hasn't been taken yet. When you find a name that isn't already in use, you can sign up over the Web by providing the contact information for the domain name and a credit card number for payment.

The following are some of the more popular free home page sites:

- **MSN Home Pages:** Microsoft's MSN.com gives you up to 12MB of disk space to create a Web site. MSN.com provides templates that let you build Web sites that include advanced features such as a photo album, file cabinet, discussion board, and chat room. For more information, check out `homepages.msn.com`.

- **Yahoo! GeoCities:** Yahoo! GeoCities (`geocities.yahoo.com`) is one of the best-known free home page services, hosting more than 1 million home pages. Each free site can use up to 15MB of disk space, and you can increase the allocation to 25MB for a mere $4.95 per month.

- **America Online:** AOL offers up to 12MB of space for home pages, and you don't have to be an AOL subscriber. Just visit `hometown.aol.com` to sign up.

Many other free home page services are available. Some cater to specific types of home pages, such as artists' pages, churches, and chambers of commerce. Others are for general use. You can find a good directory of free home page services by going to Yahoo! (`www.yahoo.com`) and searching for *free web pages*.

Software for Creating Web Sites

Before you begin to create your Web site, you need to acquire the right software for creating and editing Web pages. Walk the aisles of any store that sells computer software, and you quickly discover that you have many options to choose from.

If you want to create a professional-quality Web site, are computer savvy, and are willing to spend the time it takes to learn how to use complicated but powerful software, you may want to invest in a professional-quality Web development program, such as Macromedia Dreamweaver 4, Microsoft Visual InterDev Professional 6, or Adobe GoLive 5. These programs (which cost $300 and up) let you incorporate advanced Web design features, such as templates and style sheets, to give the pages in your site a consistent look; navigation bars to automatically link the pages in your site; and special effects, such as buttons that change shape or color when the user points at them with the mouse.

If your budget and needs are more modest, you can choose an inexpensive (less than $150) Web site development program such as Microsoft FrontPage 2002 (which you can purchase separately or as a part of Microsoft Office XP), Adobe PageMill 3, or HotDog Professional 6, from Sausage Software. These programs don't have as many advanced features as their more expensive counterparts, but you can use them to create great-looking Web sites.

You can also create Web pages using Microsoft Office. Each of the main Office programs — Word, Excel, PowerPoint, and Access — has features that let you create Web pages. For basic Web pages, use Word or PowerPoint. For pages that present data in the form of spreadsheets or charts, use Excel. To create pages that let you view information from a database, use Access.

Part V
The Part of Tens

The 5th Wave   By Rich Tennant

"Guess who found a Kiss merchandise site on the Web while you were gone?"

In this part . . .

1f you keep this book in the bathroom (where it rightfully belongs), the chapters in this part are the ones destined to gain the most readership. Each of these chapters offers up ten (more or less) things that are worth knowing about various aspects of using Internet Explorer.

Without further ado, here they are, direct from the home office in Fresno, California. . . .

Chapter 20

Ten Tips for Using Internet Explorer Efficiently

T he Internet can be a fun place to explore. But because it's so big, losing your way is easy. Fortunately, Internet Explorer is filled with nifty little tricks that can make your Internet explorations more fruitful. The tips presented in this chapter can help you explore the Internet more efficiently so that you don't get lost in the woods. Many of these tips are covered elsewhere in this book; I gathered them here merely for your convenience, at no extra charge.

Stashing Goodies on the Favorites Menu

The Internet Explorer Favorites menu lets you gather up your favorite Web pages into a single location so that you can get to them easily. If you find yourself visiting a Web page frequently, add it to the Favorites menu so that you can go to that page directly from any other Web page. For example, if you like to visit www.dummies.com to find out what the latest *For Dummies* books are, add www.dummies.com to your Favorites menu. You can go directly to the Dummies.com page at any time simply by choosing it from the Favorites menu.

To add an item to your Favorites menu, follow these steps:

1. **Go to the page that you want to add to your Favorites menu.**

2. **Choose Favorites⇨Add to Favorites.**

   Doing so brings up the Add Favorite dialog box.

3. **If you don't like the description of the page listed in the Name text box, you can type a new description.**

4. **Click the OK button.**

For more information about working with Favorites, see Chapter 5.

Customizing Your Links Toolbar

An even faster way to access the pages you use most is to add them to your Links toolbar. The Links toolbar, at the top of the Internet Explorer window, contains buttons that let you go to frequently used Web pages with a single click of the mouse.

When you first install Internet Explorer, the Links toolbar includes links to Web sites that Microsoft thinks you should visit often, such as Microsoft's own corporate Web site, the Microsoft Windows Web site, and other Microsoft sites. But you can easily add your own sites to the Links toolbar. Follow these steps:

1. **Go to the page that you want to add to your Links toolbar.**

2. **Drag the page icon from the Address bar to the Links toolbar.**

   This step is a little tricky. The page icon appears right next to the Web page address on the Address toolbar. Point the mouse at this icon and then press and hold the left mouse button. Next, move the mouse to the position on the Links toolbar where you want the link to appear. When you release the mouse button, a button for the page appears.

To remove a link from the Links toolbar, right-click the link and then choose the Delete command.

For more information about customizing the Links toolbar, refer to Chapter 5.

Creating Desktop Shortcuts

Yet another way to go quickly to a Web page you use frequently is to create a desktop shortcut for the page. You can call up the page at any time by double-clicking the shortcut on your desktop.

To create a desktop shortcut, follow these steps:

1. **Go to the page that you want to create a shortcut for.**

2. **Right-click in an empty portion of the page and choose the Create Shortcut command.**

   Doing so brings up a dialog box informing you that a shortcut will be created.

   If the Create Shortcut command doesn't appear on the menu, right-click somewhere else on the page. The Create Shortcut command doesn't appear if you right-click a link, picture, or other object on the page.

3. **Click the OK button.**

   The shortcut is created on your desktop.

Be careful about creating too many desktop shortcuts. If you create too many shortcuts, your desktop can become cluttered.

Discovering Weird Places to Click

The Internet is a mousy place. You can click your way through link after link to get wherever you want to go. However, there are more places to click than you're probably aware of. In many cases, the links on a page aren't as obvious as you would hope. Move the mouse pointer over different areas of the page to find out. If the mouse pointer changes to a hand, you've found a hidden link.

Another way to exercise your mouse skills is to try right-clicking various objects on Web pages. Right-clicking an object on a page summons a pop-up menu of commands that apply to the object. For example, right-click a picture on a Web page to get a menu of commands that lets you save the picture to a file, print the picture, or use the picture as your Windows desktop wallpaper.

Finally, try working out the mouse on the Internet Explorer toolbars. You can use your mouse to rearrange the location of the toolbars by dragging the toolbar handle (the vertical bar located at the left edge of each toolbar). You can customize your toolbars by right-clicking between the buttons of any toolbar to bring up a pop-up menu that lists customization options. And don't miss the little extension arrows that appear at the right edge of the toolbars. Click these arrows to reveal additional toolbar buttons.

If you play with your toolbars too much and want to restore them to their original settings, choose View➪Toolbars➪Customize and click the Reset button in the dialog box that appears.

Searching Tips

When you need to look something up on the Internet, you can turn to one of the Internet's many search services, such as Yahoo!, Lycos, AltaVista, or Microsoft's own MSN Search. Unfortunately, if you don't use these search services wisely, you can spend hours looking for something without ever finding it.

Here are some tips for using Internet Explorer's search features efficiently:

✔ Use the Search bar. It enables you to display search results in a separate pane on the left side of the Internet Explorer window while viewing Web pages at the same time.

✔ Choose your search keywords carefully. If you search for broad terms like *animals* or *history,* you get — as Carl Sagan would have said — billions and billions of results to sift through. If your search words are too narrow, you don't get any results. It's usually best to start with search words that you think may be too narrow and then move to more general words if you don't get the results you want. The Internet is a huge place, and you'll be surprised by how many results you get from searches that you may at first think are too specific. (For example, I recently searched for *bald starship captain* and got 283 results, most of them correctly identifying Patrick Stewart from *Star Trek: The Next Generation.*)

✔ Use the advanced search page available on most search services rather than the search text box found on search service's home pages. The advanced search pages let you use advanced search features to help you make more efficient searches, such as searching for pages that contain all the words you type in the search field or any of the words you type in the search field. You can also search for pages that contain two words in close proximity to one another.

✔ Don't give up if you don't find the information you're looking for right away. If one search service doesn't turn up the page you need, try the same search using another service.

✔ To access search services quickly without having to wade through the search pane, add to your Links toolbar a link to the search service.

✔ When you do find a Web page that is interesting, add it to your Favorites menu so that you don't have to trudge through a complicated search to find the page again later.

Customizing Your Start Page

By default, Internet Explorer configures itself to use www.msn.com as its start page. The MSN.com home page is a great place to start your explorations of the Internet. But the best thing about the MSN.com page is that you can scustomize it to show the information you're most interested in. By personalizing msn.com, you can get stock quotes, news headlines on the subjects that interest you, sports scores, movie reviews, and other useful information all on one page, so you don't have to waste time surfing through page after page to find the information you need.

To personalize the MSN.com start page, click the Change Content link. You can choose the items you want to add to your personalized home page.

If you would rather switch to an altogether different start page, you can do that, too. Choose Tools⇨Internet Options, click the General tab, and then change the home page Address field to the address of any page you want to use for your start page.

For more information, see Chapter 15.

Dealing with Those Annoying Ad Windows

Many Web pages have an annoying habit of popping up advertisements in separate windows. Eventually, your entire desktop can become cluttered with little ad windows. You can dismiss an ad window by clicking the window's Close button, but sometimes the windows keep popping back up.

Here's a little trick that sometimes suppresses those annoying windows that insist on reappearing after you dismiss them: Rather than close the persistent window, minimize it. The window is sent to your taskbar, where it remains until you leave the site. If the window remains on your taskbar after you leave the site, you can safely close it.

Typing Web Addresses the Easy Way

If you've been using the Internet for a while, you probably have the keystrokes for www. and .com ingrained in the motor-memory of your fingers. If you're tired of typing these keystrokes for just about every Web page you visit, you can leave them off when you use Internet Explorer. Just type the middle portion of the Web address — the part that comes between www. and .com, and press Ctrl+Enter rather than just Enter to go to the Web site. When you press Ctrl+Enter, Internet Explorer automatically adds www. to the beginning and .com to the end of the Web address.

Using Other Software to Improve Internet Explorer

Although Internet Explorer is a great web browser, you can get even more out of the Internet by using other software to add features that Internet Explorer doesn't offer. The following are several types of programs you can use along with Internet Explorer:

✔ Internet security programs can make your Internet excursions safer by preventing hackers and other unscrupulous nuts from sneaking in to your computer while you're online. Two great security programs are BlackICE Defender (www.networkice.com) and Norton Internet Security, from Symantec (www.symantec.com). Both security programs cost about $50.

✔ Cookie managers help you control the proliferation of *cookies* — little files that many Web sites leave behind on your computer. Some cookies are necessary. For example, online stores that let you add items to a shopping cart before you check out place cookies on your computer to keep track of which items you have selected. Other cookies are questionable. Some are put there to keep track of what Web sites you visit or to gather personal information about you. A cookie manager program can alert you to cookies being stored on your computer and can selectively remove cookies you don't want to keep. Some popular cookie managers are Cookie Crusher (www.thelimitsoft.com), Cookie Pal (www.kburra.com), and Cookie Cruncher (www.rbaworld.com).

✔ Parental control programs, such as NetNanny (www.netnanny.com) and CyberPatrol (www.cyberpatrol.com), let you filter out inappropriate Web sites and keep track of how much your kids are using the Internet.

Chapter 21

Ten Things That Sometimes Go Wrong

*A*ctually, it's probably accurate to say that more like 10,000 things *can* go wrong, but this chapter describes some (okay, so I list nine, not ten — but who's counting?) of the things that often get out of kilter.

"I Don't Have Internet Explorer!"

No problem. Internet Explorer 6 is available from many sources, and it's free. If you have any type of access to the Internet, you can find Internet Explorer 6 at the Microsoft Web site, at this URL:

```
www.microsoft.com/ie
```

If you don't have access to the Internet or you don't want to contend with a horrendously long download (it can take hours), you can purchase Internet Explorer at your local computer store for a modest charge. Or, you may be able to find it bundled with a computer magazine at your local grocery store.

"I Can't Connect to the Internet!"

Modem connections are finicky. Most of the time, they work fine, but once in awhile they choke. You double-click the Internet Explorer icon, the Connection Manager dialog box appears, and you type your name and password, but you can't get any further. Arghhhhh!

Many, *many* things could be wrong. Here are a few general troubleshooting procedures that can help you solve the problem or at least narrow down the possibilities:

- ✔ Make sure that the phone cable is securely connected to the telephone wall jack and to the correct jack on the back of the modem. Phone cables sometimes jar loose. They go bad sometimes, too, so replacing the cable may solve the problem. If you're not sure which jack is the correct one, consult the manual that came with the modem.

- ✔ Make sure that the modem isn't in use by another program, such as a fax program or the Windows HyperTerminal program.

- ✔ Make sure that your teenager isn't talking on a phone that shares the same phone line as the modem. (With three teenage daughters, this happens often at my house.)

- ✔ Try calling your Internet access number on a regular phone to see whether it answers. If you get a busy signal or if it just rings on and on, something may be wrong with the local access number. Try again later, and call your Internet Service Provider's customer service department if the problem persists.

- ✔ Double-check the phone number in the Connection Manager dialog box. If your Internet Service Provider supplies an alternative phone number, try that one instead.

- ✔ If you can afford to wait, try accessing the Internet again later. It could be that your ISP's server is experiencing a temporary problem that will be corrected soon.

If you just installed the modem or if the modem never has worked right, you should make sure that the modem is configured to use the proper communications port within your computer. To change the port setting, follow these steps:

1. **Click the Start button on the taskbar and choose Control Panel.**

2. **Double-click the Phone and Modems icon, and then select the Modems tab in the dialog box that appears.**

3. Select the modem and click the Properties button.

4. Change the Port setting for the modem.

5. Click OK twice.

6. Try dialing in again.

Sometimes, removing and reinstalling the modem within Windows solves the problem. If all else fails, try these steps:

1. Click the Start button on the taskbar and choose Control Panel, and then double-click the Phone and Modems icon.

2. Click the Modems tab, click the modem to select it, and then click the Remove button.

3. Click Add.

4. Follow the Install a New Modem Wizard to reinstall the modem.

"I Forgot My Password!"

Didn't I tell you to write it down and keep it in a safe place? (Sigh.) If you really did forget your password and you didn't write it down anywhere, you have to call your Internet Service Provider for assistance. If you can convince the person on the other end of the line that you really are who you say you are, she can reset your password for you.

To avoid this kind of time-consuming mess, write down your password and store it in a secure location. Here's a list of several not-so-secure places to hide your password:

- In a desk drawer, in a file folder labeled *Not My Internet Password*.

- On a magnet stuck to the refrigerator. (No one, including you, will ever be able to pick it out from all the other junk stuck up there.)

- On the inside cover of this book, in Pig Latin so that no one can understand it.

- Carved on the back of a park bench.

- On the wall in a public rest room.

- Tattooed on your left buttock, backward so that you can read it in a mirror.

"I Got an Unexpected Error Message!"

Sometimes, when you try to follow a link to a cool Web page or you type a URL yourself and press Enter, rather than get the page you expected, you face a dialog box with a message that looks something like this:

```
Internet Explorer cannot open the Internet site
          http://www.whatever.com
A connection with the server could not be established.
```

Sometimes, no dialog box appears, but rather than the page you're looking for, you get just a page with some bland text that says something like

```
HTTP/1.0 404 Object Not Found
```

These error messages and others like them mean that your Internet Explorer couldn't find the page you tried to access. Several possible explanations may account for this error:

✔ You typed the URL incorrectly. Maybe it should have been `www.whoever.com` rather than `www.whatever.com`.

✔ The page you're trying to display may no longer exist. The person who created the page may have removed it.

✔ The page may have been moved to a new address. Sometimes you get a message telling you about the new address, sometimes not.

✔ The Web site that hosts the page may be having technical trouble. Try again later.

✔ The page may be just too darn popular, which causes the server to be busy. Hit the refresh button a couple of times. If that doesn't work, try again later.

"The Internet Explorer Window Disappeared!"

You know that you're signed in to the Internet, but you can't seem to find Internet Explorer anywhere. The window has mysteriously vanished!

Here are a few things to check before giving up in despair:

✔ Find the taskbar, that Windows thingy that usually lurks down at the bottom of your screen. The taskbar has a button for every program that's running. If you find the Internet Explorer button on the taskbar, clicking the button should bring the window to the front. (You may have to move your mouse all the way to the bottom edge of the screen to make the taskbar appear. Also, if you moved your taskbar, it may be on the top, left, or right edge of the screen rather than at the bottom.)

✔ If no Internet Explorer window appears on the taskbar, you may have closed Internet Explorer but remained connected to the Internet. To make Internet Explorer come alive again, click the Internet Explorer icon on the taskbar or click the Start button and choose Internet Explorer from the Programs menu. Because you're already connected to the Internet, you don't have to reconnect.

✔ You may have been disconnected from the Internet for one reason or another. Normally, when that happens, a dialog box appears, informing you that you have been disconnected and offering to reconnect. If no dialog box appears, you can reconnect by clicking Start, choosing Settings⇨Dial-Up Networking, and then double-clicking the icon for your Internet connection.

You can tell whether you're connected to the Internet by looking for the little connection icon in the corner of the taskbar next to the clock; it looks like two little computers strung together with kite string. If the icon is present, you're connected. If the icon is missing, you're not.

"I Can't Find a File I Downloaded!"

Don't worry. The file is probably around; you're just not looking in the right place. Internet Explorer offers a Save As dialog box that you must complete before downloading a file, so presumably you know where the file has been saved. However, you can all-too-easily click OK without really looking at this dialog box when it appears.

Fortunately, all you have to do is choose File⇨Save As to recall the Save As dialog box, which by default opens the same folder the dialog box was last opened to. Just check the Save In field at the top of the dialog box to find out the folder where you saved your file.

If you can't remember the name of the file you downloaded, here's a trick that may help you find it:

1. **Open a My Computer window for the folder in which you saved the file.**

    Click My Computer and then navigate your way through your drives and folders until you come to the one where you saved the file.

2. **Choose View⇨Details to display a list of detailed file information for each file in the folder.**

3. **Choose <u>V</u>iew⇨Arrange <u>I</u>cons⇨By <u>D</u>ate.**

   The list of files is sorted into date sequence, with the newest files appearing at the top of the list.

4. **Look at the files at the top of the list.**

   With luck, one of these files rings a bell.

Another trick that may help if you can remember the filename is to click the Start button, choose Search, and then search for the missing file.

"I Was Disconnected in the Middle of a 2-Hour Download!"

Wow. Tough break. Unfortunately, the Internet doesn't have any way to restart a big download, picking up where you left off. The only solution is to download the entire file again.

Don't blame me — I'm just the messenger.

If you do lots of downloading, you may want to look into special Internet download programs that can resume interrupted downloads, such as Go!Zilla (www.gozilla.com).

"I Can't Find That Cool Web Page I Saw Yesterday!"

I've faced this problem myself. The Web is such a large place that you can easily stumble into a page you really like and then not be able to find it again later.

If you can't seem to retrace your steps, you may still have a record of where you were. Click the History button to display links to all the pages you recently visited. With some luck, you can find the page in the History folder.

To avoid the frustration of misplacing the Web sites you love, use the F<u>a</u>vorites⇨<u>A</u>dd to Favorites command whenever you come across a Web page you think you may want to visit again. That way, you can always find the page again by choosing it from the Favorites menu. If you later decide that the page isn't so great after all, you can always delete it from your Favorites.

"I've Started a Nuclear War!"

If you're minding your own business, enjoying a nice game of Global Thermonuclear War at www.wargames.com, and you suddenly hear air-raid sirens and see mushroom clouds on the horizon, don't panic. See whether you can interest the computer in a nice game of chess instead.

Just kidding. Nothing you do can start a nuclear war from the Internet. Experienced computer hackers have been trying to start nuclear wars on the Internet for years, and no one has succeeded . . . at least not yet.

Chapter 22

Ten Safety Tips for Kids on the Net

* *

In This Chapter

▶ Safety tips for kids and their parents

▶ Ways to help make the Internet a safe place for everyone

* *

The Internet is an inherently risky place for kids (and adults, too). Your kids can just as easily find, along with pictures of Neil Armstrong on the moon, images that you probably don't want them to see. And although chatting online can be fun and enlightening, it can also be unhealthy and possibly even dangerous.

This chapter lists ten important safety tips that parents should drill into their kids' heads before they allow them to go online.

I really don't want to be an alarmist here. Overall, the Internet is a pretty wholesome place. Don't be afraid to let your kids venture out online, but don't let them go it alone, either. Make sure that they understand the ground rules.

Don't Believe That People Really Are Who They Say They Are

When you sign up with an Internet Service Provider, you can type anything you want for your user ID. You also get to create your own user ID for instant-message services, such as AOL Instant Messenger (AIM) and MSN Messenger. And no one makes you tell the truth in e-mail, newsgroups, or chat rooms. Just because someone claims to be a 16-year-old female is not reason enough to believe it. That person can be a 12-year-old boy, a 17-year-old girl, or a 35-year-old pervert.

Never Give Out Your Address, Phone Number, Real Last Name, or Credit Card Number

If you're not sure why Rule No. 2 exists, see Rule No. 1.

Never Pretend to Be Someone You're Not

Here's the flip side of not believing who someone says she is: Other people may believe that you are who you say you are. If you're 13 years old and claim to be 17, you're inviting trouble.

We all like to gloss over our weaknesses. When I'm online, I don't generally draw attention to the fact that a substantial portion of my hair is gone and that I'm a bit pudgy around the waistline. (Well, okay, I'm a *lot* pudgy around the waistline.) But I don't represent myself as a super athlete or a rock star, either. Just be yourself.

Save Inappropriate Postings to a File So That You Can Show Them to an Adult

If someone sends you inappropriate e-mail — not just something that makes you feel angry or upset, but something that seems downright inappropriate — choose File⇨Save As to save the message as a file. Then show it to an adult.

If Someone Says Something Inappropriate to You in a Chat, Save the Chat Log

If someone is vulgar or offensive in an online chat, save the chat log to a file. Then show it to an adult. In MSN Messenger, you can save the chat to a file by choosing File⇨Save.

Watch Your Language

The Internet isn't censored. In fact, it can be a pretty rough place. Crude language abounds, especially on Usenet and in chat rooms. But that doesn't mean that you have to contribute to the endless flow of colorful metaphors. Watch your language while chatting online or posting messages.

Don't Obsess

The Internet can be fun, but there's more to life than going online. The best friendships are the ones in which you spend time in the presence of other people. If you find yourself spending hour after hour online, maybe you should cut back a bit.

Report Inappropriate Behavior to an Adult

If something seems amiss in your Internet experience — for example, if you think that someone is harassing you beyond what should be normal or if someone asks you questions that make you uncomfortable — tell an adult.

You can also complain by sending e-mail to the administrator of the perpetrator's Internet Service Provider. If the perp is clever, you may not be able to figure out his true e-mail address. But you often can. If you receive harassing mail from idiot@jerk.com, try sending a complaint to postmaster@jerk.com.

If You Feel Uncomfortable, Leave

Don't stick around in a chat session if you feel uncomfortable. Just leave.

Similarly, don't bother to reply to inappropriate e-mail messages or newsgroup articles.

Parents, Be Involved with Your Kids' Online Activities

Don't let your kids run loose on the Internet! Get involved with what they're doing. You don't have to monitor them every moment they're online. Just be interested in what they're doing, what friends they have made over the network, what they like, and what they don't like. Ask them to show you around their favorite Internet pages.

Glossary

Address Book: A file that stores the Internet e-mail addresses of the people with whom you correspond regularly. Outlook Express maintains an address book for your e-mail.

AFK: *Away from keyboard,* an abbreviation commonly used when chatting. See also *IRC.*

America Online: A popular online information service that also provides Internet access. America Online is often referred to as *AOL.* To send e-mail to an AOL user, address the message to the user's America Online name followed by the domain name (@aol.com). For example, if the user's AOL name is Barney, send an e-mail message to Barney@aol.com.

anonymous FTP: An FTP site that allows access to anyone, without requiring an account.

AOL: See *America Online.*

applet: A program written in the Java language and embedded in an HTML document. An applet runs automatically whenever someone views the Web page that contains the applet.

ARPANET: The first incarnation of the Internet, built by the Department of Defense during the Summer of Love.

article: A message posted to a Usenet newsgroup.

ASCII: The standard character set for most computers. Internet newsgroups are *ASCII-only,* meaning that they can support only text-based messages.

attach: Sending a file along with an e-mail message or newsgroup article. Internet Explorer automatically encodes and decodes attachments.

attachment: A file attached to an e-mail message or a newsgroup article.

AutoComplete: A mostly useful but sometimes annoying feature of Internet Explorer that anticipates what you are trying to type and tries to complete your typing before you finish. AutoComplete works in the Address bar and in form fields.

AVI: The Microsoft standard for video files that can be viewed in Windows. AVI is one of the more popular video formats on the Web, but other formats, such as QuickTime and MPEG are also widely used.

bandwidth: The amount of information that can flow through a network connection. Bandwidth is to computer networks what pipe diameter is to plumbing: The bigger the pipe, the more water allowed through.

baud: See ***bits per second.*** (A technical difference does exist between *baud* and *bits per second,* but only people with pocket protectors and taped glasses care.)

binary file: A non-ASCII file, such as a computer program, a picture, a sound, or a video.

BITNET: A large network connecting colleges and universities in North America and Europe through the Internet. BITNET mailing lists are presented as Usenet newsgroups under the `bit` hierarchy.

bits per second (bps): A measure of how fast your modem can transmit or receive information between your computer and a remote computer, such as your Internet Service Provider. You won't be happy browsing the Internet using anything less than a 28,800 bps modem (commonly referred to as a *28.8 modem*). Note that the term *Kbps* is often used to designate thousands of bits per second. Thus, 28,800 bps and 28.8 Kbps are equivalent.

BRB: *Be right back,* an abbreviation commonly used when chatting. See also ***IRC.***

browser: A program, such as Internet Explorer, that you can use to access and view the World Wide Web. Internet Explorer is, at its core, a browser.

cable modem: A high-speed Internet connection that is always connected to the Internet and works outrageously faster than a dial-up connection.

cache: An area of your computer's hard disk used to store data recently downloaded from the network so that the data can be redisplayed quickly.

cappuccino: An Italian coffee drink that blends espresso, steamed milk, foam, and (if you're lucky) a dash of cinnamon. Not to be confused with ***Java.***

certificate: An online form of identification that gives one computer assurance that the other computer is who it claims to be. Certificates are a common form of security on the Internet.

CGI: *Common Gateway Interface.* A method of programming Web sites, mostly used to handle online forms. CGI uses script programs that run on the server computer, as opposed to Java or VBScript programs, which run on client computers.

chat: See ***IRC.***

chat room: A place where two or more Internet users gather online to hold a conversation. See also *IRC.*

chat server: An Internet server that hosts a chat.

compressed file: A file that has been processed by a special *compression program* that reduces the amount of disk space required to store the file. If you download the file to your computer, you must decompress the file using a program, such as WinZip or PKUNZIP, before you can use it.

compressed folder: A Windows XP feature that automatically treats compressed zip files as though they were folders.

CompuServe: A popular online service that provides Internet access. To send Internet mail to a CompuServe member, address the mail to the user's screen name followed by cs.com, as in Gopher¢.com. (Some CompuServe users have CompuServe Classic accounts, which use a numeric user ID composed of two groups of numbers separated by a comma. To send mail to a CompuServe Classic user, address the mail to the numeric user ID followed by @compuserve.com. However, use a period rather than a comma in the user ID. For example, if the user's ID is 55555,1234, send e-mail to 55555.1234@compuserve.com. You have to use the period because Internet e-mail standards don't allow for commas in e-mail addresses.)

Cone of Silence: A top-secret security device employed by agents of CONTROL to prevent spies from KAOS from eavesdropping on sensitive conversations.

connect time: The amount of time you're connected to the Internet or your online service. Internet Service Providers that limit your monthly connect time or charge you by the hour are going the way of the dodo bird. However, some providers automatically disconnect you if you stay connected but don't do anything for a certain length of time.

Connection Manager: A gizmo that comes with Internet Explorer to take care of dialing in to your Internet Service Provider and logging you on to the Internet.

Content Advisor: An Internet Explorer feature that lets you block Web sites based on their ratings. See also *rating.*

cookie: A file that a web server stores on your computer. The most common use for cookies is to customize the way a Web page appears when you view it. For example, customizable Web pages such as www.msn.com use cookies to store your viewing preferences so that the next time you visit that Web page, only the elements that you request are displayed.

cyberspace: An avant-garde term used to refer to the Internet.

decode: The process of reconstructing a binary file that was encoded using the uuencode scheme, used in e-mail and newsgroups. Outlook Express automatically decodes encoded files.

decompression: The process of restoring compressed files to their original states. Decompression is usually accomplished with a program, such as WinZip and PKUNZIP. (You can download the shareware version of PKUNZIP at www.pkware.com.)

decryption: See *Tales from Decrypt.* Just kidding. Decryption is the process of unscrambling a message that has been encrypted (scrambled so that only the intended recipient can read it). See also *encryption.*

dial-up connection: An Internet connection that uses a modem and a telephone line to connect to the Internet. Faster alternatives include *cable modem, DSL,* and *ISDN.*

dial-up script: A special file that contains the instructions used to log you in to your ISP so that you can connect to the Internet.

"Dixie": A happy little tune that you can whistle while you're waiting for a Web page to finish downloading.

DNS: *Domain Name Server.* The system that enables us to use almost intelligible names, such as www.microsoft.com, rather than completely incomprehensible addresses, such as 254.120.0.74.

domain: The last portion of an Internet address (also known as the *top-level domain*), which indicates whether the address belongs to a company (com), an educational institution (edu), a government agency (gov), a military organization (mil), or another organization (org). Recently, a slew of new top-level domains has been approved for use, including .biz (for business), .info (for informational Web sites), .pro (for professionals), .name (for individuals), and a few others.

domain name: The address of an Internet site, which generally includes the organization domain name followed by the top-level domain, as in www.janethatesbill.com.

download: Copying a file from another computer to your computer via a modem.

DSL: *Digital Subscriber Line.* A high-speed connection that, like a cable modem connection, is always connected to the Internet and runs much faster than a dial-up connection.

Dynamic HTML: An advanced type of HTML that is supported by Internet Explorer and that enables you to create Web pages in which every element on the page (text and graphics alike) can be dynamically changed as the user interacts with the page.

e-mail: *Electronic mail,* an Internet service that enables you to send and receive messages to and from other Internet users.

e-mail address: An address used to send e-mail to someone on the Internet. An e-mail address consists of a username followed by a domain name. For example, if your user ID is `JClampett` and your domain name is `beverly.hills.com`, your e-mail address is `JClampett@beverly.hills.com`.

emoticon: Another word for a *smiley* — an expressive face you can create with nothing more than a few keystrokes and some imagination. `:-)`

encode: A method of converting a *binary file* to ASCII text, which can be sent by Internet e-mail or posted to an Internet newsgroup. When displayed, encoded information looks like a stream of random characters. But when you run the encoded message through a decoder program, the original binary file is reconstructed. Outlook Express automatically encodes and decodes messages, so you don't have to worry about using a separate program for this purpose.

encryption: Scrambling a message so that no one can read it, except, of course, the intended recipient, who must *decrypt* the message before reading it.

ETLA: *Extended three-letter acronym.* A four-letter acronym.

Explorer bar: The left one-third or so of the Internet Explorer main window, which Internet Explorer periodically uses to display a special toolbar when you click the Search, History, or Favorites button.

FAQ: A *frequently asked questions* file. Contains answers to the most commonly asked questions. Always check to see whether a FAQ file exists for a forum or Usenet newsgroup before asking basic questions. (If you post a question on an Internet newsgroup and the answer is in the FAQ, expect to be flamed for sure.)

Favorites: A collection of Web page addresses that you visit frequently. Internet Explorer enables you to store your favorite Web addresses in a special folder so that you can recall them quickly.

File Transfer Protocol (FTP): A system that allows the transfer of program and data files over the Internet.

first-party cookie: A cookie that is created by the web server that hosts the page you are viewing. See also *cookie.*

flame: A painfully brutal response to a dumb posting on an Internet newsgroup. (On some newsgroups, just having aol.com in your Internet address is enough to get you flamed.)

Flash: A program created by Macromedia that is often used to create animations on Web pages. To play a Flash animation, you need the free Flash player, which you can download from www.macromedia.com.

freeware: Software you can download and use without paying a fee.

FTP: See *File Transfer Protocol.*

FTP site: An Internet server that has a library of files available for downloading with FTP. Internet Explorer lets you browse FTP sites as though the sites were folders on your own hard drive.

GIF: *Graphic Interchange Format.* A popular format for picture files. The GIF format uses an efficient compression technique that results in less data loss and higher-quality graphics than other formats, such as PCX. However, GIF files are limited to 256 colors and cannot reproduce photographic-quality images, like JPEG files can.

History bar: A place where you can sip a martini while discussing the Civil War. Just kidding. Actually, it's a variant of the Explorer bar, which lists pages you have visited recently so that you can conveniently return to them.

home page: (1) The introductory page at a Web site; sometimes refers to the entire Web site. (2) The first page displayed by Internet Explorer when you start it. By default, the home page is set to www.msn.com, but you can change the home page to any Web page you want.

host computer: A computer to which you can connect via the Internet.

HTML: *Hypertext Markup Language.* A system of special tags used to create pages for the World Wide Web.

HTTP: *Hypertext Transfer Protocol.* The protocol used to transmit HTML documents over the Internet.

hyperlink: A bit of text or a graphic in a Web page that you can click to retrieve another Web page. The new Web page may be on the same web server as the original page, or it may be on an entirely different web server halfway around the globe.

hypermedia: A variation of hypertext in which hyperlinks can be graphics, sounds, or videos as well as text. The World Wide Web is based on hypermedia, but the term *hypertext* is often loosely used instead.

hypertext: A system in which documents are linked to one another by text links. When the user clicks on a text link, the document referred to by the link is displayed. See also *hypermedia.*

IBM: A big computer company.

ICRA: *Internet Content Rating Association,* the organization that developed and oversees the use of Internet ratings.

information superhighway: Al Gore's pet name for the Internet.

instant message: An Internet feature that lets you exchange messages with other Internet users in real time, like an online phone conversation but using text rather than voice. See also *MSN Messenger.*

Internet: A vast, worldwide collection of networked computers — the largest computer network in the world.

Internet address: An address for a person or place on the Internet. See also *e-mail address, Web address.*

Internet Connection Wizard: A program that comes with Internet Explorer to help you get connected to the Internet.

Internet Explorer: The Microsoft program for browsing the Internet.

Internet Relay Chat: See *IRC.*

Internet Service Provider: Also known as an *ISP.* A company that provides access to the Internet.

IP: *Internet Protocol.* The data transmission protocol that enables networks to exchange messages; serves as the foundation for communications over the Internet.

IRC: *Internet Relay Chat.* A system that enables you to carry on live conversations (known as *chats*) with other Internet users.

ISDN: A digital telephone line that can transmit data as fast as 128 Kbps. For most people, a cable modem or DSL connection is better.

ISP: See *Internet Service Provider.*

Java: An object-oriented programming language created and designed by Sun Microsystems to be used on the World Wide Web. Java is one way to add sound, animation, and interactivity to Web pages. Although Internet Explorer supports Java, Microsoft prefers that you use VBScript instead.

JavaScript: A scripting language used with Netscape Navigator that enables Web-page authors to embed Java programs in HTML documents. *JScript* is the Internet Explorer version of JavaScript.

JPEG: *Joint Photographic Experts Group.* A popular format for picture files. JPEG uses a compression technique that greatly reduces a graphic's file size with only a small loss of quality. For photographic images, this loss is usually not noticeable. Because of its small file sizes and high quality, JPEG is a popular graphics format for the Internet.

JScript: The Microsoft implementation of JavaScript for use with Internet Explorer.

KB: An abbreviation for *kilobyte* (1,024 bytes).

Kbps: A measure of a modem's speed in thousands of bits per second. Two common modem speeds are 28.8 Kbps and 56 Kbps.

LAN: See *local area network.*

link: See *hyperlink.*

Links toolbar: A special Internet Explorer toolbar that lets you quickly access a handful of the sites you visit most frequently.

Linux: A free version of UNIX that is used on many web servers throughout the world.

LISTSERV: A server program used for mailing lists, which are basically e-mail versions of newsgroups. See also *mailing list.*

local area network: Also referred to as a *LAN.* Two or more computers that are connected to one another to form a network. A LAN enables the computers to share resources, such as disk drives and printers. A LAN is usually located within a relatively small area, such as in a building or on a campus.

LOL: *Laughing out loud.* A common abbreviation used to express mirth or joy when chatting on MSN Messenger, in e-mail messages, or in newsgroup articles.

lurk: To read articles in a newsgroup without contributing your own postings. Lurking is one of the few approved forms of eavesdropping. Lurking for a while in a newsgroup before posting your own articles is the polite thing to do.

mailing group: A list of e-mail addresses. You can send mail to everyone on the list by specifying the list name.

mailing list: An e-mail version of a newsgroup. Any messages sent to the mailing list server are automatically sent to each person who has subscribed to the list.

MB: *Megabyte.* Roughly a million bytes.

Media bar: A special toolbar for working with media files.

message rule: An Outlook Express feature that lets you automatically delete messages that you don't want to read or move certain types of messages to folders other than your inbox.

Microsoft: The largest software company in the world, at least for now. Among other things, Microsoft is the maker of Windows and the Microsoft Office suite, which includes Word, Excel, PowerPoint, and Access. Oh, and I almost forgot — Internet Explorer, too.

MIME: *Multipurpose Internet Mail Extensions.* One of the standard methods for attaching binary files to e-mail messages and newsgroup articles. See also **uuencode.**

modem: A device that enables your computer to connect with other computers over a phone line. Most modems are *internal* — they're housed within the computer's cabinet. *External* modems are contained in their own boxes and must be connected to the back of the computer via a serial cable or a USB cable.

moderated newsgroup: A newsgroup whose postings are controlled by a moderator, which helps to ensure that articles in the newsgroup follow the guidelines established by the moderator.

MPEG: *Motion Picture Experts Group.* A standard for compressing video images based on the popular JPEG standard used for still images. Internet Explorer includes built-in support for MPEG videos.

MSN: The Microsoft Network, a commercial online service. A few years ago, Microsoft thought that MSN would become the center of the online universe. Now, MSN is little more than a glorified Internet Service Provider.

MSN Messenger: An instant-messaging program that lets users exchange messages with one another in real time, kind of like a phone call but using text rather than voice.

NetMeeting: A program that comes with Internet Explorer and enables you to have online meetings with other Internet users.

Netscape: The company that makes the popular *Netscape Navigator* browser software for the Internet. Internet Explorer and Navigator are duking it out for the title of Best Web Browser.

Network Wizards: An organization that monitors the growth of the Internet. Check out its Web page at www.nw.com to find out how big the Internet really is.

news server: A host computer that stores newsgroup articles. You must connect to a news server to access newsgroups; your Internet Service Provider probably has a server to which you can connect. Microsoft uses its own news servers for its product-support newsgroups.

newsgroup: An Internet bulletin board area where you can post messages, called *articles,* about a particular topic and read articles posted by other Internet users. Thousands of different newsgroups are out there, covering just about every conceivable subject. You can access newsgroups with Outlook Express.

OIC: *Oh, I see.* A commonly used abbreviation in chats or e-mail messages.

online: Connecting your computer to a network, an online service provider, or the Internet.

Outlook Express: A scaled-back version of the Microsoft Outlook program that comes with Internet Explorer. (You can get the full Outlook program with Microsoft Office XP.)

Perl: A type of script that can be used to program Web sites. Perl uses script programs that run on the server computer, as opposed to Java or VBScript programs, which run on client computers.

PKZIP: A popular shareware program used to compress files or to expand compressed files. You can get your copy at www.pkware.com.

PMJI: *Pardon me for jumping in.* A commonly used abbreviation in newsgroup articles.

PNG: Portable Network Graphics, a type of graphics standard for network image files.

posting: Adding an article to a newsgroup.

PPP: *Point-to-Point Protocol.* The protocol that enables you to access Internet services with Internet Explorer.

protocol: A set of conventions that govern communications between computers in a network.

public domain: Computer software or other information that is available free of charge. See also *shareware*.

QuickTime: A video format popularized by Apple for its Macintosh computers. Internet Explorer provides built-in support for QuickTime movies, so you don't need separate software to view QuickTime files.

rating: A voluntary system of rating the content of Internet sites, similar to the ratings used for movies and television. Internet Explorer lets you block Web sites based on their ratings.

ROFL: *Rolling on the floor laughing.* A common abbreviation used in chats, newsgroup articles, and e-mail messages. You may see variations, such as ROFLPP and ROFLMAO. Figure those out yourself — this is a family book.

RSAC: *Recreational Software Advisory Council,* the organization that developed and oversees the use of Internet ratings. Now known as the Internet Content Rating Association (ICRA).

script: A type of program that is often embed in HTML documents. Internet Explorer allows scripts that are written in one of two languages: VBScript and JScript.

Search Assistant: An Internet Explorer feature that helps you look for various types of information on the Internet, such as Web pages, e-mail addresses, or encyclopedia articles.

Search bar: A special toolbar that appears in the left one-third or so of the Internet Explorer main window when you click the Search button. See also *Explorer bar*.

Secure Sockets Layer: *SSL.* The preferred method of security for sending confidential information, such as credit card numbers, over the Internet.

server: A computer or computer program that provides services to other computers or programs on the Internet or on a local area network. Specific types of Internet servers include news servers, mail servers, FTP servers, and web servers.

service provider: See *Internet Service Provider*.

shareware: A software program that you can download and try — free of charge. The program is not free, however. If you like the program and continue to use it, you're obligated to send in a modest registration fee. See also *public domain*.

shortcut: An icon that can represent a link to a location on the Internet. You can place shortcuts just about anywhere, including on your desktop, in a Windows folder, or even in a document.

signature: A fancy block of text that some users routinely place at the end of their e-mail messages and newsgroup articles. Outlook Express lets you use signatures. See also *stationery.*

SLIP: *Serial Line Internet Protocol.* A method for accessing the Web, now largely replaced by PPP connections.

smiley: A smiley face or other *emoticon* created from keyboard characters and used to convey emotions in otherwise emotionless e-mail messages or newsgroup postings.

spam: Unsolicited e-mail or newsgroup postings that do not relate to the topic of the newsgroup. Spam is the electronic equivalent of junk mail.

SSL: See *Secure Sockets Layer.*

stationery: An Outlook Express feature that lets you add a background graphic, signature, and font style to your e-mail messages and newsgroup postings.

taskbar: A Windows feature that displays icons for all open windows, a clock, and the Start button, which you use to run programs. Normally, the taskbar appears at the bottom of the screen, but it can be repositioned at any edge of the screen you prefer. If the taskbar isn't visible, try moving the mouse to the bottom of the screen or to the left, right, or top edge of the screen.

TCP/IP: *Transmission Control Protocol/Internet Protocol.* The basic set of conventions the Internet uses to enable different types of computers to communicate with one another.

Telnet: A protocol that enables you to log in to a remote computer as though you were actually using a terminal attached to that remote computer.

third-party cookie: A cookie that is created by a web server that hosts an advertisement on the page you are viewing rather than by the server that hosts the page itself. See also *cookie.*

thread: An exchange of articles in a newsgroup; specifically, an original article, all its replies, all the replies to replies, and so on.

TIFF: *Tagged Image File Format.* A format for picture files. TIFF files are large compared with other formats, such as JPEG and GIF, but they preserve all the original image's quality. Because of their large size, TIFF files aren't all that popular on the Internet.

TLA: *Three-letter acronym.* Ever notice how just about all computer terms can be reduced to a three-letter acronym? It all started with IBM. Now, there's URL, AOL, CGI, and who knows what else.

Uniform Resource Locator: Also known as a *URL.* A method of specifying the address of any resource available on the Internet, used when browsing the Internet. For example, the URL of Hungry Minds, Inc., is `www.hungryminds.com`.

UNIX: A computer operating system that is popular among Internet users. The Internet was developed by UNIX users, which is why much of the Internet has a UNIX look and feel — especially when you leave the World Wide Web and venture into older parts of the Internet, such as FTP sites.

upload: To copy a file from your computer to the Internet.

URL: See *Uniform Resource Locator.*

Usenet: A network of Internet newsgroups that contains many of the more popular newsgroups. You can access Usenet from Outlook Express, which comes free with Internet Explorer.

uuencode: A method of attaching binary files, such as programs or documents, to e-mail messages and newsgroup articles. The other method is *MIME.*

virus: An evil computer program that slips into your computer undetected, tries to spread itself to other computers, and may eventually do something bad, like trash your hard disk. Because Internet Explorer doesn't include built-in virus detection, I suggest that you consider using one of the many virus-protection programs available if you're worried about catching an electronic virus.

Web: See *World Wide Web.*

Web address: An address of a Web page. A domain name by itself (for example, `www.microsoft.com`) takes you to the home page for a Web site. A complete Web address may include folders and filenames, as in `www.microsoft.com/ie/default.htm`.

web browser: A program that can find pages on the World Wide Web and display them on your home computer. Internet Explorer is an example of a web browser.

Web host: A computer that stores Web pages that can be accessed over the World Wide Web. See also *web server.*

Web page: An HTML document available for display on the World Wide Web. The document may contain links to other documents located on the same server or on other web servers.

web server: A server computer that stores HTML documents so that they can be accessed on the World Wide Web.

wide area network: Commonly called *WAN.* A computer network that spans a large area, such as an entire campus, or perhaps a network that links branches of a company in several cities.

Windows XP: The newest version of the Microsoft Windows operating system. Windows XP (along with its predecessors Windows Millennium Edition, Windows 98, and Windows 95) is the main operating system for Internet Explorer, although versions of Internet Explorer exist for Windows NT, Windows 3.1, and Macintosh computers.

WinSock: Short for *Windows Sock*ets. The standard by which Windows programs are able to communicate with TCP/IP and the Internet. Fortunately, you don't have to know anything about WinSock to use it. In fact, you don't even have to know you're using it at all.

WinZip: A Windows version of the popular PKZIP compression program.

World Wide Web: Abbreviated *WWW* and referred to simply as *the Web.* This relatively new part of the Internet displays information using fancy graphics. The Web is based on *links,* which enable Web surfers to travel quickly from one web server to another.

XML: *eXtensible Markup Language.* A definition of the rules used to create markup languages, such as HTML.

zipped file: A file that has been compressed using the PKZIP or WinZip program.

Index

• Z •

FOR DUMMIES
BOOK REGISTRATION

Register This Book and Win!

We want to hear from you!

Visit **dummies.com** to register this book and tell us how you liked it!

✔ Get entered in our monthly prize giveaway.

✔ Give us feedback about this book — tell us what you like best, what you like least, or maybe what you'd like to ask the author and us to change!

✔ Let us know any other *For Dummies* topics that interest you.

Your feedback helps us determine what books to publish, tells us what coverage to add as we revise our books, and lets us know whether we're meeting your needs as a *For Dummies* reader. You're our most valuable resource, and what you have to say is important to us!

Not on the Web yet? It's easy to get started with *Dummies 101: The Internet For Windows 98* or *The Internet For Dummies* at local retailers everywhere.

Or let us know what you think by sending us a letter at the following address:

For Dummies Book Registration
Dummies Press
10475 Crosspoint Blvd.
Indianapolis, IN 46256

...FOR DUMMIES

BESTSELLING BOOK SERIES